ALSO BY SUSAN EISENHOWER

Partners in Space: U.S.–Russian Cooperation After the Cold War
Mrs. Ike: Memories and Reflections on the Life of Mamie Eisenhower
Breaking Free: A Memoir of Love and Revolution
The Making of a Soviet Scientist (coauthor with Roald Sagdeev)

HOW IKE LED

HOW IKE LED

The PRINCIPLES *Behind* EISENHOWER'S BIGGEST DECISIONS

SUSAN EISENHOWER

THOMAS DUNNE BOOKS
NEW YORK

First published in the United States by Thomas Dunne Books,
an imprint of St. Martin's Publishing Group

www.thomasdunnebooks.com
www.stmartins.com

Designed by Devan Norman

Library of Congress Cataloging-in-Publication Data

Names: Eisenhower, Susan, author.
Title: How Ike led : the principles behind Eisenhower's biggest decisions / Susan Eisenhower.
Identifiers: LCCN 2020006777 | ISBN 9781250238771 (hardcover) | ISBN 9781250238788 (ebook)
Subjects: LCSH: Eisenhower, Dwight D. (Dwight David), 1890–1969. | Eisenhower, Dwight D. (Dwight David), 1890–1969—Military leadership. | United States—Foreign relations—1953–1961—Decision making. | United States—Politics and government—1953–1961—Decision making. | Political leadership—United States—Case studies. | Command of troops—United States—Case studies. | Generals—United States—Biography. | Presidents—United States—Biography.
Classification: LCC E836 .E429 2020 | DDC 973.921092—dc23
LC record available at https://lccn.loc.gov/2020006777

Our books may be purchased in bulk for promotional, educational, or business use. Please contact your local bookseller or the Macmillan Corporate and Premium Sales Department at 1-800-221-7945, extension 5442, or by email at MacmillanSpecialMarkets@macmillan.com.

First Edition: 2020

10 9 8 7 6 5 4 3 2 1

I dedicate this book to my strategy and leadership students at the Eisenhower Institute at Gettysburg College, and to the rising generations across the country. It is my hope that they might know more of this man— a principled leader.

CONTENTS

You have completed your mission with the greatest victory in the history of warfare. You have commanded with outstanding success the most powerful military force that has ever been assembled. You have met and successfully disposed of every conceivable difficulty incident to varied national interests and international political problems of unprecedented complications. . . . You have been selfless in your actions, always sound and tolerant in your judgments, and altogether admirable in the courage and wisdom of your military decisions. You have made history, great history for the good of all mankind, and you have stood for all we hope for and admire in an officer of the United States Army. These are my tributes and with them I send my personal thanks.

—Gen. George C. Marshall,
chief of staff of the army,
to Gen. Dwight D. Eisenhower on May 8, 1945

HOW IKE LED

General Dwight D. Eisenhower (U.S. Army Pictorial Service)

INTRODUCTION

The rolling hills and the orchards of southern Pennsylvania are especially lush in late summer. Farmers' roadside stands burgeon with some of the season's most succulent picks. The still, heavy air, the rattle of cicadas, and the hum of occasional bees bring a sense of timeless tranquility.

Amid the neat stone farmhouses and open fields of soybeans and corn, one must remind oneself that the Battle of Gettysburg was one of the bloodiest and most significant battles of the Civil War. It was one of the key turning points of a conflict that split our nation in two. Lee, Meade, and Pickett left their historical marks on this land. And a little less than one hundred years later, my grandparents, Dwight and Mamie Eisenhower, chose this place as their home. In 1950 they bought a Civil War–era farmhouse and 189 acres of land in the distant shadow of South Mountain. For a little more than ten short years the newly rebuilt house, along with the land Ike restored, served as the first and last private home my grandparents shared. It was the centerpiece of family life.

As president, and later in his retirement, Ike brought many old friends and colleagues to this farm, including British prime minister Winston Churchill and French president Charles de Gaulle. Sometimes he also used the farm as a place for political discussions, and as a retreat for taking the measure of key people, including Soviet premier Nikita Khrushchev, Indian prime minister Jawaharlal Nehru, Chancellor Konrad Adenauer of Germany, and Mexican president Adolfo López Mateos, to name just a few. It was here too that the United States and the Soviet Union stood back from an ultimatum that might have led to war.[1]

I grew up in the years of Dwight Eisenhower's presidency. As one of his four grandchildren, I was subject to an odd combination of family intimacy and life in the public spotlight. My siblings and I had Secret Service protection for those eight years, so it was clear to us and everyone we encountered that we were not living a conventional childhood.

An incident during my middle-school years was a stark reminder of this fact. My history teacher once requested that I ask my grandfather a few questions about his time in office. I felt uncomfortable about carrying these questions to Granddad, but out of respect for my teacher I did so. One question related to the 1956 Hungarian uprising. Ike did not like mixing "business" and "home time" (or having any of his grandchildren placed in the awkward role of go-between). That is why, perhaps, he replied somewhat tartly when I asked why he hadn't intervened: "What—and risk starting World War III?"

In a flash I understood the gravity of the decisions my grandfather had had to make.

Yet it was not until my grandparents had died that I really began to think of them as public figures. And when I did, I could see clearly that knowing that side of them was critical for my own appreciation of them as people, as well as for my understanding of the history of World War II and the postwar period.

In 1996 I wrote a family biography that was centered on my grandmother, Mamie, and her marriage to Ike. Writing *Mrs. Ike: Memories and Reflections on the Life of Mamie Eisenhower* was an adventure for me. I learned about my grandparents' lives before I knew them, through their stories as they recounted them and the observations of others who knew them. And just as important, I gained a sense of who they were as they emerged as public figures.

But in my professional career as a Washington policy strategist, it is my grandfather who has come to mind most often. It has been nearly impossible for me to undertake any topic that has not been touched by his legacy in some way. For that reason I started to read about his career and the times in which he lived—perhaps somewhat defensively at first. (In high school and college, my siblings and I were accustomed to years of professorial swipes, and sometimes downright rude lectures on Eisenhower's alleged shortcomings.)

What occurred over time was not just the rise of Eisenhower's reputation, but for me the remarkable process of getting to know the other side of this someone I loved. It has made me regret that when he was alive I did not know fully the multidimensional person he now is for me. Discovering the "other side" of Ike has left me, frankly, in awe of how he handled some of the most consequential decisions ever undertaken by a general or a president—all while retaining a genuine capacity for empathy and kindness, which belied or survived the hard and painful decisions he'd been compelled to make. I don't know how he did it, but I saw firsthand that he never became callous, hard, or cynical.

In Gettysburg I still feel close to my grandparents, and I still go to these rolling hills for reflection. Yet so much has changed since that time—not just the disappearance of the Stuckey's souvenir shops or the Rexall drugstore on Gettysburg's main square—the fabric of our society today has a different texture than it did in the 1950s: some of it stronger but much of it very badly frayed.

Engaging one's deepest self was easier in those days—with long waits between letters and long-distance phone calls deferred until Sunday when the rates were cheaper. Today, tethered to smartphones and transfixed by Twitter and Instagram, we lurch from one demand to another with scarcely a moment to think. Our impulses are reactive, not considered. They are short-term rather than strategic. We have lost our capacity to act in the present while thinking into the future. We are struggling.

I have always been one to look forward. Increasingly, however, it has been impossible for me to do this without looking back—at our nation's journey since my grandfather's years. What is profoundly striking is how far we have veered from the guiding principles of those days.

This became increasingly obvious to me as I worked on this book. It has required countless hours of reading firsthand accounts and academic scholarship on Dwight Eisenhower and his professional responsibilities. The books on this subject have been sources of fascination for me, and I have nothing but appreciation and gratitude for the many who have, as one author described it to me, "lived with Ike for years." I know that feeling, and in undertaking this project I have sought to add what I knew of the man to the many outstanding contributions on his life and times.

What I have written is not a biography, nor does it pretend to cover fully Eisenhower's wartime or presidential years. Rather it is a primer, a sampler perhaps, for the many readers who may not remember or know much about Dwight Eisenhower and his approach to the important questions of his day. While it is impossible to write about every crisis or assess every controversy in a short book, my intention is to convey that he was a leader during transformational times, and that later as chief executive he was arguably the most bipartisan president we have had in modern American history. I have used, where possible, Ike's own words, and I have also given primacy to the assessments of his associates. They are the people who knew him best, professionally.

Ike was not a leader in the way we customarily "teach" leadership in our country. He was a *strategic* rather than an operational one. During the war his role was to receive all the inputs—across the entire enterprise: both internal and external, political and practical, fundamental and future oriented. His job was to "strip down" a problem to its essence, prioritize it among many, and ensure that any plan reflected those factors in a coherent form, ready for execution. His decisions were undertaken with the *entire* enterprise in mind.

Eisenhower had the thirty-thousand-foot responsibilities. In fact, it is noteworthy that his job description, when he was given the supreme command of Operation Overlord, was in essence to invade the mainland of Europe and bring about the destruction of Nazi forces. No other leadership job in the Western Alliance looked anything like his. And the opinion that truly mattered rested with his superiors' assessment of his performance. Ike, in his own words, described what was expected of him:

> A Supreme Commander in a situation such as faced by us in Europe cannot ordinarily give day-to-day and hour-by-hour supervision to any portion of the field. Nevertheless, he is the one person in the organization with the authority to assign principal objectives to major formations. He is also the only one who has under his hand the power to allot strength to the various major commands in accordance with their missions, to arrange for the distribution of incoming supply, and to direct the operations of the entire air forces in support of any portion of the line.[2]

Eisenhower's talent for envisioning a whole, especially in the context of the long game, may explain why he did not necessarily need combat experience to be a brilliant strategic leader. It is also why he never lost the confidence of his superiors during the conduct of World War II, even if his subordinates groused about some of his decisions—many of which, not surprisingly, related to resource allocation and personal authority. Eisenhower's subordinates simply did not have the same considerations he did.

Ike had to worry about the direction of the war, the assets he had at his disposal, the liabilities he had to mitigate, and a timeline that had to be met. He had finite human and material resources. He also had to scale up a war effort that, for the American cohort alone, began as a small group in 1942 and culminated in a force of more than three million people under his command only two years later. The performance of key subordinates was his responsibility at a time of nationalist tensions within the wartime alliance. And he had to factor in the worthiness of his military options and view them in the context of the political, social, or resource priorities made clear to him by Franklin Roosevelt, Winston Churchill, and the Combined Chiefs of Staff (COSSAC). He also had to be adept enough to sense the moment when the plan had to change.

Again, as president Eisenhower was the nation's chief strategic leader. Influenced by his success during the war, he developed a process—a staff system—that would assure the collection of all possible facts and facets of any issue; an organization that would also serve to coordinate the implementation of the president's own direction. Eisenhower was deeply troubled when his successors, starting with John F. Kennedy, dismantled it. Ike feared that the nation's chief executive, whose job it is to "connect the dots," would be so overwhelmed by diverse and second-order inputs that he would resort to governing like an *operational* leader rather than a *strategic* one. Eisenhower predicted that without a system for unbiased analysis and policy integration, avoidable mistakes would be inevitable. His views, many historians say, have been vindicated over the years—starting with the Bay of Pigs fiasco, a failed attempt by the Kennedy White House to invade Cuba and initiate an uprising. It was impacted significantly by JFK's last-minute decision to cancel air support and relocate the landing beaches.[3]

Even as a young man, Eisenhower had a strong preference for big-picture thinking in warfare and beyond. Before graduation from West Point, Ike's class of 1915 participated in a "staff ride" of the Gettysburg battlefield: "Each student was instructed to memorize the names of every brigadier in the opposing armies and know exactly where his unit was stationed at every hour during the three days of the battle," he wrote. "Little attempt was made to explain the meaning of the battle, why it came about, what the commanders hoped to accomplish, and the reason why Lee invaded the North the second time. If this was military history, I wanted no part of it."

Later one of his mentors, Gen. Fox Conner, chief of operations during World War I, recommended a reading list in the hope that it would change his protégé's mind about the usefulness of studying military history. And, during their time together in Panama in the 1920s, Conner would school Eisenhower with provocative questions about earlier battles. "What conditions existed when the decisions were made? What might have happened if a different decision had been made?" And "What were the alternatives?" he would ask.[4]

To understand Eisenhower is to understand that in war and peace his primary aim was to foster unity of purpose and to approach every issue from an "architectural perspective"—in other words to begin any significant undertaking by framing it and building a strong foundation for future betterment. He was keenly aware that no president has the time to finish fully any major initiative, so a sustainable approach, approved on a bipartisan basis, must be advanced at the outset.

Another key element of Eisenhower as a leader should be viewed in the context of his character and the impact he had on others. I was drawn to assess how he made people feel, and to ponder whether his relationship with the American people furthered American goals or subverted them. In addition to his obvious talent in the use of force, Eisenhower also believed deeply in "soft power," which has all but disappeared as a tool of influence in our country today.

I never had the chance to discuss these things directly with my grandfather—I was seventeen when he died—but his passing left an enormous void in my life, as it did for all our family members. So, in 1984, when I first came to Washington, I tried to meet everyone in the city and beyond who had known him. Many had served in the Eisenhower administration, or with him during the war. While a number of key people had already died, the many I met and came to know validated my instincts about Ike as a person and taught me much about strategy and leadership.

Striking to me was the way they talked about "the Boss," and the wistfulness they displayed in thinking about how far our country had already come in disavowing the mechanisms of good governance. They lamented, as I did even then, that much of our public life had already become highly politicized, regardless of how we see the 1970s and '80s now as "the good ol' days."

The revolving door had made it too easy to put one's own selfish desires ahead of the job that was there—and still is—to be done. Those decades were marked by crises and scandals, including exploding debt, union busting, a savings and loan crisis, and the Iran-Contra affair.

Even in the 1980s one could feel that it was fast becoming politically old-fashioned to develop a plan for *all* Americans, as both political parties increasingly focused on only their bases of support.

Gen. Andrew Goodpaster, Ike's trusted White House staff secretary and defense liaison, and later supreme commander of NATO and superintendent of West Point, was my mentor. Well over six feet tall, he had a commanding presence and spoke with quiet, unshakable authority. For years we had adjacent offices at the Eisenhower Institute, which we founded together. The countless hours I spent in his company were often punctuated by stories, expressions, or anecdotes that came from his time with my grandfather.

Over more than a decade, Goodpaster had plenty to say about current affairs, as he watched the country move from one with a clear-cut national security strategy to a more muddled and opportunistic approach. He talked often about a strategy "for the long haul," and it was from him that I learned to think of the challenges facing this country as a tent.

"It is critical to determine," he would say, "which of all the areas of national affairs are the 'long poles' and which ones are the 'short poles.'" It should be noted that the long poles, if they are not kept sturdy through reinforcement and timely maintenance, can bring down the whole tent.

One of the long poles was our foreign relations, and in that General Goodpaster and my father, John, gave me all the encouragement a young professional could hope for in pursuing a dialogue between the United States and the Soviet Union in the mid-to-late 1980s. Mikhail Gorbachev had come to power in the USSR—and the window for improving U.S.–Soviet relations had just started to open.

A decade and a half after we started these initiatives, General Goodpaster would sometimes come into the office with a look of concern. "Did you read the paper this morning?" he would ask me. "This is just not serious. Most of the stories in the paper are second- or third-order issues." Such conversations confirmed to me that we had known and were deeply influenced by the same man.

Sometimes Goodpaster, or "Andy" as we called him, would use some of Granddad's favorite maxims, and we would both laugh. "Take your job seriously, but never yourself," was one of Ike's warnings. Or "All generalizations are false including this one." Or "There's no such thing as an indispensable man or woman." Or the one I liked especially for its ironic humor: "Let's not make our mistakes in a hurry." Goodpaster, however, often told me the question most asked by President Eisenhower at cabinet meetings was "What's best for America?"—for the country as a *whole*?

Goodpaster's long association with Dwight Eisenhower could be seen in other ways, too. In the 1990s he and I, along with a few others, resigned from the board of a Washington-based think tank over the fact that they were accepting money from defense contractors to pay for national security studies. Today such principled departures are all but unheard of, and such "conflicts" are commonplace. But back in those days, Goodpaster held the view that such practices were unacceptable and only aided and abetted the potential for the "unwarranted influence" of the "military-industrial complex"—a concept articulated by the Boss in his farewell address to the nation in 1961. Goodpaster believed this phenomenon was real, and that it had the potential to deform our democratic processes—especially the development of policy making.

Former attorney general Herbert Brownell, Ike's chief civil rights adviser, also took me under his wing, along with others such as Maxwell Rabb, Ike's cabinet secretary and Arthur Flemming, the former secretary of Health, Education, and Welfare.[5] Arthur Flemming, who had worked on both domestic (HEW) and defense (Office of Defense Mobilization) matters during the Eisenhower administration personified for me Ike's view of the interconnectedness of domestic and national security issues. I had so much to learn from Secretary Flemming, in fact, that for years we had lunch together regularly at Twigs, a quiet little restaurant at the Capital Hilton on 16th Street where he had his own permanently reserved table.

I knew numerous other people, too, who had served their country in one capacity or another with Ike; many from the war years like Gen. Elwood "Pete" Quesada, commander of tactical bombing on D-day, and Gen. Alfred Gruenther, former supreme commander of NATO (and Ike's favorite bridge partner).

I was eager to learn about the service of these remarkable people, and I was intrigued by their current views. I also wanted to hear what they had to say about Eisenhower's leadership style, how he tackled issues, and what it was like to work for him.

This quest eventually led me to the Supreme Court of the United States, where Chief Justice Warren Burger, was willing to meet me for fifteen minutes, his assistant told mine. When we were seated in his spacious office, he began to warm up. Over the course of two and a half hours he told me stories about what he learned from serving in the Justice Department during the Eisenhower administration, while they crafted the framework of the civil rights revolution that was gathering force.

He was impressed, he told me, that President Eisenhower had deployed the 101st Airborne Division in Little Rock to desegregate Central High School. The use of the 101st instead of the National Guard sent an unmistakable signal of resolve, not just to Little Rock and the state of Arkansas, but far beyond its state boundaries. Little Rock also showed the international community that the United States was, resolutely, a country of laws. I was intrigued when the chief justice told me that his decision on the Kent State shootings was positively influenced by Eisenhower's handling of Little Rock.[6]

All these distinguished people, including my grandfather's youngest brother, Milton, wanted to make sure I knew and remembered some key points about their experience in working for Ike. They also wanted me to know how he had organized things—and why it produced results.

They often spoke of Ike's intellectual honesty, his unmistakable adherence to specific strategic concepts, and his judicious use of power—which included not just the political and constitutional power he wielded, but also the power he had over other people. They described to me his charisma, his energy, and what that meant in the context of being part of his team.

Arthur Burns, a former Columbia University economist and later Ike's chairman of the Council of Economic Advisers (later still, chairman of the Federal Reserve Board under Nixon), may have been the first public official who ever described for me, in such vivid ways, one of the president's qualities that had already been flagged by Ike's classmates at West Point. Eisenhower was, according to his 1915 yearbook, "As big as life and twice as natural."

When I first visited Dr. Burns at his office in Washington in 1985, where he worked after serving as the U.S. ambassador to West Germany, he described to me the overwhelming power of Dwight Eisenhower's presence, his magnetism, his warmth and his vibrancy—or what State Department official Robert Bowie called his "electricity." I, of course, knew of this quality firsthand, but I was intrigued by the apparent impact Ike's personality and physical magnetism had on his team.

Burns was quick to tell me, however, that beneath the cheery demeanor and the easy, jocular way Eisenhower interacted with people, there was a mind that worked like a steel trap. He was a man of deep conviction and a firm set of ideas honed during the "crisis years" of World War II. I can attest to the fact that everyone in Eisenhower's orbit felt this power and had an instinctive desire to live up to his expectations and to win his approval.

When Ike walked into a room, and I experienced this myself, his energy radiated. His personal power could, as some of his colleagues noted, "fill an empty space."

For that reason I could never understand, as a kid, how Ike's political opponents characterized him during his presidency as passive, bumbling, or ineffective. Didn't they know this was the same person who'd stood down Hitler? Never was there anything I saw in him that could have been described as passive or out of touch—even in the very last months of his life. Indeed, Henry Kissinger, who had opposed Eisenhower on a number of issues, once described to me his first and only meeting with Ike just after Nixon's election and just months before his death. Kissinger said he was unprepared for the former president's sharpness, and the mental energy he exuded even as he lay in his hospital bed, physically diminished by a series of heart attacks.

I remember vividly, too (and recounted in *Mrs. Ike*), an incident just after one of Granddad's many heart attacks in 1968. Gen. Leonard Heaton, his physician and surgeon general of the army, came into his hospital room as our immediate family was gathered around Granddad, who was lying flat, his body emaciated from his ailments. We thought, in those precious moments, that we were saying our last good-byes. Heaton told his patient that it was time for us to leave the room so he could get some rest. With that, Ike roared from his bed: "How many stars do you have?" Heaton, surprised, said "Three, Sir."

Granddad retorted: "Well I've got five, and I tell you they are going to stay."

Ike's personal power was part of what drew people to him. But his straightforward approach to things also won him admirers. Bill Robinson, a newspaperman and later chairman of Coca-Cola, once recounted to William Ewald, a White House staffer and later an Eisenhower historian, some of his first impressions of Ike.

Robinson had kept notes from an encounter he had with Eisenhower after the war, in 1947. He described the general's style:

> There was no pose, no pretense, no attempt to establish anything for the record. . . . He was natural, alive, alert, spirited, and gave the impression of having an intense amount of unloosened energy, both intellectual and physical. . . . [No] public man whom I have ever known, or had ever known about, had such intellectual honesty as Eisenhower. I also had the impression that here was a man who was realistic, practical and disciplined.[7]

Bill Ewald himself also recalled another kind of honesty. After the presidency, he was tapped to help coedit Ike's White House memoirs with my father, John.

Ewald's job in that effort was to provide documents and look for details that would assure "fidelity to the facts," as the former president worked on drafts of the manuscript. Ike had an extraordinary memory, as well as an organized mind that made it possible for him to dictate not only letters but whole book chapters in nearly paragraph-perfect form. In 1945, for instance, one month after the Germans' unconditional surrender, he even gave his famous twelve-minute Guildhall Address from memory before a London crowd of millions.

One day, Ewald challenged, indeed contradicted, the former president on his recall of a specific event. "He was absolutely certain he had done one thing, though I had brought him documentary evidence that he hadn't," Bill recalled.

Ike's frustration and anger began to rise, and he got up from his chair and left the room. ("Imagine, contradicting the general about what was, after all, his own history. Conceivably, he could even, though it seemed unlikely, *be* right," Ewald worried. He was sure he would be fired, "and I felt I deserved it.")

A few moments later Ike returned. "If that's the way the record is," he said, "that's the way it should read."

"Whatever his foibles," Ewald concluded, "this iron respect for the truth underlay the feeling that I came to have for Dwight Eisenhower."[8]

Those associated with Ike knew that honesty was embedded in his thinking. It resided at the very core of his values. I don't think you can assess Eisenhower the general or Eisenhower the president without understanding this.

Ike's capability as a long-range thinker also explains one other quality that I later found remarkable. He could be utterly in the moment, while at the same time absorbing and assessing what the consequences of an experience, event, or trend could have in the decades to come.

On visiting Ordruf, a Nazi concentration camp near Buchenwald on August 12, 1945, Eisenhower put in place, virtually on the spot, a policy of far-reaching impact. So overwhelmed was he by the "savagery" and "bestiality" of what the Nazis had done in this "horror camp," he insisted that from then on the Holocaust's atrocities must be chronicled and preserved for all time—on the basis that at some point in the future there would be people who would say it never happened.

It is hard to imagine someone instinctively thinking about fifty years from now as he is standing, confronted for the first time, by a profoundly shocking discovery. But without Eisenhower's immediate response at Ordruf, one can only imagine how the lies of Holocaust deniers might have taken root after the war.

Ike's leadership approach was also informed by an understanding of human nature, the determination to establish an effective mode of operation and organization, as well as the conviction that it is necessary not just to inspire but also to challenge his associates' shortcomings—starting with his own. He was always mindful, however, that not all personal growth and change can happen under the glare of public scrutiny. He would also show the effectiveness of advancing his set of principles publicly—and even privately—if the results were likely to be more effective.

While there may be many who will still challenge some of

the decisions Ike made, no one can dispute that he brought sincerity, idealism, and utter dedication to the performance of his duty.

Bill Ewald, in referring to Eisenhower, once observed that self-sacrifice and selflessness—on which the highest form of duty is based—"is the possession of the objectivist; the man who sees that the truth is greater than himself."[9]

Eisenhower's leadership—one of head *and* heart—was projected in the context of a higher cause, one that rested on accountability and humility. The importance of serving something bigger than yourself is a truth that Ike would tell from power—through the full force of his personal, political, and military will.

General Eisenhower meets paratroopers of the 101st Airborne Division in Newbury, England, prior to their boarding for the invasion, June 5, 1944. (U.S. Army)

1

ACCOUNTABILITY WITHOUT CAVEATS

On July 11, 1944, Dwight Eisenhower's naval aide, Capt. Harry Butcher, asked his boss, supreme commander of Allied Forces Europe, if he could keep the note that Ike had carried in his wallet on D-day. Operation Overlord was the mightiest amphibious military operation in history, and a turning point of World War II. Eisenhower was uncomfortable about relinquishing the short statement, and he did not understand why Butcher wanted it. Ike had written such a note, he told the captain, for every major military operation for which he had responsibility.

It read:

> Our landings in Cherbourg-Havre area have failed to gain a satisfactory foothold and I have withdrawn the troops.

> My decision to attack at this time and place was based on the best information available. The troops, the air and the Navy did all that bravery and devotion to duty could do. If any blame or fault attaches to the attempt, it is mine alone. July 5.

Ike thought so little of the historical significance of his simple "in case of failure" communiqué that when Butcher asked him to date it, he wrote "July 5," thinking only of the current month—rather than June 5 when Allied forces were poised to storm the Normandy coast.[1]

This unused communiqué is often thought of today as a symbol of Ike's leadership—the willingness to take full and complete responsibility for his decisions—even though one of the most important variables, in this case the weather, was out of his control. It is correct that Eisenhower would have released the statement had the invasion forces been thrown back into the sea; but they weren't and Ike wanted to keep the note private. As he had told Butcher in 1942, when his naval aide began his duties as the headquarters diarist, there should be no effort to apply PR spin to things. "We are not operating or writing for the record," Ike had told him. "[We are here] to win the war."[2]

Eisenhower wrote such "communiqués" as much for himself as for any kind of public release, should the worst happen. He was not trying to burnish his reputation in writing it, he was reminding himself, and if necessary others, that he alone was responsible for the outcome of the mission. It was a personal and public form of accountability.[3]

Much has been written about D-day and the vast undertaking aimed at the heart of Nazi German power. It is worth remembering that the Germans saw this endeavor as the existential moment of the war. The German High Command knew full well that the outcome of the war rested on making sure the Allies failed in any amphibious assault—for behind any successful beachhead lay the nearly unlimited military and industrial resources of the United States.

Before the fateful assault known as Operation Overlord, or D-day as we call it, General Eisenhower was called upon to make an array of difficult decisions. Many of them would be life-or-death calls; all would have lasting impact on the continent of Europe and across the United States.

In addition to the frightening uncertainties of the Normandy weather in launching any attack, General Eisenhower had to make a number of consequential calls, from the role of tactical and strategic bombing and their likely targets, to the resolution of various issues related to Allied squabbling and doubts about the mission.

Ike later wrote in his diary that on June 6:

> There was no universal confidence in a completely successful outcome. Indeed, most people thought that even should we, in some two or three years eventually win, we would pay a ghastly price in battling our way toward Germany. . . . Some newspapers went so far as to predict 90 percent losses on the beaches themselves. Even Winston Churchill, normally a fairly optimistic individual, never hesitated to voice his forebodings about the venture.[4]

The assault on Normandy from across the English Channel, and the subsequent battles for France and Western Europe, were complex operations in which military strategy fused with geopolitical considerations. Since 1942, the Americans, most notably Gen. George C. Marshall—chief of staff of the army—argued for this direct approach. Eisenhower, too, favored it. The British, however, with the Dunkirk evacuation and the failed Dieppe raid still fresh in their minds, were skeptical, if not downright hostile to the idea.

There were a number of strategic considerations on both sides. But perhaps one of the most compelling arguments for mounting a direct assault, sooner rather than later, had rested on our eastern ally, the Soviet Union, and its attitude to the opening of a second front. The upper echelons of decision makers in the American war effort argued that there was a danger that the Soviet Union might make a separate peace with Hitler, not unlike World War I when the Russians withdrew from their alliance with Britain and the United States, to significant effect. No doubt this was a key factor when President Franklin Roosevelt promised Soviet leader Joseph Stalin that the Allies would open a second front that would include the Normandy landings and Operation Anvil, an invasion of southern France that would augment D-day and post-D-day forces. In return Stalin agreed to open an offensive on the eastern front, in support of our assault, to assure that the Germans could not relocate their forces to the West.

It was not until the Tehran Conference in December 1943 that a full commitment was made to cross the English Channel and storm the French coastline. By this stage of the war some of the most significant battles of the European theater had already been fought on the eastern front, in Kursk, in Moscow, and in Stalingrad. The pressure was now on the Western Allies to move quickly to secure Western Europe, in conjunction with the Soviet advances in the East, in a chokehold movement that would bring the end of Nazi power.

Many things were at stake. The survival of the Jewish people, the necessity to bring an end to Germany's increasing use of advanced weaponry on Great Britain, including the V1 and V2 rockets, and the urgent necessity to halt Germany's research and development of an atomic bomb. Before end-of-the-war political decisions were made, there were also legitimate concerns, especially in London, about potential Soviet advances into Western Europe.

Within weeks of the Tehran Conference, at the insistence of Marshal Joseph Stalin, the Western Allies named a supreme Allied commander of the Normandy campaign. While many had assumed that Gen. George C. Marshall would take on this crucial role, President Roosevelt requested that Marshall stay in Washington at his side, and he appointed General Eisenhower instead.

Up to this point Eisenhower had commanded forces in North

Africa and also in Sicily, and he had weighed in on the Normandy concept. In 1943, while still in Africa, Brig. Gen. William E. Chambers of the Combined Chiefs of Staff (COSSAC) brought a copy of the Normandy invasion plan to Eisenhower for his opinion—as he was the only Allied general who had already launched large-scale amphibious operations. On reading the document, Ike told Chambers that in his view the attack on a three-division front was fatally weak. "Were this my operation," he said, "I would insist on broadening it to a five-division front with two divisions in floating reserve." Ike had no idea that this mission would later become his own.[5]

Chambers returned to London and reported on Eisenhower's critique to Gen. Frederick E. Morgan, the plan's author. The Combined Chiefs rejected Eisenhower's suggestions and adhered to the original plan because of troop and sea-lift limitations.

Not long after Christmas 1943, Eisenhower—now appointed supreme commander—was sent back to Washington by General Marshall to have a few days' rest and to attend meetings before returning to London. Ike was understandably concerned that time had been lost with regard to enlarging the plan.

The strategic decision to land in Normandy, rather than somewhere else along the French coast, was not in contention. Considerable analysis had already been undertaken to determine the best place to strike. Among a number of factors, Normandy was chosen because it was in some ways an illogical place to land, thus enhancing the chance for a surprise attack. Pas de Calais, farther east along the coast, was actually considerably closer to Great Britain, thus requiring a shorter time for naval vessels to cross the Channel. Normandy may have also been seen by the Germans to be a less likely place for the assault since there was no port along that coast, an asset vital for the arrival of men and supplies. Little could Berlin imagine that the Allies would bring with them their own artificial ports, called Mulberries.

There were many complicated considerations for selecting the actual landing sites, such as the texture of the sand, the topography, the German defenses, including deeply embedded bunkers and mines, and Hitler and the German High Command's perception of where the Allies were likely to attack.

With the invasion beaches identified and agreed to, Eisenhower remained adamant that the weakness of the Allied forces envisioned in the plan threatened their success in meeting Allied objectives—the city of Caen for the British and Canadians, and Cherbourg, a major port, for the Americans. Time was short, however, and Eisenhower's proposed change in plan would basically double the force, requiring further surveys, more mapping, a new logistical plan, and the acquisition of additional shipping, probably from the Far East.

Before leaving for Washington, Eisenhower sought and received British general Bernard Law Montgomery's endorsement of his revised plan, and in London "Monty" and American general Walter Bedell Smith, Eisenhower's chief of staff, argued for these revisions: "You will be right in telling them [the Combined Chiefs] I will not yield on this matter," Eisenhower told the two generals.[6]

Monty and Smith called upon Prime Minister Winston Churchill and made Eisenhower's case. But even by the time Ike had returned from Washington for the final invasion preparations, this crucial question was still unresolved. According to army historian Gen. S. L. A. Marshall, "Eisenhower stood firm" on the necessity for a revised plan, "and the opposition had either to yield or to relieve him. Of the yielding came the addition of the Utah Beach operation and the two-division U.S. airborne strike inland from it, which together proved decisive."[7]

American forces were to land on Utah Beach, establish a beachhead, then pivot north and proceed up the Cotentin Peninsula to capture Cherbourg. To facilitate that landing, American paratroopers would drop behind Utah Beach and secure the single-lane causeways that crossed marshland, now lakes that had been flooded by the Germans as part of their coastal defenses. If the paratroopers were unable to secure these causeways, the Utah Beach segment of the operation would be in trouble. In that case the troops landing on Utah Beach would be unable to move inland, thus jeopardizing other oncoming troops who would land on the beaches in synchronized groups every half hour.

The success of Operation Overlord depended on establishing a solid beachhead. Eisenhower outlined the objectives of each of his services: Airpower would be deployed to curtail and wear away the Luftwaffe, the German Reich's air force, and bomb vital transportation depots and rail lines to assure that the Germans could not use them to reinforce their positions. The naval plan was to provide for minesweeping, bombardment of the coast, and protection against submarine forces.[8]

The logistical plan depended on the capture of the port of Cherbourg, but also on the utilization of glider forces that would deliver men and equipment, along with the artificial Mulberries to be assembled at Arromanches and Omaha Beach. The plan was comprehensive; every detail had been considered and worked out.

Eventually Eisenhower and his generals won the argument with COSSAC to enlarge the force, but time was running out until the most advantageous landing dates arrived. The invasion required a full moon, relatively calm seas, and skies clear enough to assure that the aircraft could find their targets. The assault had to occur in partial light because the Germans had reinforced mines and other obstacles along the beach.

Despite preparations, jurisdictional matters continued to be hard-fought battles. Some of the disagreements revolved around key strategic elements of the plan, such as the critical shortages of troop landing craft. To amass enough for the expanded plan, Eisenhower had to "beg, borrow, and steal" from other operations and military theaters. This critical shortage was the reason for a monthlong delay of the assault.

Another concern was the so-called Transportation Plan—an effort to redirect strategic bombing away from industrial targets in Germany to transportation and depot targets in France. Eisenhower and his deputy commander, British air marshal Arthur Tedder, were insistent that the Transportation Plan was necessary if the Allies were to stop a German counterattack after the landings.

Since the strategic bombing forces were resistant to taking orders from an overall supreme commander, the issue was whether or not Eisenhower would be given full control over *all* the forces. Military tradition, culture, and national pride were the sticking points. Eisenhower, exercising what S. L. A. Marshall described as "clear vision and tough-mindedness," finally prevailed by issuing the order to proceed with the Transportation Plan over the persistent reservations of the British War Council. Eisenhower's order stood.[9]

On May 15, a month later, and less than three weeks before the invasion date, Eisenhower's SHAEF (Supreme Headquarters Allied Expeditionary Forces) held a conference at Saint Paul's School in London to brief the British chiefs of staff and the War Cabinet on D-day preparations. This was the highest-ranking group of attendees at any briefing of the war to date. It offered the opportunity to iron out any last-minute details or difficulties, and that day both Churchill and King George VI spoke.

What struck the Americans, Eisenhower later wrote, was that Churchill, while giving a rousing speech, said, "'Gentlemen, I am hardening toward this enterprise,' meaning to us that, though he had long doubted its feasibility and had previously advocated its further postponement in favor of operations elsewhere, he had finally, at this late date, come to believe with the rest of us that this was the true course of action in order to achieve the victory."[10]

All matters seemed to be set for the deployment of this vast armada, scheduled for June 5. And Eisenhower thought that the last remaining issue he would have to deal with was making the decision on the actual date and hour of the assault. This would be dependent on lunar windows and, of course, the weather forecast for the few vital days necessary for establishing a beachhead.

Two weeks later, on May 29—and a week before D-day was actually launched—Eisenhower's commander in charge of airborne forces, Britain's air chief marshal Trafford Leigh-Mallory, approached Eisenhower about the paratroopers and glider units, which would land with troops, equipment, and supplies. Leigh-Mallory had been concerned about this element of the operation for some time, but now he put it more bluntly. He strongly recommended that the airborne operation, specifically behind Omaha and Utah Beaches, be abandoned. He argued that the drop zones were unsuitable and that the airborne troops would meet heavy resistance, as intelligence had noted that the Germans were reinforcing the area where the 82nd Airborne would be dropping; similar concerns entailed the 101st Airborne, which were to link up forces behind Omaha and Utah Beaches.

Leigh-Mallory warned that given these hazards, the result of dropping the airborne units would be a "futile slaughter" of these young Americans. He predicted the loss of at least 70 percent of the glider forces and 50 percent of the paratroopers, leaving the few surviving men without tactical power and no capacity to affect the outcome of the invasion.

Eisenhower took Leigh-Mallory's recommendation very seriously. The British air chief marshal was commander of airborne operations, his technical expert, and the person whom he had empowered with the planning of this phase of operations. Eisenhower believed in the importance of delegation and the requirements of assembling a team on which he could count. Leigh-Mallory was one such person. Ike described him as a man "noted for his personal courage" as well as his "frankness" and "sincerity."[11]

Nevertheless, "It would be difficult to conceive a more soul-racking problem," Eisenhower later wrote. "If my technical expert was correct, then the planned operation was worse than stubborn folly, because even at the enormous cost predicted we could not gain the principle object of the drop . . . this meant that the whole operation suddenly acquired a degree of risk, even foolhardiness, that presaged a gigantic failure, possibly Allied defeat in Europe."[12]

Eisenhower asked Leigh-Mallory to put his recommendation in writing to "protect" him in case he, Eisenhower, disregarded his advice. In those days generals were being fired left and right for errors of judgment, and if Eisenhower decided to use the airborne troops anyway and Leigh-Mallory was correct, then he did not want the air chief marshal to be blamed for the fiasco since there would be no written record of his warning.

Ike told Leigh-Mallory that he needed two hours to assess his recommendation and that he would write him with his final decision. He retreated in solitude to his trailer.

Once there, Eisenhower ran through each argument to assess the implications, one way or the other. He reminded himself that if Leigh-Mallory was right, and he went ahead with the drop, he would likely carry to his grave "the unbearable burden of a conscience justly accusing me of the stupid, blind sacrifice of thousands" of men. Aside from this personal burden, Ike recalled, given the critical importance of GI morale, the effect of such a disaster would ripple through the entire invasion force.[13]

After a thorough assessment of each of the factors, Eisenhower concluded that if he cancelled the airborne operation then he would have to cancel the Utah Beach segment. Without taking such a step he would condemn the troops landing on Utah Beach to a greater catastrophe than the predictions for the airborne troops.

"In long and calm consideration of the whole great scheme we had agreed that the Utah Beach attack was an essential factor in prospects for success," Eisenhower later reflected.

The supreme commander could do nothing, he thought, but trust that the two years of careful planning and the insistence he had placed on greater forces and resources would carry the day. He reminded himself that Leigh-Mallory's assessment was just an estimate. Some of his other senior generals, especially generals Omar Bradley and Matthew Ridgway, expressed considerably more confidence in the outcome of these operations than did the British officer. Still, Eisenhower faced, in effect, a deadlock among the high echelons of his command.

A few hours later Eisenhower telephoned Leigh-Mallory and told him that the airborne operation would proceed as planned and that he would confirm it in writing.

May 30, 1944
To Trafford Leigh-Mallory
Top Secret

Dear Leigh-Mallory,
Thank you very much for your letter of the 29th on the subject of the airborne operations. You are quite right in communicating to me your convictions as to the hazards involved and I must say that I agree with you as to the character of these risks. However, a strong airborne attack in the region indicated is essential to the whole operation and it must go on. Consequently, there is nothing for it but for you, the Army Commander and the Troop Carrier Commander to work out to the last detail every single thing that may diminish these hazards.

It is particularly important that the air and ground troops involved in the operation be not needlessly depressed. Like all of the rest of the soldiers, they must understand that they have a tough job to do but be fired up and determined to get it done.

I am, of course, hopeful that our percentage losses will not approximate your estimates because it is quite true that I expect to need these forces very badly later in the campaign.
Sincerely,"[14]

Eisenhower and Leigh-Mallory knew as well that the paratroop divisions were new units, created specifically for combat in World War II. Ike was also left with the hard fact that only 15 percent of his D-day troops had ever been in combat. Leigh-Mallory's dire predictions added another significant worry to the last-minute arrangements before the start of the assault.

As the invasion drew closer, Eisenhower had many meetings with key advisers and political figures, including Prime Minister Winston Churchill. He also met with French general Charles de Gaulle, who was irate that he had not been briefed sooner about the plans, due in no small measure to British security and censorship, which had curtailed diplomatic business. Though not an elected leader, de Gaulle insisted that only he could speak for France after a successful assault.

Eisenhower also had to attend to critical correspondence and a range of orders that needed immediate attention from all senior commanders in the campaign. One such letter was to General Marshall, only ten days before D-day, regarding a miscalculation of ammunition requirements—a very serious matter; another, an order to his field commanders about the preservation of historic monuments. "It is the responsibility of every commander to protect and respect these symbols wherever possible."[15]

Schedule permitting, Ike spent as much time as he could visiting the men who would be executing the plan. He saw their morale as a critical input to success. During the buildup to the Normandy campaign Eisenhower visited twenty-two divisions, twenty-one airfields, and four major units of the naval fleet. On May 27 Eisenhower visited Gen. Leonard T. Gerow's Fifth Corps—which, on D-day, would take the brunt of the resistance on Omaha Beach. That day he also visited the Canadian First Army.

So determined were the Allied forces to make the Germans think the landing would be in Calais that in the run-up to Operation Overlord, the Allies dropped twice as many bombs on Calais as they did on Normandy. Even after the Allies established a beachhead on the coast, Ike was adamant about the necessity to keep the Germans thinking that the main attack would still be in Calais. That included the continued closure of southern England. He worried that if the travel ban was lifted too quickly after the assault it would confirm for the Germans that the main attack had been at Normandy. If they could be successfully fooled, the Germans might well continue to keep the lion's share of their troops farther east.

The deception plan, which had been under way for some time, was code-named Operation Fortitude. Construction of fake encampments, complete with inflatable tanks and jeeps—and the presence of Gen. George S. Patton—had miraculously deceived the Germans until this point.

Given the size of the invasion forces, it is hard to imagine that the Allies managed to keep their intentions secret. The Germans knew an assault was imminent, but where it would come remained shrouded in uncertainty—an impossible feat had the Allies not had virtual air supremacy and control over the seas between Britain and France. This made it possible to misdirect the Germans and camouflage the presence of mounting Overlord forces consisting of 12,000 airplanes, 7,000 vessels, 24,000 paratroopers, and 160,000 soldiers who were soon to storm the Normandy coast.[16]

As the days until June 5 grew closer, Ike's team at Southwick House, the headquarters of Adm. Bertram Ramsey near Portsmouth, met twice a day, at 9:30 p.m. and 4:00 a.m. As D-day got closer, Group Capt. James Stagg, chairman of a meteorological committee, ordered the part of his team in Greenland to step up its efforts. Before the eve of the D-day preparations, the weather team in Greenland had been releasing hydrogen balloons once a day to determine conditions in the upper atmosphere. With the invasion nearing, they stepped up their tests to every hour. However, while vitally important, these measurements did not quell the growing dissension among the members of the panel of meteorologists.[17]

Over some months Ike had been keeping track of the weather and the forecasts he had been receiving, to compare their accuracy after the fact. He was sufficiently impressed with the Allied meteorologists that as the hours grew shorter, he felt he could consider the most important weather forecast in history with some degree of confidence. The problem remained that the meteorologists themselves did not agree.

The date scheduled for D-day was June 5—but on June 4 Stagg predicted that June 5 would be a day of high winds, low clouds, and big, turbulent seas. A June 5 invasion looked bleak, even though Ike and his commanders considered this forecast at their conference table at Southwick House on a day of sunny skies and calm winds. Nevertheless the decision to delay the invasion—though complicated to carry out—was prudent as well as fateful.

Postponing the launch date left only two other possibilities in June: the next few days—the sixth and the seventh—or two weeks later. But with each passing day the risk of discovery and the potential for security breaches mounted, as did a significant drop in morale. Two million men were awaiting the order, a significant percentage of whom were crowded onto bobbing transport ships tied up at the docks.

The next day winds and rain lashed the windows of Southwick House as the Allied commanders sat at their long table, listening to Stagg's latest report. This time he offered some hope: A clearing might be on the way.

While Eisenhower and the other commanders were heartened by this prospect, many of them still had deep reservations about the forecast during this weather window. Each of the operations under their command required reasonable conditions for success. Nevertheless Eisenhower gave a tentative go, ordering that it be confirmed at the 4:30 a.m. meeting.

With little sleep, he and his commanders reassembled in the mansion's library in the middle of the night. This time Stagg predicted that the rain would stop in the next two to four hours and that there would be a twenty-four-to-thirty-six-hour period when the winds would die down and the waves would be manageable. He warned that the front would not sustain good weather for long—but there *was* this opportunity. Eisenhower asked each of his commanders for his views one more time, but it appeared that still there was no clear consensus. Then he said: "Well, let's go."

The decision to invade on that date was a gamble. Eisenhower was counting on his men to establish a beachhead in Normandy within at least twenty-four hours. If not, the operation could fail, without a palatable plan B.

His three words set in motion the mighty machinery of Overlord. From western and northeastern Great Britain, the Allied armada advanced into well-choreographed places in line. The invasion, set for June 6, was finally under way.

"I suppose nobody can really describe those last few days before the big show started," wrote Ike's valet, Sgt. Mickey McKeogh. "Your nerves got tight . . . you could feel the tightness all through you, and you could see it in the faces of other men around . . . in the way they moved and the way their voices sounded—the tightening you felt in yourself."[18]

Later in the evening of June 5, Eisenhower began to make trips up and down the southern coast of England, visiting airborne troops. The late-summer light was dimming, and C-47 transport planes, as well as the gliders and their tow planes, were moving into line. The dusk began to settle. The men stood in small groups near their planes, talking in low voices and smoking their cigarettes. Invariably Ike would drive up to each of these groups, get out of the car, and walk toward them. According to eyewitnesses, he'd flash that "magnificent smile" and encourage the troops to gather around him.[19]

Perhaps the picture that best captures these visits, and Eisenhower's style, is the famous photo of Ike talking to the 101st Airborne paratroopers before their departure for France. What could have been running through his mind as he looked each young man in the eye, knowing full well that Leigh-Mallory had warned him that they might be senselessly slaughtered? Was the firmness of his jaw and the look of determination in his eyes indicative of a rousing pep talk he was giving these troops? It would not be until many decades later that we found out what the tallest of those paratroopers in the picture had to say. A survivor of the war, Wallace Strobel, later told us of this encounter.

"Where are you from," Ike asked the tall paratrooper—number 23. "From Michigan, Sir."

"How's the fly-fishing in Michigan?" General Eisenhower responded.

"It's great, Sir," Strobel replied.

When the picture was snapped, Eisenhower was making a hand gesture similar to that of a fly fisherman about to cast his line.

Eisenhower went on to say that he had been to Michigan to fish on several occasions. After a discussion of this for a few minutes, the supreme Allied commander asked: "Are you ready and have you been briefed properly?"

"Yes, Sir, we've been well briefed and we are ready."[20]

"Good," Eisenhower said, and moved on to the next small group of paratroopers.

Ike often added "Good luck" or "I know you are well prepared" as he left a gathering of men. But just as often some of the guys would shout: "Don't worry about us, Sir. We're going to whip Hitler!"

Years later, my father—a well-known military historian and his father's confidant—told *The Baltimore Sun*: "[Ike] was always trying to talk to troops about things back home, things that were familiar to them. If Ike found out that someone was from Kansas, he'd talk about cattle and farming, so it's natural that with Wally he discussed fishing."

I, too, asked my father about Ike's visits with the troops and his approach to those exchanges. "Your grandfather knew that these men were perfectly well aware that soon they would be in the middle of a desperate fight," he told me. "He wanted to remind them of what they had to live for."

Wally Strobel remembered looking out of his aircraft as the C-47 gained altitude on its way to German-occupied France. He could see the figure of the supreme Allied commander, still on the runway, as he watched the planes take off, headed for the epic battle to liberate Europe.

Strobel's eyes had not deceived him. That night Eisenhower stood on the tarmac until the last of the planes left. When they had gone, the general got back into his car, and his driver, Sgt. Leonard Dry, took him back to his headquarters. They arrived sometime after midnight—just before many of the men Eisenhower had seen were flying toward France, preparing to jump over the Normandy countryside to unknown fates.

Reflecting on those momentous days, Harry Butcher reported that Eisenhower surprised everyone with his apparent calm: "He was almost fatalistic about it." Someone had to make the decision and it was his responsibility to do it.[21]

Even so, Ike slept only a few hours that night. When Mickey Keogh went to his room at seven fifteen that morning of June 6, the supreme Allied commander was awake—and it was clear he had not slept. Beside his bed was an overflowing ashtray that had been empty when he had retired only four hours earlier. "His face was drawn and tired, and he had only half a smile. I asked him how he felt and he said 'Not too bad, Mickey.'"

Still, Ike was not in the mood to talk much that day and spent most of the time by himself, except for periodic reports of developments on the coast.[22]

As the news began to filter in, he was told that things looked better than expected for the paratroopers behind Utah Beach. One of the long-awaited reports came from Leigh-Mallory himself, who called to say that the airborne landings had been, by and large, a success. With a note of graciousness, the British air chief marshal apologized for adding to Ike's burdens in the previous days. According to army sources, the drop losses would turn out to be about 4 percent overall and about 10 percent on the first day of action. A beachhead had also been established along the five-beach front, after a dire fight on Omaha Beach in the early waves of landings.[23]

History tells us how this pivotal day ended. But as S. L. A. Marshall noted, the invasion's success rested with General Eisenhower's airborne decision: "The [paratrooper] night-drop proved to be the lynchpin of the whole operation, the decisive amendment to a COSSAC plan that without it would have been marked for defeat."[24]

The tireless efforts of the Allied countries working together to execute the revised plan, and the bravery of the men who carried out the orders, have become legendary. But D-day and the battle for Normandy would not be the end to the war. The Allies fought their way through France and central Western Europe with successes and setbacks, culminating in the Battle of the Bulge, the Germans' last-ditch effort to avert their inevitable defeat. With enormous sacrifice, eleven months after D-day the Allied forces won the unconditional surrender of Germany.

For Ike it had been three years of one-hundred-hour weeks and the unrelenting necessity to make far-reaching decisions, without adequate information. In so many instances these were the difference between life and death, success or failure. The scale of the sacrifice was unimaginable. Even though Eisenhower was a trained soldier, the carnage, the destruction, and the utter futility of this wastage must have left an imprint on his very soul.

Eight years later, in July 1952, some of the men who served under Eisenhower got a glimpse of what those critical decisions, and the loss of those boys, really meant to their supreme commander.

Early that month, Ike and Mamie attended the 82nd Airborne convention in Chicago. They accepted the invitation but, given the personal nature of the visit, asked for some privacy, recalled John R. "Tex" McCrary, one of the organizers of the event.

The luncheon was attended by, among others, a roomful of World War II paratrooper veterans. Seated at the table with the Eisenhowers was the only living Medal of Honor holder of the 82nd Airborne, former sergeant Leonard Funk. When the program began, the guests grew quiet and the room darkened, illuminated only by candlelight. According to those who attended, the candles on the podium made the Medal of Honor gleam in the dark.

The chaplain gave a twenty-minute eulogy about the bravery and the sacrifice of the 82nd and their acts of heroism on that fateful day. But it was Leonard Funk who brought Ike to tears.

With a candle in one hand, Funk stammered for a minute and then recovered his calm. Clarence Adamy, AMVETS national service director, who was in the room that day, recalled that Funk's remarks were "a brilliant expression of faith in the general." Funk told the gathering that General Eisenhower had had to decide whether or not to drop airborne forces behind the beaches on June 6. If he didn't "neutralize" the area the oncoming American troops might fail to land, thereby jeopardizing the whole invasion. "It was a terrible decision for a man to make," Funk concluded. "Ike not only made it, but had the courage to come personally to face the men he was sending to almost certain death."[25]

As Ike listened to this Congressional Medal of Honor recipient speak, his emotions rose and his eyes welled up, as "unashamed" tears fell down his cheeks. He covered them completely with his large hands, spread widely over his handkerchief.

Then Ike got up, stood "eye to eye" with Funk, and saluted the former sergeant. He turned to the podium, his eyes still glistening. "Eisenhower spoke for fifteen minutes," McCrary recalled, "with the clarity of his Guildhall Address—a speech about duty, honor, country—and our comrades in arms. At the end, [he got] the most eloquent applause—absolute silence for about 30 pin-drop seconds and then everyone on their feet"—followed by an overwhelming ovation.[26]

In 1952 the "unused communiqué" had not yet become widely known. Ike had not been looking to be anyone's hero when he wrote that note assuming full personal responsibility for the D-day decision. Personal accountability was what he demanded of himself. Nor did he expect such accolades from his GIs for his command during that critical time. He knew simply that the men he was facing that day at lunch were the ones who had survived—while so many others had perished.

Ike's note, written privately in the early hours of June 5, 1944, just after he'd made the fateful decision to launch the largest combined military operation in history, signified a truth—to self. Should things go badly, he would be the man—very rightly—to bear the full burden of a historic defeat.

The Eisenhower family. Back row: left to right, Arthur, Edgar, Dwight, Roy, Earl, Milton; front row: David and Ida. Abilene, Kansas, June 1926.

2

INNER STRUGGLES

Unlike today, when people tailor even their most intimate moments for consumption on social media, Eisenhower believed that the task of overcoming any challenge must be a personal matter—a burden to be borne alone. While he never suggested to family members or close associates that they should address their own difficulties and challenges in his way, Eisenhower himself chose such an approach for personal as well as professional reasons. Coming to terms with one's internal storms and contradictions required a form of privacy that would enable him to keep his relationships straightforward and uncomplicated. America's commentators who assumed that Ike was just a "lucky guy" misread his attempt and significant success in gaining mastery over himself. In 1999 the late George W. S.

Trow, a longtime writer for *The New Yorker*, offered an example of that view:

> There can rarely have been a man who cut with such effortless ease through the history of his time. It is hard to think of a situation in which Dwight Eisenhower wasn't lucky—so lucky he's become kind of invisible. He was like water. He flowed so easily within the events he dominated that he became indistinguishable from them. And like some natural element, he had no natural heirs, and established no school. His school, of course, was the sequence of his own life, and his ability to walk from sphere to sphere staying, one thinks, pretty much the same, and yet subtly changing. . . . He'd walked through a charnel house with perfect composure.[1]

Trow's theory is that while Ike, in terms of prestige, popularity, and sheer power stood above all others during and after the war—in the 1950s—his poise did not speak to "much suffering about him." Trow saw no signs of struggle, no valiant effort to overcome something desperately painful, no evidence of self-doubt. He asserted that this period of history, and Eisenhower's place in it, afforded him unimaginable power.

Like many other commentators at the time, Trow never understood what was behind Eisenhower's apparent success at making public life look so effortless. What was missing to many of America's intellectuals was the recognition that Eisenhower's greatest value as a leader was that he overcame his struggles and also heart-numbing pain—in private. His deepest instincts told him that these must be personal matters, informed by the deepest parts of one's inner self. It was up to him, he believed, to keep his own counsel. This he did during the war and the presidency—and even after the death of his first child. Ike and Mamie's three-year-old son, Doud Dwight (nicknamed Ikky), died of scarlet fever just after New Year's Day 1921. Ike later called this loss the "the greatest disappointment and disaster of my life."[2]

In 1952 Ike once wrote Mamie's mother with a version of this very notion of personal introspection: "If I have one instinctive passion in my dealings with others, it is the right of every individual to his own privacy in heart and mind. Humans are more emotional and sentimental beings than they are logical and intellectual. When, therefore, they are shocked or hurt in their deepest selves, others should . . . as I see it stand by but refrain from probing, advising or even—in a verbal sense—sympathizing."[3]

At the same time as he sought such privacy in his inner deliberations, he disdained whiners and perennial pessimists, as well as those who indulged in showmanship, publicity seeking, bragging, and any other public displays of this kind—at home we often used the term "show ponies." Sometimes he would assess a subordinate's efficiency with warnings if the man had a tendency to keep track of privileges or had a propensity to preen or look for credit. Entitlement was not an attitude that Dwight Eisenhower could countenance.

When his was fast becoming a household name, Eisenhower advised Harry Butcher and others at Allied headquarters to get the newsmen to write about someone else, despite endless requests for interviews with the general. Ike complained to Mamie once that he did not want his name associated with being a publicity seeker: "We have one of those in the army and that's more than enough."[4]

To Eisenhower, drawing attention to oneself was not evidence of personal confidence or strength—quite the reverse. His strength came from balance, and such psychological equilibrium required the melding of humility, determination, and human empathy. At the same time, he thought through these personal matters alone without, to any degree, seeking the emotional counsel of family or friends.

However, if it was hard to read Eisenhower's inner thoughts, he outwardly demonstrated his inner drive. He believed passionately in the necessity for preparation. On this point former U.S. ambassador Lawrence Taylor once aptly observed to me: "Eisenhower prepared himself for leadership even though he didn't know if his time would ever come."

Ike vowed in his early years to make each of his commanding officers regret his departure for his next assignment. A determination to focus on and succeed at even the most mundane tasks stood him in good stead when World War II began. Eisenhower's knowledge of tanks—he commanded a tank corps training unit in Gettysburg, Pennsylvania, during World War I—and then his intimate familiarity with the French terrain, gained while living in Paris in the 1920s, writing *A Guide to the American Battlefields of France*—gave him invaluable experience. This was ironic when one considers that both of those jobs were what Eisenhower's peers regarded as secondary assignments. Nevertheless, Ike put his best self into succeeding at the tasks. He was awarded the Army Distinguished Service Medal for his outstanding work at Gettysburg. He was just thirty years old.

Ike was highly competitive, but he was driven to be better—for himself as much as for any cause. Even in leisure sports, he played against himself. As my brother, David, later recalled, Ike's "worst rounds of golf were often his most serene, his best rounds the most agitated." His fury, however, was always directed at himself.

"One afternoon he shocked [our] mother, Barbara, for eighteen holes with unpredictable and terrifying outbursts of wrath, agony, and self-reproach. In the car returning to the residence, he sat studying the scorecard, tabulating the numbers and rechecking. 'Barbie,' he beamed, 'this was the best round I've shot in over six months.'"[5]

Much has been written about Ike's formative years. But no account of it is more powerful than Ike's own rendering of it in his memoir, *At Ease: Stories I Tell to Friends*. Ike's skill as a writer makes his Huck Finn childhood come alive; with stories of playground fistfights, poker games around campfires, and plenty of sibling mischief. The third son of seven boys, six of whom lived into adulthood, Ike was a competitive kid. He was also an intellectually curious student, whose class yearbook predicted that he would one day become a renowned history teacher at Yale. His interest in history was so intense that his mother had to lock some of his books in a closet, so he would concentrate on his immediate responsibilities.

It is ironic that after World War II, when Eisenhower was appointed president of Columbia University, there was sniping from the academic community that a general had been selected as their president. Even though Ike may have been the successful supreme commander of the Western Alliance in the European theater of World War II, academics then (as now) were wary of the military and could not imagine him having any intellectual underpinnings.

Harry Carman, dean of Columbia College at the time, recalled one history department annual dinner. He invited the new university president, telling Eisenhower that he did not have to give a speech—he could just observe the others, or join in the informal "chat." The conversation at one point that evening turned to a question posed among the professors: Why hadn't the Allies attacked the soft underbelly of Europe, rather than attack through Italy?

"We suddenly heard a voice saying, 'soft underbelly of Europe?' Southern Europe is a mass of mountains and impenetrable passes and valleys," Eisenhower said. "And he began with Philip of Macedonia and without missing a word he gave us a history of warfare in the Balkans. It was very impressive," Carman recalled. "And we couldn't restrain ourselves. When he finally stopped talking we all clapped."[6]

If Ike missed his calling as a history professor, his older brother Edgar, the editors of the Abilene High School yearbook speculated, would one day be a two-term president of the United States.

Both boys were close in age, and both were highly competitive. In a small town like Abilene, they were intent on defending the reputation of those who lived on their side of town—the proverbial "wrong side of the tracks."

Two years older than Ike, Edgar was bigger and more dominating. However, once Ed recounted a fight Ike got into with Wes Merrifield from the north side of town: "To look at them together on the street you have thought that Wes would have killed him. But my brother could take a punch, and he could deliver one."

Edgar mused that in this Ike was like their father, David, a stubborn fighter. "He refused to go down easily."[7]

Somewhere, too, young Ike learned reflexively that when he was knocked down he must pick himself up and smile. This disarming, counterintuitive response required discipline—but proved in the coming decades to be a remarkable metaphor for the way he conducted his professional life.[8]

In the broadest sense, the keys to Dwight's upbringing can be put in simple terms: his family, his community, and the benefits of living in a country setting that fostered independence, self-discovery, and time to think.

The most important influences revolved around his family and the example set by his parents, especially his mother, Ida Stover Eisenhower. Their spirituality was informed by the teachings of the River Brethren community, which formed in parts of Pennsylvania in the eighteenth century, and who were thought to have split from association with the Mennonite and other Brethren groups. The Bible was read at home twice a day, and Ida often hosted Bible gatherings as part of her place in this community. But something else permeated their home—a sense of service to something bigger than themselves. This was not a casual motivational idea but fundamental to who they were as people.

Ike's mother, Ida, was, as I once termed her, "the wellspring of Ike's idealism." Ike had always had an idealistic streak, even as a boy. And as he matured and finally assumed supreme leadership, he never lost his drive to forge a lasting, sustainable peace from the wreckage of the war—and never flagged in his belief that it was possible.

Ida herself was a woman of courage and hope. She left for the Plains after the early deaths of her parents to attend Lane, a Brethren college in Lecompton, Kansas. There she met David Jacob Eisenhower, and they were eventually married in the college chapel. Both were of modest means, but they had those deep religious bonds in common, as well as a strong work ethic. They devoted themselves to their faith in God, to their family and community—and to the importance of continuing education. While David had two serious business setbacks as a young man—hoping to make his own way outside the close-knit community—he never lost his abiding interest in history, government, and human affairs.

Many years ago I attended the reopening of the newly renovated Carnegie Library in Abilene, Kansas. That day they showed the original visitors' book that was signed by those who had attended the library's first opening in 1907. Next to the townspeople's names, the guest roster encouraged signers to indicate what book they were currently reading. David Jacob Eisenhower, who was a simple engineer at the Belle Spring Creamery in town, noted that he was currently reading a book, *Uncle Sam's Secrets*, published in the late nineteenth century, which focused mainly on how our federal government works.

Ida was, no doubt, less concerned with how institutions in Washington functioned than on her growing brood of boys and her charitable works. The Eisenhower boys were an energetic bunch and in constant need of direction.

Years later, in looking back on his childhood, Ike would reveal an admiration, almost a reverence, for his mother's managerial skills and his father's role as chief disciplinarian—even though he probably met his father's stick more than his other brothers did.

Some scholars have suggested that David Eisenhower was a martinet—and even abusive at times. Perhaps such theories reflect our society's tendency to judge people based on today's values, rather than the ideas that prevailed at the time—in this case "Spare the rod, spoil the child." It was never suggested by any member of my family—including my grandfather or my father, who knew his grandparents well—that Ida and David Eisenhower were anything other than hardworking, God-fearing believers who deeply loved their children. If David was hard on the boys at times, and determined to teach them discipline, it is not surprising. The family motto was "Sink or Swim, Survive or Perish." That was life on the prairie in the early 1900s.

Ida was, as my father used to tell us, "the patron saint of the family." She was calm, gentle, and ready to teach—through showing and living—the qualities that would lead to harmony and cooperation. She was also an ardent pacifist, a choice she made for herself having been a child in the immediate aftermath of the Civil War. Even in her later years she retained memories of the devastation in the Shenandoah Valley, where she grew up.

As a kid it impressed me greatly when Granddad would tell my siblings and me that his mother would rotate her boys through a range of household chores, from washing clothes and cleaning the house, to doing the sewing and taking responsibility for some of the cooking and all the washing-up. She also quietly showed her boys what fairness meant. Of all his brothers, Ike may have been the most attentive to this lesson. At dinner, for instance, when it was time for the pie to be cut, Ida made sure that the boy whose task it was to cut the pie was always given the last slice.

With a gift for Christian empathy, Ida helped develop in Ike the capacity to see things not only from his own point of view but also from the perspective of others. General Goodpaster and I remarked on how often Ike would ask his associates (and even his grandchildren) to tell him how "it looks to the other guy." His insistence on evaluating the perspective of others may have been the result of rigorous training: Deception plans in military operations, for instance, cannot be successful without a robust analysis of how the enemy sees the situation. But I believe that Ike came to the military with the seeds of this skill already well and truly planted.

It was the differences in his parents' personalities that may have provided the "secret sauce" that produced six extraordinarily successful sons. When the news media started to write about Ike's origins, family members were often asked for interviews. In an exchange of letters with Edgar, Ike offered his own private assessment of their parents' approach. On June 30, 1953, he wrote: "So far as the discipline and conduct of the family was concerned, [Dad] was, of course, the czar—I think mother was the one who talked more of standards, aspirations and opportunities. Dad believed more, I think, in sheer training and discipline. He was not one to be trifled with, unless you were prepared to take the consequences."[9]

These two strong-willed people contributed significantly to Ike's emotional intelligence, but the composition of his family might have also been crucial. Being third among these six sons gave Ike some freewheeling independence and a perch from which to watch his other brothers. They were athletic, competitive, and highly charged.[10]

Ida and David also conveyed to Ike and his brothers a respect for the dignity of a man's work, even the most humble among us. Again, Ike may have been the quickest learner. His older brother Edgar, for instance, was humiliated and embarrassed by one of the boys' chores—to sell their garden-grown vegetables door-to-door, across the railroad tracks in the wealthy part of Abilene. Ike had no such qualms. He enjoyed the satisfaction that came from his labor. He kept that feeling his entire life. He had empathy for the ordinary man's lot in life, which was evident especially by the way he connected with his GIs.

During the war Mickey McKeogh and Harry Butcher both commented on how adamant Ike was about the treatment of his fighting men. For example, the supreme Allied commander made it clear that GIs should get all the latest movies before they came to him. Mickey also remarked on Ike's great interest in what the GIs ate.

On the inspection visits Ike made throughout the war, he often went out of his way to go to the canteens and to visit hospitals. While there, he would make a thorough assessment of the kitchens he encountered, giving close examination to the pots and pans and the quality of the food.[11] As Mickey later explained, General Eisenhower saw food and morale as being tightly connected.

One amusing example of this food issue occurred during this period. Eisenhower had a stateside visitor who wanted to stop by to say hello. It was Bing Crosby. When Crosby asked what he missed about the food, Eisenhower replied, "Hominy grits." To headquarters' astonishment, a week later countless boxes of hominy grits inundated their facilities—"tons of it" in the words of an astonished mail carrier. Ike immediately sent the grits to the GI mess hall. But given the overwhelmed facilities, he was heard to say that he would never again tell a radio personality anything personal of this sort. Apparently Crosby had mentioned that Eisenhower missed hominy grits on his show and America responded![12]

Even after the war, people from all walks of life saw his respect for the working man. When Ike retired from the army after more than thirty years and became president of Columbia University in 1948, the campus soon saw him demonstrate this.

Patrick Kennedy, one of the gardeners on the maintenance staff at Columbia, remembered that when Eisenhower took over as president of the university, he convened an unprecedented gathering of the campus workers. Still in their work clothes, they assembled at Low Library. Kennedy recalled that Ike told them: "Each individual has a job to do, and . . . one job depends on the next."

Kennedy recounted that Ike flashed that "wonderful grin of

his" and then said: "Now if you fellows ever meet me around the campus, don't ignore me just because I come from the sticks"—an obvious reference for these New Yorkers to his prairie hometown upbringing.

Kennedy was proud of the fact that the president of the university had specifically asked these modest workers to call him "Ike."[13]

Throughout the war and even into his presidency, Eisenhower was a regular visitor to Abilene, Kansas—seeing old friends and checking in with the locals, with appreciation and a genuine interest in the recent developments in town. It is astonishing that throughout his life he continued to reply to the newsy letters of his high school buddies, as well as the townspeople who thought of him as their own.

Perhaps it was Ike's place in the family that afforded him this capacity to emotionally factor in and assimilate the needs of others. Or perhaps the compassion his mother showed others—and also him—had had a lasting impact.

Ida, however, was always thoughtful and perfectly correct in the even-handed way she thought of her boys. After the war, when a newspaperman asked her if she was proud of her son, she replied: "Which one?"

As for Ike? She said on more than one occasion: "Of all of my sons, Dwight had the most to learn." Perhaps it was not clear that her third son had assimilated his parents' lessons, but time would show that he had absorbed a lot. The biggest challenge young Ike faced was in controlling his outsize personality and the fearsome temper that came with it. He was an emotional youngster, with an intense sensitivity to injustice. His diaries reveal a passionate nature and deeply held feelings.

One of the incidents in Ike's youth that he later said had a lasting impact on him revolved around Halloween. When he was in elementary school, his two older brothers were given permission to go out and trick-or-treat. Ike wanted desperately to go, but was denied permission by his parents. In a spectacular display of what we would today call a "meltdown," Ike went into a rage—and essentially blacked out as he bloodied his fists by repeatedly hitting them against a tree. His parents, rightly concerned, took measures. His father probably gave Ike's backside a few strokes of a hickory stick, and he was sent to his room—the one he shared with the two brothers who were out on the town.

As Ike lay in bed sobbing pitifully, his mother came upstairs and sat quietly for a few minutes, waiting for him to settle down. When his tears had turned to occasional whimpers, Ida talked to him in a gentle but firm way. Did he know that his behavior had hurt only himself?

After a few quiet words she ended with a paraphrase from the Bible: "He who conquereth his soul is greater than he who taketh a city."[14]

As his mother bandaged his hands, she continued to talk to her son, again calmly urging him to understand that in his anger he had hurt only himself; that the object of his anger (in this case his brothers) probably didn't even know of his resentment.

Eisenhower later wrote that the conversation was "one of the most valuable moments of my life." He determined from that incident that he would learn how to forget resentment, and he vowed to himself to "avoid" allowing himself to hate anyone. If necessary he would simply put such people out of his mind.[15]

For Ike, conquering his own soul was no small undertaking. Even in adult life he would often have to check his temper, ultimately utilizing a range of tricks to avert blowing off steam. Yet if he had not learned how to take control of his inner space, nurturing it and caring for the complex feelings that often roiled in his head, if he had not learned to redirect his passion and the power it had over him, he would have never taken a city, let alone a continent.

To the outside world Dwight Eisenhower might have moved through his era "like water," as George Trow suggested, but it was only because he had been able to tame the inner storm that at times threatened to engulf him. Maybe he was a lucky man. But as with so many other people of great success, there was the alignment of favorable conditions with the luck he made for himself.

General Eisenhower visits the remains of a Nazi concentration camp near Gotha, Germany, April 12, 1945. (U.S. Army)

3

BEYOND ETHNIC KINSHIP

Some might think it ironic that a man of German extraction would be called upon to defeat his ancestors' homeland in the most devastating war in history. In contrast, during World War II one of our Allies, the Soviet Union, sent all its ethnic Germans into exile. Those farmers had been part of the same eighteenth-century migration that had brought Eisenhower's forbears to American shores. It was all part of the efforts by William Penn and Catherine the Great to entice hardworking German farmers to migrate to their respective countries. In this twentieth-century war, the Soviets surmised that their ethnic Germans could not be trusted. The U.S. military, on the other hand, had many distinguished leaders of German origin—and those who descended from them fought for the United States, in the devoted service of an American identity and a set of values that were stronger and more enduring than any near or distant kinship.

The Eisenhowers immigrated to the United States in 1741, but their deepest roots were in the Odenwald Mountains of Germany. Ike's earliest ancestors farmed land in the Palatinate, an individual state within the German realm. Between the Rhine, Main, Neckar, and Tauber Rivers, this region was also mined for iron ore. (In German *Eisenhauer*, the family's original spelling, means "iron hewer" or "iron artisan.")

A number of landmarks survive the earliest years of the Eisenhauers' lives in Germany. An Eisenhauer tomb of Ike's direct ancestor from the 1500s can still be seen, as well as the stone remains of the farm where the family lived. In 1617—perhaps driven off the land—they left the Odenwald Mountains and went into the valley to Eiterbach to seek other work. It was there in 1691 that Hans Nikolaus was born, the head of Ike's branch of the Eisenhauer family.

In this context it is worth remembering that during that era the Palatinate was a lawless, dangerous place. From 1685 until 1733, the region was under siege by French king Louis XIV, who declared war on Germany and overran the area after Elector Charles of the Palatinate died in 1685. Villages were burned, property was pillaged, and the local population was threatened by roving gangs in the towns, and wolves and dislocated wildlife in the countryside. High taxes burdened the livelihood of everyone, and murder was commonplace.

Perhaps because of those conditions Hans Nikolaus's family eventually moved to Karlsbrunn, another mining region in the Saarland. From there the Eisenhauers, including Hans Peter, Hans Nikolaus's son and Ike's direct ancestor, sailed for America, via the Dutch port of Rotterdam in 1741.

The family, along with other members of the Palatinate community, settled in Lancaster County in the mid-1800s, eventually moving to Elizabethville, Dauphin County, Pennsylvania, not far from Harrisburg. In his lifetime Hans Peter had three wives and eventually produced seventeen children. It was his youngest son who led the great River Brethren migration to Kansas in the 1870s, taking his children, among them Ike's father. The community was not an insignificant group. Several hundred people, with fifteen railcars of furniture, farming equipment, and personal possessions, boarded the train for a new life on the Plains. With half a million dollars between them—a king's ransom in today's dollars—the community would purchase virgin land from the Kansas Pacific Railroad and establish farms on the outskirts of Abilene.[1]

The Brethren community was certain to have had a moral impact on the notoriously corrupt cowtown, just as the power of the community was to leave an indelible imprint on its sons and daughters. They were simple, modest people with an abhorrence for alcohol, tobacco, and dancing. They were also deeply committed to brotherhood, sacrifice for their neighbors, and a rejection of war. It is no wonder given this that Ike's own parents were distraught and saddened when he chose to attend West Point so that he could get a free education. There his ideals were given form and purpose: It was at West Point that he determined that his deepest desire was to serve his country.

Ike was clearly conscious of his Germanic roots. Both his father and his mother's sides of the family were from German-speaking lands, and within the Brethren community he lived among many who still spoke German, including the elders of his own family—a language his father, David, however, eschewed. And in the state of Kansas, with a large percentage of farmers of German descent, much of the food and many of the customs still harked back to their ancestral roots in the old country.

As late as 1928, Ike commented on his German heritage. The kinship he had felt as a kid was given voice, most strikingly, the summer he and Mamie and their friends Bill and Helen Gruber took a car trip through Europe just after he had completed *A Guide to the American Battlefields of France* for Gen. John J. "Black Jack" Pershing. The route that had taken them through the German Alps was breathtaking in its beauty. Ike, the diary keeper for this leg of the trip, wrote: "We seemed to experience very definite exhilaration upon leaving Belgium and entering the Fatherland. Maybe that's because both Bill and I have our family roots in this country as our names testify."[2]

After the trip through the Rhine Valley, they stopped for tea at the landmark castle in Heidelberg. And then their Buick headed for the Black Forest. Ike and Mamie probably did not know that Ike's ancestral farm was within easy distance of Heidelberg. Nor could they have imagined that little more than ten years later, the war would break out and Ike would be given the command to crush the German enemy.

At the end of the tour Ike and Mamie returned to Washington. He would become an aide to Chief of Staff of the Army Gen. Douglas MacArthur, a position that eventually led to an assignment in the Philippines as the general's right-hand man.

Despite the posting in Asia, Ike stayed abreast of the situation in Europe, where events were unfolding in an alarming way. Were those the developments that Ike's mentor, Gen. Fox Conner, had predicted? Political events in Germany, in particular, were moving quickly. Concerns about the rise of fascism and repression reached them even as far away as the Philippines.

At the time Ike knew well the Frieder brothers, two men who owned and operated a cigar/tobacco business in the United States. The Frieders spent considerable time in the Philippines and were regulars at the Manila Hotel, where card games were the norm on hot, humid afternoons. Many of Manila's expats played in that afternoon game, and sometimes the president of the Philippines himself, Manuel Quezon, would join them.

In 1934 into 1935, the conversations at the card table took on some urgency, as discussions regularly turned to the persecution of the Jews in Europe. Alex Frieder and his brothers—along with Ike—used these occasions to persuade Quezon to allow eventually as many as two thousand Jews to immigrate to the Philippines. History might well have told a very different story if Dwight Eisenhower had accepted the group's lucrative offer to leave the army and stay in Manila to manage that refugee effort. But Ike stood firm in his conviction that the place he could best serve his country was as an army officer. He felt certain that the United States was moving toward war.

By 1940, a year after the Eisenhowers' return to the United States, the country was well and truly preparing for war—even if politically it still retained a posture of rigid neutrality. Ike, as chief of staff of Lt. Gen. Walter Krueger's Third Army, played the winning role in the Louisiana Maneuvers throughout 1940–41, a four-hundred-thousand-person-strong war game staged in that southern state. Assembled to test doctrine, military leadership, and training logistics, Eisenhower's success as the architect of victory brought him to the attention of Army Chief of Staff George C. Marshall, and won him his first star.

Just after Pearl Harbor on December 7, 1941, Ike was called to Washington to work in the war plans division of the War Department. Marshall watched Dwight Eisenhower and gave him increasing responsibility to test his capabilities as a leader. Marshall was looking for subordinates who could assume responsibility and execute a plan without constant referrals back to headquarters. In other words, he needed to know to whom he could delegate responsibility.

Eisenhower was tapped in the early days to work on the U.S. response in the Far East. Once he dispatched an entire division (fifteen to twenty thousand men) to Australia without asking Marshall's permission. Rather than take offense at this, Marshall determined that Ike was exactly the kind of man he was looking for: someone who could make decisions and live with the consequences.

In June 1942, Eisenhower was sent to serve as commander of the American forces in the European theater—eventually being given commanding responsibility in the North African and Sicily campaigns, culminating in his appointment in 1943 as supreme Allied commander of Operation Overlord that coming June.

The execution of the war was what Eisenhower and others referred to as "the emergency." The Nazis were our enemies, and from the outset Eisenhower took a principled position with respect to how he, and we, should view them.

While Eisenhower was in command in North Africa, a U.S. general asked Ike for permission to have a private dinner with some captured German generals, to discuss strategy and other past developments. Ike would not even consider it.

"I don't think war is a game," he told a colleague and friend years later on remembering the incident. "I don't belong to the school that believes the generals can be above the mess, and act as if they belonged to some superior society. I never spoke to a German general [during the war], except to Jodl and that was to order him to my office to be sure he understood the terms of surrender."[3]

The long war, which had strained every ounce of emotional and physical energy, must have made the herculean fight to defeat Nazi Germany even harder in the last days of the conflict. Millions had perished and many of the continent's city lay in ruins. In desperation, the enemy was taking even more extreme measures. Eisenhower was impatient and angered by the Nazis' brutal refusal to capitulate and to observe the conventions of war.

On December 17, 1944, during the Battle of the Bulge, the Germans' last offensive of the war, the so-called Malmédy Massacre occurred. There German SS troops used machine guns and pistols to mow down 150 American prisoners of war. This was not the only crime this battle group had committed. According to official U.S. Army history, by December 20 SS Standartenfuhrer Joachim Peiper's command had killed three hundred American unarmed prisoners of war, including medics, as well as at least one hundred unarmed Belgians. In his book *The Bitter Woods*, my father wrote that "The Malmédy Massacre was like electric shock through the US commands."[4]

By the evening of the massacre, the inspector general of the First Army "was aware of the atrocity . . . by late evening of the seventeenth the word that the enemy was killing prisoners had spread throughout the American divisions on the front. Surrendering to the Americans was now a riskier business for any German, and for SS men in particular."[5]

Sgt. Mickey McKeogh noticed the effect that this massacre had on everyone, including the supreme Allied commander. "It made everyone bitter," Mickey wrote. "It must have made people at home bitter . . . it made the General more bitter, it seemed to me, than it did anyone else."[6]

In early April, Eisenhower went to Gen. Omar Bradley's headquarters in Wiesbaden, and from there they went to Patton's headquarters. Mickey, who was with him, remembered the beauty of the countryside and the peacefulness of this area of Germany. Perhaps thinking back to that trip across the alps in 1928, Eisenhower looked out the window while they were en route and shook his head, telling Mickey: "'It [is] hard to understand why, with a country [this] beautiful . . . the Germans didn't stay in it. In their own yards.' . . . He shook his head, as if he were puzzled."

He shook his head again and added, "They could have stayed in their beautiful country and they didn't. They had gone out and asked for trouble . . ." Eisenhower looked at the countryside and added grimly, "[And] they're sure getting it."[7]

On April 12, 1945, after a series of conferences, Eisenhower, Bradley, and Patton took a side trip into the Third Army sector. American troops were advancing without German resistance. In fact, it was apparent that the enemy, on hearing the guns in the distance, abandoned their posts while trying to cover their tracks. Small villages seemed deserted, their windows boarded up and their inhabitants were in hiding for fear of reprisals. "The Nazis' 'orgy of murder' changed to a desperate struggle to destroy the evidence," wrote the historian Michael Korda.[8]

The first of their stops was at an old salt mine, Merkers, near Gotha, discovered a few days earlier. They went down in an elevator, two thousand feet deep, to find hidden crates of art treasures and personal effects the Nazis had stolen from museums and homes across the European continent. In addition to this unforgettable sight, the dingy tunnels and makeshift storage rooms also contained what was thought to be the last gold reserves of the Nazi regime, an estimated $250 million—in twenty-five-pound gold bars. U.S. troops were already at work inventorying the vast treasure trove, destined for safekeeping in Frankfurt.[9]

After this tour the generals were escorted to a sub-camp of Buchenwald, Ordruf, near Gotha, an outpost where political prisoners and Jews had been subject to forced labor, indiscriminate murder, and systemized killing. Ordruf was one of many camps that were being discovered as Allied forces continued their advance across Germany. In the next couple of days other, larger camps would be discovered. As the liberation of occupied territories was under way on both the eastern and western fronts, stories had begun to run rampant about the Nazi atrocities.

Though the generals had heard about such places, the visit to Ordruf was to have a profound effect on everyone who visited the camp that day, and this experience would have lasting impact on our understanding of the Holocaust.

Eisenhower was unprepared for both the sights and the smells of these hellholes. Even miles outside the camp, the stench of rotting flesh was overpowering. As they entered, they saw corpses piled up like cords of wood, hastily dug trenches, and emaciated survivors who looked like walking cadavers. Not long after entering the camp, the generals and their retinue of Signal Corps men and newspaper reporters encountered a couple of survivors who were eager to brief the camp's visitors. Eisenhower toured "every nook and cranny" of the facility, even though some members of the "visiting party" were unable to go through the "ordeal." He looked in disbelief at the various indescribable ways the Germans had made use of and then discarded these human beings.[10]

McKeogh was shocked by the look on Eisenhower's face when he returned to Patton's headquarters that evening: "The Boss's face was black when they came back. He said he had never seen anything equal to what they had seen that day; that no punishment was too great for a people who could do things like that. . . . He looked sick when he talked about them—and very angry."[11]

From Patton's headquarters, Eisenhower sent a message to General Marshall about the experience. He wrote:

> The things I saw there beggar description. While I was touring the camp I encountered three men who had been inmates and by one ruse or another had made their escape. I interviewed them through an interpreter. The visual evidence and the verbal testimony of starvation, cruelty and bestiality were so overpowering as to leave me a bit sick.

> In one room, where they were piled up, there were twenty or thirty naked men, killed by starvation. George Patton would not even enter. He said he would get sick if he did so. I made the visit deliberately, in order to be in a position to give *firsthand* evidence of these things if ever, in the future, there develops a tendency to charge these allegations merely to "propaganda."[12]

At the same time Eisenhower ordered anyone not engaged on the front line to go to the camps and, wherever possible, chronicle what they saw. My father, John, was with a unit in Europe by this point, and he was sent—along with others from his group—to Buchenwald to bear witness to the atrocities. There were twenty thousand survivors of the camp, one thousand of whom were boys under the age of fourteen. The liberators noted that the Nazis had made "souvenirs" of the tattooed skin of their victims. And those not sent to the "strangulation room" had been forced to wait their turns in unheated barracks, with less than one blanket per person—as typhus and tuberculosis raged. The Germans were disposing of bodies at a rate of four hundred per day during a ten-hour day—"a striking example of 'German industrial efficiency,'" an army report added.[13]

My father, an amateur photographer, chronicled these horrific scenes, showing the haunting results repeatedly over the years to my siblings and me, and later to our children and grandchildren.

Writing to Marshall again, Eisenhower requested that members of Congress and influential newsmen be dispatched to Germany to see these atrocities for themselves. He remarked on the unexpected scope of the camps and what he called the "indescribable horror" that prevailed. "I assure you," he added, "that whatever has been printed on them to date has been an understatement."[14]

That same week Ike also personally sent Winston Churchill photos from Ordruf: "I think they will tell their own story," he wrote in his short cover note. The British, too, took advantage of the supreme Allied commander's desire to open the camps to influential people. Churchill responded to Eisenhower's note on

April 21 with an interest in sending a parliamentary delegation, or "an Atrocity Inspection Team" as he termed it. More than one group was able to make visits before the last sprint to victory two and a half weeks later.[15]

Eisenhower's experience of his visit to Ordruf never left him, nor could he find the right words to convey what he had seen: "I have never been able to describe my emotional reactions when I first came face to face with indisputable evidence of Nazi brutality and ruthless disregard of every shred of decency," he wrote in his memoir *Crusade in Europe*. "I had known about it only generally or through secondary sources. I am certain, however, that I have never at any other time experienced an equal sense of shock."[16]

According to Third Army reports, the people of Gotha denied any knowledge of what had occurred at the camp, not far from their town. When this was reported to Eisenhower he ordered that the townspeople be marched through the camp at the point of a bayonet and be made to bury the camp's dead. This order stood for other villages as well.

After the townspeople had returned to their homes, the mayor of Gotha and his wife hanged themselves.

Camps were being located and identified almost daily in the last weeks of the war, and Ike persisted in his policy. On April 18 he wrote a letter of encouragement to George Patton: "Thank you a lot for informing me about the new camp you found near Weimar. I suggest that every visitor coming into that region should be urged to see the place if it is at all possible to arrange trips for them."[17]

The war was coming to an end, and the supreme commander's schedule was packed tight with conferences and a myriad of issues that demanded decisions. The SHAEF team was tired—but eager for the last push that would bring the cataclysm to an end. Gen. Walter Bedell Smith was dispatched to carry out the negotiations with Gen. Alfred Jodl, chief of staff of the German army, and Adm. Hans-Georg von Friedeburg of the German navy, to press them for an unconditional surrender. The Germans still had to be persuaded that it was all over and that the Western and Eastern

Allies had Nazi Germany's neck in a noose. During the negotiations with Friedeburg, Smith kept a map specifically positioned nearby so that the admiral could see it out of the corner of his eye.

The map showed troop placements and other notations of future movement. While not accurate (intentionally), the map was designed to give the impression that the Western and Eastern Allies already were poised for the total annihilation of the German forces. Smith noted that Friedeburg's eyes darted toward the map several times.[18]

"Finally I handed it to him," General Smith recalled. "'Obviously,' I said, 'you do not entirely realize the hopelessness of the German position.'"

On May 6 Jodl arrived at SHAEF headquarters in Reims. After meeting with Friedeburg for a while, Jodl informed Smith that he wanted to surrender only to the Western Allies, but not to the Russians.

General Eisenhower instructed Smith to press for a surrender on both the western and eastern fronts. He would accept nothing else. Eisenhower also made it clear that if the Nazis did not surrender in forty-eight hours, the Allied front would be sealed and no more Germans would be permitted to surrender to the Western Allies.

Jodl communicated with the new German government, conveying that it was over.

The surrender took place in the early hours of May 7. Hitler was dead, and the German army had disbanded and was scattering in all directions. Jodl appealed to the Allies' sympathy for the hardships to which the German people had been subjected: "I can only express my hope that the victors will treat them with generosity," he said.

There was silence on the Allied side.

Jodl sat down, a defeated man, in the somber acknowledgment that: "The most terrible war in human history had finally come to an end."[19]

Walter Bedell Smith signed the surrender document in Eisenhower's place. "General Eisenhower had not wished to be present at the surrender and he had assigned me the responsibility of representing him. But he wanted to say a brief, stern word to those representatives of the tyranny against which his great crusade was directed."

Smith then took the Germans upstairs to Eisenhower's office. He recalled that the meeting lasted for not much more than a minute. A stony Eisenhower asked Jodl if he understood completely the meaning of the documents he had signed. Then he told the Germans that he would hold them officially and personally responsible if the terms of the surrender were violated.

"When Jodl replied that he understood, General Eisenhower said curtly, 'That's all.'" The Germans were immediately ushered out of the room.

Wordsmiths at SHAEF headquarters put their pens to paper to come up with the wording for the victory dispatch that would be sent to announce the end of the war in Europe. These flowery missives were shown to the supreme Allied commander for his comments and additions. He looked them over and rejected them all. Instead he wrote the Combined Chiefs of Staff: "The mission of this Allied Force was fulfilled at 0241, local time, May 7th, 1945."[20]

There were difficulties in resolving the German surrender on the eastern front, thus making a coordinated announcement of victory with the Soviet Union impossible. Sporadic fighting was still being reported in Czechoslovakia.

From the north German town of Flensburg, the seat of the last Nazi government, those who had been part of that government complained that not all German units were communicating with them, but the Allies saw this as a cover for continuing German resistance. The next day Eisenhower accused Flensburg of failing to meet the terms of the Reims surrender on the agreed timeline. Eisenhower ordered that Adm. Karl Dönitz, Field Marshal Wilhelm Keitel, and Gen. Alfred Jodl be arrested immediately.

In the last hours more than a million German soldiers scrambled to control their own fates. Some tried to cross the lines to be captured by the Americans; others left for Austria. But 8,500 soldiers surrendered to the Russians. The Americans handed over those they'd caught in the Russian zone—nearly two hundred thousand troops.

It was not until May 11, 1945, that all was quiet—and the war, which had ruined Europe and consumed well more than thirty million lives, was finally over.

After victory had been announced on May 8, letters from all over the world began to pour into Ike's SHAEF headquarters—from strangers and friends alike. Among them was a June 1 letter from Ike's old friend from the Philippine days, Alexander Frieder.

"I knew you could do it!" Frieder began his letter. "Little did you and I think, when we were back in Manila, that your moment would come in such a dramatic manner."

Frieder went on to say that from his perspective the "after-work" in Europe was likely to be of almost equal importance to the campaign to defeat the Nazis. While Frieder acknowledged the indispensable importance of Eisenhower's visit to Ordruf and the consequent chronicling of the Nazi atrocities, the key part of his letter rested with his deepest concern. On this Frieder gave his old friend some unsolicited advice:

> I hope you don't fall prey to the clamor, that most certainly will arise from various and sundry sources, of sentimentalists, propagandists, pacifists and the like who will try to paint a picture of the guiltlessness of the German people, and use the false praise and apparent friendliness of the German people toward their conquerors and thereby soften in your whole German rehabilitation program. Twice in a generation those bastards upset the world with their warped mentality and barbarous ideology.[21]

In Ike's reply he thanked Frieder for his letter on the victory in the European theater: "You can well imagine my relief," he wrote, "that the fighting and killing are no longer parts of our problems." He went on to say: "Please don't ever get worried about my falling prey to the blandishment of the defeated German. I am well acquainted with their history and I most certainly hope that the world will not again make the same mistake with respect to them, that it did twenty-five years ago."[22]

While Eisenhower's response was vague on the one hand, one could well read into this note his already determined path—to assure that the victims would not be the ones inadvertently punished in the postwar period. He was determined that war criminals would be held accountable for the atrocities, and that over time the German people would know what they had done to others and also to themselves. Through this reckoning Eisenhower was committed to assuring that the Germans would never do it again.

In June, Ike returned to Washington for consultations and to attend a number of celebrations. On June 18 he gave a press conference at the Pentagon. The press gathering was an extensive session that covered a range of issues, from the contributions of the American serviceman and the future of SHAEF to the resettlement of displaced persons.

The press asked Ike what he thought about all the publicity on the German atrocities: "Do you think the publication of them is going to be very useful?"

"I think I was largely responsible for this," Eisenhower replied. "When I found the first camp like that I think I was never so angry in my life. . . . You could go to their burial site and see horrors I would really not want to begin to describe. I think people need to know about such things, it explains something about my attitude to the German war criminal. I believe he must be punished and I will hold out for that forever. I think [the coverage of the atrocities] did well. I think the people at home ought to know what they are fighting for and what kind of a person they are fighting. Yes, it did good."

Later in the conference Eisenhower expressed little regard for high-ranking German officers who denied knowledge of the camps and the atrocities. "If they didn't know," he said, "they deliberately closed their eyes to it all. As far as I am concerned those people are just as guilty as [the people who knew]."

When asked about what the German population as a whole knew, Eisenhower was unable to say. "But I let them know about [the atrocities] because I made them go out and give [the Holocaust victims] a decent burial. We made a film an hour long and we made many Germans look at it, and it is not pretty."[23]

The rest of Eisenhower's work in the postwar reorganization of Europe was as Frieder had predicted—as challenging as many trying periods during the war itself. The issues of displaced persons were complicated, and there were heartbreaking problems that demanded solutions. It was Eisenhower's decision, however, to resettle the Jewish populations first, even if it meant requisitioning German housing to provide them proper roofs over their heads. Scarce resources, logistical practicalities, and a determination to avoid any impression that the United States was adopting oppressive tactics in caring for the lives of millions of displaced Europeans would prove to be one of the most complicated postwar problems the Allies faced.

In November 1945, back in Washington again for consultations, Eisenhower fell ill with a respiratory infection. He would not return to Europe again in this capacity. That fall, he would take up a new position as chief of staff of the Army.

In the coming years Eisenhower would have to "process" the innumerable things he saw and felt during that terrible period: the unspeakable actions of the Nazi Germans; the destruction of so much of Western civilization's patrimony; and most important, the futile and unconscionable cost of war—the enormous loss of human life and all that represented. Tens of millions of people had been killed, and much of Europe lay in ruins.

No doubt Eisenhower also had to reconcile some fundamental questions for himself about good and evil. Surely there was nothing inherently evil about the German people themselves. He had come from that stock. But he was deeply disturbed by the human capacity for barbarism. The Germans had to know what had happened by their own hand and done in their names by a group of thugs who had come to power and very nearly destroyed their country as well as the continent of Europe. They had to be held accountable.

At the same time the war had shown him just how fragile human beings are, and far too often, just how weak. Complacency, fear, greed, desperation, and the pursuit of unbridled power can become drivers of amorality and twisted logic. Human emotions can inspire inhuman responses.

Accountability, renewal, and eventually reconciliation could be the only way forward.

Little more than six years later, in July 1951, Eisenhower was serving as the first supreme commander of NATO forces. All sights were set on the future. That summer he and Mamie, along with Mamie's mother, Elivera Doud, and a few friends, went to the army's rest spot near Garmisch, Germany. The villa they stayed in was run by a Bavarian named Wilhelm Gruendl. Gruendl and Eisenhower, over the course of nearly eleven days, had many chances to talk and to build a rapport.

One evening Gruendl was persuaded to sing and play some Bavarian music. Dressed in lederhosen, the traditional Bavarian costume, the hotelier made a striking impression, as he played the accordion and yodeled to the delight of the Eisenhowers.

The next morning Mamie led Gruendl out to the veranda, where Ike had set up his easel. Eisenhower, who had taken up painting as a form of relaxation, invited Gruendl to sit for a portrait. The former supreme Allied commander and future president of the United States painted the young Bavarian in his native costume, reminiscent of the previous evening's cultural odyssey.

Years later, after Eisenhower had been elected president, the *Stars and Stripes* did a story on the relationship that had developed between the two men: "What did you talk about while you were sitting for your portrait?" Gruendl was asked. He replied that they did not talk about politics at all. The general simply spoke of his German ancestors, Gruendl reported, and the origin of the Eisenhower family some centuries ago.[24]

Moved by Eisenhower's portrait of his father, Gruendl's son, Claus, later went on to establish an Eisenhower Museum near Garmisch, with Ike's likeness of Wilhelm as its centerpiece. Later

Claus purchased Dwight Eisenhower's first childhood home in Abilene, Kansas, going on to restore it and to serve as its steward.

Less than two years after that visit to Garmisch, Eisenhower was inaugurated as the thirty-fourth president of the United States. Like the Truman administration, the rebuilding of Germany and the pursuit of reconciliation with those who had not been Nazis was a top priority. During Eisenhower's years at NATO and then as president, Eisenhower built a strong relationship with West Germany's postwar giant, Konrad Adenauer. The German chancellor visited the Eisenhower farm during Ike's presidency, and they worked closely together in bringing an end to the horrific legacy of the war.

At a meeting not long after the surrender, Eisenhower had told his staff "The success of this occupation [of Germany] can only be judged fifty years from now. If the Germans at that time have a stable, prosperous democracy then we shall have succeeded."[25]

Ike used his presidency to further that goal. It was his administration, against some fierce opposition, that assured the accession protocols of West Germany into the North Atlantic Treaty Organization (NATO)—exactly ten years after the end of the most devastating war in history. West Germany had made strong economic advancements and was working hard to establish a middle class and a functioning democracy, while fully aligned with the West as a strong advocate of European reconciliation. Thus anchored in NATO, West Germany also stood as an integral pillar of our defensive force against the prospect of Soviet aggression.

Eisenhower would use the rest of his life to do all he could to avert another catastrophe like the one he'd witnessed during the war—the collapse of civilization.

The power of connections, of reaching out, would be advanced by his administration in countless creative ways. Through diligence, an unshakable long-term commitment to European security, and a belief that good can prevail over evil, the homeland of the Eisenhowers would yet become the kind of place that would have made a young Ike and his forebears—at last—very proud.

William R. Stuhler, Major Brett, Paul V. Robinson, DDE. Brief stopover of the Transcontinental Motor Convoy to visit the Firestone Homestead, Columbiana, Ohio, July 13, 1919.

4

"BORN TO COMMAND"

Today's American culture tells us that those most likely to rise to the most important positions of responsibility are the ones who graduate at the top in their classes and have long lists of extracurricular activities. Such countless engagements on a CV are somehow equated with leadership—though they may actually have as much to do with a fear of commitment, a preoccupation with image, or the inescapable desire to assure others that one can master everything at once.

It is ironic, perhaps, that many great, victorious military commanders in our history—Civil War general Ulysses S. Grant; Gen. John Pershing, World War I commander of U.S. forces; and Dwight Eisenhower, World War II supreme Allied commander in Europe—graduated from West Point well below the top of their classes. And in the cases of Grant and Eisenhower, both had disciplinary records that raised many an eyebrow. Grant, as a matter of fact, was at the bottom of his class in disciplinary matters, whereas Ike was a bit below the middle. It is worth noting here that Ike and Grant had something else in common. Neither of them had intended to become a solider. Both went to West Point for the free education.

This fact says something about Eisenhower and perhaps many of the nation's other exceptional leaders. In their cases their poor disciplinary performance may have been less about failure than an indication that their personalities questioned the importance and utility of everything. They were not "company men" or "insiders"; nor were they followers disguised as leaders. Grant, Pershing, and Eisenhower were not people to subscribe automatically to the status quo.

Ike was known to push the envelope when it came to questioning the rules at West Point. While at the academy, for instance, he and a classmate, guilty of an infraction, were ordered to appear before an upperclassman to be disciplined. They were told to report either in "full dress coat" or complete dress uniform. Eisenhower and his classmate couldn't help themselves: They turned up wearing *only* their dress coats. Ike was also caught for leaving the post to canoe into the nearest town for cigarettes and coffee. Smoking was forbidden at the academy, so Eisenhower took it up. Other demerits were accrued for "being asleep in a chair" at inspection, having shoes under his bed not properly shined, and most serious of all: violating the dancing rules by spinning his partner with such gusto that her ankles showed.[1]

Ike's attitude may have been linked to his frustration that a physical injury on the football field precluded his playing the game. But some of Ike's rebelliousness may have also been influenced by the experience of being a plebe, a first-year cadet at West Point. By tradition they were hazed (without violence) as part of the ritual intended to get them to follow orders, no matter how minor, trivial, or apparently silly. But Ike was not indifferent to the humiliation that was often felt by the plebes who were patently unused to such treatment.

"Most new upperclassmen took great pleasure in doling out

the harassment they had received as plebes," wrote the Eisenhower biographer Carlo D'Este. "Eisenhower was an exception and was never comfortable in the role of tormentor."[2]

Once while Ike was an upperclassman, a plebe ran into him as he was dashing down the hallway. The embarrassed-looking newbie looked up. Ike scowled and demanded to know what the young man had done before coming to the academy. "You look like a barber," he said.

"I was a barber, Sir," the plebe answered.

Ike moved on. But that night he recounted the story to his roommate, "I am never going to haze another plebe as long as I live. I've just done something that was stupid and unforgivable. I managed to make a man ashamed of the work he did to earn a living."[3]

While Ike might have been "a handful"—an independent thinker—he was older than his other classmates by virtue of the years he spent putting his brother, Edgar, through college before applying to the Point. Perhaps that is why he was said to look with "distaste" on his fellow cadets who were "haunted by the fear of demerits and low grades."[4]

But perhaps, unseen to his classmates and instructors, was a more profound change that was under way in him: a growing sense of duty that sprang from his training at West Point as it merged with a seriousness of mission and purpose he had absorbed from his childhood.

Eisenhower later recalled that when he took the oath of office as a cadet, "a feeling came over me that the expression, 'United States of America' would now and henceforth mean something different than it ever had before. From here on, it would be the nation I would be serving, not myself."[5]

This feeling was so strong that when he met Mamie Doud, a beautiful young debutante from Denver, and they married in 1916, Ike warned Mamie that she must understand that for him their country would always come first.

Later, with the death of Ike and Mamie's first son, a more focused, serious, and inner-directed Eisenhower appeared.

The sense of duty that was taking hold in Eisenhower's psyche was not about following orders, nor was it the simple dictionary definition: "A moral or legal obligation. A responsibility, a job, chore, or assignment."

Duty, in Ike's higher form, was intangible; it was woven into his DNA and revolved around selflessness and self-sacrifice.

In the civilian world this concept can be rather hard to fathom. Selflessness is the polar opposite of the impulses that are said to drive a capitalist world. In such a system "self*ish*ness" is what is said to ignite the "animal instincts" that many people think are vital for business acumen.

To civilians self-sacrifice is even more foreign a concept; it is counter to human nature. I once asked my father why young adults were the ones called up for combat. He replied that the recruitment age was chosen not just because late-teenage males tend to be in good physical condition; but "Older people are less likely to follow orders." Self-sacrifice, then, runs counter to human instinct, and is increasingly rare with age.

This commitment to a higher cause did not stop Eisenhower, however, from questioning the reasons why things were done a certain way. He was not inclined toward "groupthink." In many ways, Eisenhower was a futurist, and he bristled at the conclusions people reached without reference to or consideration of changing circumstances that might soon make current thinking outdated.

A few years after graduation Eisenhower was nearly dismissed from the army for writing a controversial piece in a military journal on tank doctrine, calling into question the accepted use of tanks in warfare. In his article, "A Tank Discussion," he called for a new design for tanks. The army at that time saw tanks as a form of mobile platforms, designed to go only as fast as the marching men themselves. The speed, deliberately slow, inched alongside a formation on the move. This use of tanks made no sense to Eisenhower. He could envision a fighting machine with a six-pound gun and two machine guns, ripping through the countryside at twelve miles per hour. He asserted that in place of the current tanks, "we must picture this speedy, reliable and efficient engine of destruction . . . in the future tanks will be called upon to use their ability of swift movement and great firepower . . . against the flanks of attacking forces." They would provide not only physical sanctuary for men engaged in armored battle, but also speed and lethal versatility. Such new designs also had the potential to save countless lives.[6]

At this stage in Ike's career, especially given the doctrine of the day, none of his superiors appreciated a freethinker. The capacity to question the conventional wisdom of his time set Ike and a small number of his like-minded colleagues, such as George S. Patton, apart. (During World War II the colorful Patton would prove his prowess as a great tank commander.)

Many in the infantry regarded Ike's article as "blasphemy," and later in the year he was called onto the carpet by the infantry chief, Maj. Gen. Charles F. Farnsworth, who expressed alarm about Ike's article and the other ideas he'd been advancing. They "were not only wrong but dangerous," and from then on Ike was warned to keep his ideas to himself or face a court-martial. What had been suggested, wrote Carlo D'Este, was "heresy to the leaders of the infantry . . . [yet in time the idea] would alter the whole doctrine of land warfare."[7]

Despite the warnings, Eisenhower and Patton continued to think through more of these problems of war—anticipating in twenty years that another armed conflict would arise in the aftermath of the failed Versailles treaty.

Ike might have paid the price professionally for his assertiveness had he not graduated first in his class at Command and General Staff School at Fort Leavenworth in 1926, and later devised the winning strategy for the Third Army during the Louisiana Maneuvers in 1941—just before the United States entered the war. His performance in Louisiana required quick thinking, strong strategic capabilities, and a talent for leading men.

Eisenhower's leadership attributes were more than the capacity to think beyond conventional wisdom. There were also intangibles about him that could not be reduced to a scorecard or an efficiency report. His innate sense of fairness, his humility, and his likability must also have played a role. People naturally wanted to follow him.

Sir Brian Urquhart, a former UN undersecretary who had worked as a young officer for British general Bernard Law Montgomery during World War II, once told me of an occasion when General Eisenhower came to inspect his unit. The British were still using carrier pigeons at that stage of the war, and Urquhart's unit sent off a bird, destined for London, as a demonstration for the general. As soon as the pigeon was released the bird swooped around the encampment a couple of times and landed on the branch of a tree not far from where Ike was standing. The bird sat in the tree cooing for several awkward minutes. When General Eisenhower met Urquhart's embarrassed glance, he quipped with a broad smile: "Perhaps we should keep working on our communications." They both laughed.[8]

On another occasion, in October 1944, Gen. Raymond S. McLain was commanding the Nineteenth Corps near Aachen when General Eisenhower came to inspect his troops, not far from the front line. It had been raining heavily that day as McLain and Eisenhower drove to the troops in an open jeep. When they reached the top of the ridge where the men were assembled, Ike got out of the jeep to address them. With his usual blend of informality and his interest in the conditions to which the troops were subject, he gave a short speech. According to General McLain, when the supreme commander had finished, the troops "cheered" and "clapped." As Ike stepped down from the platform he lost his footing on the muddy ground and he slipped and fell "right on the seat of his pants."

The troops could not contain themselves, McLain recalled, and they "let out a yell and cheered again" as the supreme Allied commander got to his feet.

General Eisenhower regained his footing, "gave his broad smile to the troops and waved his hand at them. The troops roared their approval." General McLain concluded, "I am sure they would have followed him anywhere in the world that he could have asked them to go."[9]

Ike had a connection to servicemen that was obvious to the GIs. He was inspired by their bravery, and, as a leader, he let them know it.

Capt. Ned Beach, Eisenhower's naval aide during his first presidential administration, recalled that Eisenhower had decommissioned the presidential yacht *Williamsburg,* whose upkeep was, in his view, an excessive use of public funds. He made it available for servicemen returning from Korea—giving them full run of the yacht. Beach recalled one evening in 1953 when the president came to the Washington Navy Yard to greet the *Williamsburg* and the GIs before their supper and return to Walter Reed Hospital. They were combat veterans who had been seriously injured, some with "disfiguring" wounds, others with severe disabling injuries.

As Eisenhower boarded the *Williamsburg,* he stepped in among the soldiers, brushing aside his Secret Service guards with words to the effect of *Just let me be for a while, I know these men.*

The president began to speak to them about what they had done for their country and the pride they should feel about the fulfillment of their duties, as well as the obligations that still rested with them as symbols of "devotion and sacrifice."

He spoke to them with warmth and empathy, and in "a somewhat different timbre than I had ever heard before," Beach recalled. The men moved in closer, surrounding the president in an intimate circle—"[as] if an unseen magnet were pulling at them."[10]

Eisenhower also believed in the power of small gestures. Whether this was calculated or whether it was part of his instinctive humility, he had a sense that small things add up and that such gestures can have an outsize effect. For instance, Ike would not wear a helmet during the war, even though there were many times when he was very close to enemy lines. Helmets were a necessary part of the uniform for people in combat, but Ike did not want to look like the guy who was trying to pretend he was assuming the risks unique to those who were engaged daily in the actual fight.[11]

That said, Eisenhower's life *was* in danger. On a number of occasions he was so close to the front lines that he narrowly missed being hit. "We got out of one corps headquarters only a couple of minutes before the German artillery opened up on it with all they had," recalled Mickey McKeogh. Later they crossed a bridge that was under fire.[12] And toward the end of the war, the Nazis even put Germans into American uniforms for the express purpose of infiltrating the lines to seek out Eisenhower to assassinate him.

Before that moment, however, Ike would sometimes pick up soldiers while he was en route somewhere and give them lifts. This would enable the supreme commander to ask where they were from, how they were doing—and just as important, "what kind of food they were getting."[13]

By the same token, Eisenhower rarely went to bomb shelters, arguing that the GIs did not have access to them. When the attacks occurred during dinner, the danger would bring out the stubbornness that Ike had shown as a kid. He would not get up from the table. "I'll be damned if I am going to let the Germans interfere with my dinner," he would say with annoyance and sometimes genuine anger, as he continued eating.[14]

Unlike his former boss, Gen. Douglas MacArthur, who commanded troops in the Far East, Ike refused the Congressional Medal of Honor. He replied respectfully that the award was given for extraordinary valor in combat, and he thought it inappropriate for someone not facing that peril to accept it.

And for those who worked for him, Ike was, as many of them have written, the most considerate of bosses. When one of his African American housemen was in the hospital, the general visited him on numerous occasions; Eisenhower gave Mickey McKeogh twenty dollars to buy his fiancée, Pearlie, a gift (almost three hundred dollars in today's money)—and later squared things so that his valet and Pearlie could be married at Marie Antoinette's chapel at Versailles. Ike also ensured that everyone joined him in helping to keep up the morale at headquarters. Harmony among what he called his "official family" was critical for the well-being and the well-ordered running of his headquarters. He also genuinely cared about his team's welfare.

Eisenhower's job with his bosses and the top military brass required a different kind of consideration. "By his prudence, tact and fundamental fairness" Eisenhower kept together the alliance, "whose interests often diverged sharply," noted the historian Michael Korda.[15]

General Montgomery, the highest-ranking British general in the European theater, was Eisenhower's chief rival. Short, spare, and temperamentally difficult, he believed he deserved Ike's job and never let Eisenhower forget it.

One simply could not have imagined two people more different in personality, not to mention at odds in their approach to strategic matters. In a gracious essay after Ike's death, Montgomery noted: "In some extraordinary way . . . [Eisenhower] could instantly warm the hearts of all who came into contact with him. He had a most disarming smile, and it was impossible to become exasperated with him however much one might disagree with his opinions or actions . . . During our long wartime association he was my chief and I was his subordinate."[16]

General Patton, a longtime friend and brilliant tank commander, had to be dealt with in a different way. The irascible and overemotional general had to be reprimanded sometimes—such as assigning him lesser duties for a time. On other occasions Eisenhower would give him an ultimatum—which would also work for a while. Patton's promise never to create controversy again would last until Ike would have to go through the whole process all over again.

As a strategic leader, Eisenhower's interactions with Marshall, Roosevelt, Churchill, and de Gaulle were inevitably more sophisticated. His primary objective was to assure unity of purpose, and this goal informed the way he handled each situation.

With Marshall, Eisenhower never failed to keep his immediate boss informed, by lengthy letter if necessary, to explain the state of affairs. Marshall gave Eisenhower enormous latitude.

Eisenhower's relationship with the others centered on what I regard as his genius—a trait he carried with him into the presidency. He was a master in knowing when to suppress his ego and when to deploy it.

Countless times in reading about World War II, I've had the urge to offer counsel to the man in the book. Don't stand for that, I've caught myself thinking. Yet Ike was playing a longer game. He was honed in the art, strategically used, of standing back and allowing others to win a few, while saving himself for the moment of greatest impact. And he was a master of choosing his battles—not everyone or everything is worth the effort or the expenditure of personal or political capital.

By the end of the war it was clear that Eisenhower had prevailed over the key arguments advanced by presidents, prime ministers, and key military advisers and commanders—on nearly every significant point. The only exception would have been the higher-level discussion between Roosevelt, Churchill, and Stalin over the timing of the cross-Channel invasion and the postwar division of Europe. Huge strategic decisions were at stake during the war, but none perhaps had a greater impact on the psychology of a nation than Eisenhower's decision to allow the French to liberate their own city of Paris. A man of unchecked ego would have relished the thought of this ceremonial demonstration of his own personal and military power. Not Eisenhower. Focused on the ultimate goal of Germany's defeat, he needed to secure Paris firmly in the Allied orbit. The most expeditious way to do this was to assure that the French, divided internally and politically by German occupation, would accept the outcome of the liberation—and the French themselves were in the best position to do that.[17]

Eisenhower's support of Gen. Charles de Gaulle, over the wishes of his boss, President Roosevelt, paid dividends more than a decade later. During the 1960 U-2 crisis, when the Soviet Union shot down a U.S. surveillance plane, French president de Gaulle locked arms with President Eisenhower when Soviet premier Khrushchev tried to break up the Paris summit over the issue.

In the liberation of Paris, and other subsequent squabbles over command structure and strategy in the last days of the war, Eisenhower prevailed. This included his broad-front strategy after the Normandy campaign. At that time the general resisted the strategic alternative, proposed by the British, of a single thrust. He feared that a concentrated strike alone, which Montgomery wanted, would allow the enemy to attack the Allied lines on its flanks. It would not, in his view, produce the total destruction of the Nazi enemy. While Eisenhower's broad-front strategy may have prolonged the war in Europe by some months, it promised, wrote the historian Jean Edward Smith, "[Germany's] total defeat . . . [and] it assured that there would be no latent resistance to the new order, bringing the prospect of a 'long peace.'"[18]

In another difficult moment with the British after the Normandy landings, Churchill resisted the proposed decision to invade southern France, Operation Anvil/Dragoon, which was designed to augment Allied attempts to break out of the Normandy area. Churchill instead wanted those troops and equipment to be used for military action elsewhere, including in the Balkans.

Eisenhower and Churchill, who Ike admired enormously, nevertheless had a confrontation over the future of the Anvil/Dragoon operation. In a heated discussion with the supreme commander at his forward headquarters in Normandy, the British prime minister threatened to quit his job if he did not get his way. Eisenhower told Churchill that if the issue at hand was political in nature, then the prime minister should take up the matter with Roosevelt. If solely military in nature, the operation would proceed.

The next day Churchill had a letter from Eisenhower on his desk, in which Ike produced a stirring reiteration of the fundamental importance of the alliance, what they were trying to accomplish, and a reassertion of the wisdom of retaining the plan as it was already adopted. At the same time he made a point of lauding the prime minister's leadership and noting how much he, as a commander, depended on Churchill's support. This personal touch had its effect: Churchill withdrew his resignation threat.[19]

There must have been moments during the war when Ike was concerned, even worried at times, about the stresses and strains on the alliance. But if he felt it, he kept his own counsel. The disciplined use of optimism was of critical importance to the overall success of the venture.

In times of stress, perhaps the greatest struggle Ike had to contend with was the desire—the imperative—to control his temper: "Anger cannot win," he wrote in his diary in 1942. "It cannot even think clearly . . . for many years I've made it a religion never to indulge myself, but yesterday I failed."[20]

Ike had a strong incentive, however, for finding ways to keep his temper in check. Many of his contemporaries would blow up, and he knew how it made him feel. Ike noted this issue in his personal, secret diary. Of George Marshall he wrote that he had never seen a man who had "a higher pressure of anger," which was "fleeting" and then he would return to "normalcy. . . . I burn for hours," he added.[21]

Douglas MacArthur, on the other hand—a man he had worked for during the prewar period—was given to "tirades," enflamed outbursts to which Ike and his fellow officers were repeatedly subject. Such tantrums were wearing and "silly" in retrospect, he wrote.[22]

But Ike saved his private antipathy specifically for Adm. Ernest King, the wartime chief of naval operations, a man who Roosevelt once noted "shaved every morning with a blowtorch."[23]

"[King is] the antithesis of cooperation, a deliberately rude person, which means he's a mental bully . . . he's going to cause a blow-up sooner or later," Ike confided in a diary entry on March 10, 1942. Days after, Ike wrote himself an account of the man's unrestrained ego—leading one to believe that it left Ike with an ever deeper determination never to behave in such a way.

"One day this week General Arnold [Air Force General Henry "Hap" Arnold] sent a very important note to King," Ike wrote. Inadvertently the stenographer in Arnold's office addressed it, on the back outside, to "Rear Admiral." [A long, heavy arrow had been drawn in a diagonal line underneath, pointing to the word "Rear."] And that's the size of the man the navy has as its head. He ought to be a big help winning this war," Ike added somewhat sarcastically.

Eisenhower just couldn't get over the fury King felt because someone had accidentally written his name with a lower rank than he actually held.

Despite these misgivings Eisenhower understood that King would be a vital ally for him during the war. Much of what was at stake depended on the allocation of military equipment and other resources. Ike made a noteworthy effort to win King over, successfully forming a bond that yielded the kind of mutual assistance that was critical for the war effort.[24]

All these relationships could be strengthened—or jeopardized—by General Eisenhower's own approach to the unfolding events.

For instance, one of Ike's acquaintances during the war was George Allen, a close friend of Harry Truman. Allen was a rotund man with an impish twinkle and a never-ending string of one-liners, all punctuated by self-deprecating asides.

While Allen was an acknowledged raconteur, he later admitted that during the war he often projected gloom about its outcome—an expression of hopelessness that was countered immediately by General Eisenhower's optimism. Allen, while visiting England, worried out loud to the general that Hitler would take the Suez Canal and "bottle up the Mediterranean, invade and occupy Ireland, force Russia out of the war and proceed to mopping-up . . . in all directions."

Eisenhower was, according to Allen, "one of the most confidence-inspiring men it has been my good fortune to know. If he ever entertained the slightest doubt about the outcome of the war, he never betrayed it. . . . He never underestimated the difficulties, but neither did he question the ability of the United States and its Allies to meet and overcome them."[25]

Bill Robinson, another acquaintance at that time, noted that during a visit he made to headquarters during the harrowing struggle under way during the Battle of the Bulge, Ike was the only "unworried, un-harassed man I had met in four days."[26]

In a draft of *Crusade in Europe*, Eisenhower offered an insight into his thinking on the importance of this optimism, though this highly personal observation was edited out of his memoir before the final version.

"During those anxious hours," Ike had written, "I first realized . . . how inexorably and inescapably strain and tension wear away at the leader's endurance, his judgment and his confidence. The pressure becomes more acute because of the duty of a staff constantly to present to the commander the worst side of any eventuality." The commander therefore has the "double burden" of "preserving optimism in himself and in his command," and that "optimism and pessimism are infections and they spread more rapidly from the head down than in any direction."[27]

With those realities in mind he made a resolution:

> I firmly determined that my mannerisms and speech in public would always reflect the cheerful certainty of victory—that any pessimism and discouragement I might ever feel would be reserved for my pillow. . . . I adopted a policy of circulating through the whole force to the full limit imposed by physical considerations. . . . I did my best to meet everyone from general to private with a smile, a pat on the back and a definite interest in his problems.[28]

Finally, Eisenhower believed that optimism is not the only factor in morale. Assuring that there are no double standards is also key to avoiding a sense of injustice.

Gen. Henry J. F. Miller, who had earned his two stars as an army aviator, was sent to Europe as part of the Allied Expeditionary Force. During the run-up to D-day, Miller attended a London cocktail party one evening at Claridges, with another officer and an attractive woman. Perhaps to impress the lady, General Miller committed an indiscretion when he revealed that the Allies would be in France before June 15. This was not said in passing, since he apparently "offered to take bets that he was correct." On hearing of this incident, Eisenhower fired the general, stripped him of his rank, and sent him home. Miller, a longtime friend and West Point classmate of Eisenhower's, wrote the supreme commander pleading for clemency on the basis of his "outstanding service with the air forces." Eisenhower replied that only his past service to the air force had kept him from being court-martialed.[29]

Miller was not the only general Eisenhower personally fired during the war, but in some cases the individual was given the chance to work his way back into a meaningful wartime role.

Tenacity in time of battle was highly prized by the general, and he himself was "inspired" by one of the generals he had to dismiss, Leroy Watson.

"Fortitude in the face of defeat can take many forms," Eisenhower wrote in his retirement for an article on leadership for the *Reader's Digest*. Major General Watson had been in command of a division and had made "such serious mistakes of judgment" that Eisenhower had to relieve him of his duties. When such firings occurred there would inevitably be a demotion involved, as the individual would revert to his peacetime rank, in this case lieutenant colonel. "A decision such as this was heartbreaking for me, particularly when the officer in question was intelligent, technically proficient and sincere—as this man was," Eisenhower recalled. "But when the lives of thousands of men are at stake, a commander has no choice."

Firings were commonplace during the war, and those who were removed were often emotionally crushed. Eisenhower was impressed that Watson asked that he be allowed to remain in the theater so he could continue to fight, and then carried on with his duty "without bitterness."

Watson's request was granted and, according to Eisenhower he "did so well at his new job that he was promoted, eventually reaching the rank of Brigadier General in combat." In time he regained the rank of major general: "This man not only possessed inner resources of the spirit; he also had the unusual capacity to admit error and learn from it."[30]

This was not exactly the case with Gen. George S. Patton. Eisenhower made an exception for this troublesome genius. Leaders are often faced with the necessity to be flexible, indeed pragmatic, with regard to the basic principles they employ when the mission is directly involved. Eisenhower simply could not do without Patton's talents. Despite several contraventions of discipline and demeanor—including one egregious occasion when he slapped a soldier with an acute case of post-traumatic stress disorder (PTSD)—Patton was retained by Eisenhower but (as mentioned earlier) punished to make his point.[31]

Firing friends, withstanding criticism, avoiding self-doubt, and the resolute determination to avoid favoritism required a firm set of operating principles.

Eisenhower believed that nothing destroyed the morale of a fighting man more than seeing favoritism in the ranks. In thinking about his experience, he once observed: "Morale is at one and the same time the strongest and most delicate of growths. It withstands shocks—even disasters of the battlefield, but can be destroyed utterly by favoritism, neglect or injustice." He asserted that the same was true in civilian life.[32]

But favoritism can track both ways, and it is not enough to demand high standards of others without adopting them for yourself. Ike insisted, for example, that his headquarters show that there were no double standards. The story revolved around a measure called "Reverse Lend-Lease."

Our Allies owed the United States money for the armaments and other materiel we supplied them before our entry into the war and during it. To determine what a country owed, there was a Lend Lease account, and sometimes the United States would draw on it by charging goods we purchased against our Allied partners' debt.

It came to Eisenhower's attention that one of his subordinates had purchased for his headquarters a "handsome silver tea service" and "charged" it to reverse Lend-Lease. "When General Eisenhower" was told of this, Harry Butcher noted, "he blew a fuse."

Eisenhower ordered a full investigation, and it was revealed that other items such as furniture had been ordered in his name, even though some of the charges were necessary. Even four throw pillows that had made his own austere couch more comfortable were sent back as unacceptable.[33]

Eisenhower's "duty" inevitably came with both praise and criticism, which also required a philosophical anchor. The general determined that he would simply put both out of his mind. But the hard decisions that leaders have to make require courage, and the willingness to draw on emotional resources from deep inside themselves.

Bill Ewald, his presidential aide, once noted that "Courage is not the absence of fear, but the mastery of fear." He was moved by Eisenhower's internal strength, this conquest over the anxiety of the unknown.[34]

No doubt some of it was a mask, which may have been rooted in a philosophy summed up by this anecdote:

Col. William Draper, President Eisenhower's Air Force One pilot, told former president Eisenhower that after many years of service he was being forced into retirement because of a heart problem, which would necessitate a new career as an airline executive. He confided that he was worried about whether he would be able to succeed in the corporate world. On listening to Draper, Ike said to his longtime pilot, "Go ahead, *be* scared, and do it anyway."[35]

Whether Eisenhower was frightened or scared we will never know. But he once articulated his simple formula in a letter to Mamie that contained the critical word. He wrote that it was imperative on him to "struggle is to do one's best; to keep the brain and the conscience clear; never be swayed by unworthy motives or inconsequential reasons but to strive to unearth the basic factors involved and then do one's duty."[36]

Eisenhower's sense of duty, and all it meant and entailed, was a critical factor in his leadership, as earlier noted, but many of Eisenhower's other traits were developed through experience. And others, like toughness and practicality, had been with him since his youth. The "heart" that he showed in so many cases also came from that long-ago time, when young Ike had been taught restraint, humility, and fairness. But he had worked hard—inside himself—to bring about balance in all these experiences and instincts.

Some of these traits were already evident to those at West Point who looked for talent and often offered second chances. For all of Ike's false starts at West Point, his instructors had seen something in the young man. On one of Ike's West Point efficiency reports, an overall evaluation of his capabilities as a cadet and his prospects for the future said simply: "He is born to command."[37]

President Harry S. Truman congratulates General of the Army Dwight D. Eisenhower, former supreme commander, Allied powers, Europe, after the general was presented the Distinguished Service Medal by the president, during a ceremony at the White House. Mrs. Eisenhower looks on. It is the fifth DSM received by General Eisenhower, who is retiring from the army after more than forty years of active federal service. June 2, 1952. (U.S. Army)

5

HUMAN PROBLEMS

Less than a year after the end of the war—on January 2, 1946—and only two months after he assumed the job as chief of staff of the army, Eisenhower wrote to West Point superintendent Gen. Maxwell Taylor, urging that the U.S. Military Academy establish a psychology department. Though it would be a radical step for what was still regarded as an engineering school, Ike did not see how West Point could address leadership issues without one. His letter said: "I think that both theoretical and practical instruction along this line could, at the very least, awaken the majority of the Cadets to the necessity for handling human problems on a human basis and do much to improve leadership and personnel handling in the Army and at large."[1]

Ike's suggestion was prescient. Only days later—on January 6, 1946—some twenty thousand GIs stationed in Manila, the

Philippines, stormed the city hall in protest against delayed discharges. These American servicemen demanded that they be released and sent back to the United States without delay: The war was over and they wanted to go home.

This "mutiny" caught on, and other U.S. military installations abroad, especially in Asia, also saw some forms of protest. From large-scale demonstrations and donation drives to public advertisements of their grievances in major American newspapers, the disgruntled GIs and their families successfully applied political heat. The situation had been brewing for a long time, precipitated by the coming Christmas season and a grassroots campaign founded to assert these demands on Capitol Hill—especially with those members of Congress running for reelection.

Women, distraught that their husbands were waiting in Asia or Europe for release, sent photos of their children to their representatives and senators with captions reading "Please Bring Home My Daddy." There were also as many as two hundred "Bring Back Daddy Clubs" organized by servicemen's wives to pressure Congress. Some of them sent baby booties and other such items to members of Congress, to apply more pressure.

Eisenhower had just assumed his new post as chief of staff of the army on November 20, 1945, and the most immediate of the problems of the nation's return to "normal" was demobilization. This was inevitably linked to the level of military forces now required in this postwar environment. And tied to that was the selective service—the draft.

In the aftermath of the Manila incident Eisenhower ordered a report on the overseas riots and concluded, on seeing the results, that they had been prompted by "acute homesickness," not by darker motives. Military law was clear on the punishment for mutiny: incarceration and even the death penalty. Eisenhower allowed these demonstrations to pass without recommending disciplinary action, but made it clear that there would be no tolerance for further upheaval, and that all future incidents would be referred to court-martial review.[2]

In fact, the chief of staff's office, first under Marshall and then under Eisenhower, was doing the best that was humanly possible to reunite families under a difficult set of circumstances.

Earlier wars had taught the military that advance planning would be critical, so in 1944 Army Chief of Staff George Marshall had convened a commission of civilians and military personnel to review the issues related to demobilization and to propose a system that would be deemed as just and equitable. This group recommended a points system, which was put into place. A point rating was given to each GI, with differing values that were accrued according to length of service, children at home, distinguished performance, and other metrics.

Nevertheless, the problem rested in many ways on the sheer number of military personnel eligible to return. It was staggering.

As demobilization started, GIs were being transported home at a rate of 435,000 men and women per month over the next fourteen months. And by the end of 1945 alone an impressive one million GIs had returned home.

In truth, by the end of the year 1944, the Pentagon had been ahead of schedule in decommissioning and sending GIs home. Still, the public was tired of war, and a vocal minority of families thought the system had failed.

There were many difficulties in settling this important public issue. The operation, involving millions of people, was complex. It had taken years to scale up military operations that extended to all corners of the globe. Nearly the same effort was required for demobilization—in reverse—including completing the paperwork on performance, future benefits, and logistical assignments for each person.

As the Pentagon moved ever more quickly to return GIs to their homes, a policy change readjusted the points used for determining who should be able to return. The measure, while well meaning, resulted in a shortage of ships that had to be readapted as troop carriers. In some cases, given this shortage, men who had been cleared to return home were forced to wait idly at their bases.

The issues of demobilization and a continuation of the draft were intertwined, as was the all-important question of postwar troop size in Europe and Asia:

"Of course the number one problem is demobilization, and due to a bundle of misunderstandings I'll soon have to go before Congress personally to tell them the facts of life," Ike wrote in his diary on December 15. "They won't like it, but I can't help it. Selective service must be continued for the year otherwise the thing is in chaos. The extension should be indefinite, but no one has the courage to support me on that."[3]

In February, Eisenhower was called to Capitol Hill to testify before Congress on the question of retaining the draft. That day, when he concluded his remarks to the members and walked out into the corridor, he was suddenly ambushed by a group of wives and mothers who demanded that their husbands and sons come home without delay. They were so determined, so outspoken, and so physical in their pursuit that this uncomfortable encounter left an indelible impression on the army's new top officer.

According to *Life* magazine, Eisenhower "beat a strategic retreat into Representative Andrew May's office, but the women broke through and drove him into a corner. Tight-faced, the general explained patiently that there was little he could do to help. Later he admitted that the engagement left him "emotionally upset."[4]

Somewhere in this process, Eisenhower had decided that he would review personally every case of "unusual hardship" or "injustice" that was reported to the Pentagon by men who filed a complaint about their time overseas. A special office, which worked eighteen hours a day, processed the complaints that were filed for Eisenhower's review each morning.

Demobilization was more complex than the simple necessity to bring long-serving GIs home. The armed services had gone from combat troops to front-line humanitarians overseas, facing an overwhelming task of helping to resettle the displaced persons in Asia and Europe.

In Europe, the area that had been under Eisenhower's command, the figures were incomprehensible. Nearly 7,500,000

Germans had been rendered homeless due to bombing, expulsions, return from prisoner-of-war camps, and other circumstances. And those Jews and political prisoners who had not died in concentration and death camps had to be housed, fed, and given medical attention. The responsibility for much of this lay with the servicemen and women who had just won the war.

While still in Europe, Eisenhower was quite clear with George Patton's replacement as commander of the Third Army, Gen. Lucien Truscott. He stipulated that denazification was a critical matter for his command, as was the handling and treatment of those who had been "victims of Nazi persecution." He urged Truscott to "give preferential treatment to Jewish Displaced Persons."[5]

In the big scheme of things this presented a challenge all its own. How would they ensure that the Nazis' victims were cared for, and also address the needs of millions of Germans who were homeless and without work, due to the vast destruction of their cities? Concerns about civil unrest and political stability weighed on the authorities and made their way to Washington.

In 1945, less than six months after the surrender, a Roosevelt appointee to the Intergovernmental Commission on Refugees, Earl G. Harrison, issued a report on the status and living conditions of displaced persons. After a trip to inspect some of the DP camps in Germany and Austria, he filed his report to President Truman. He blasted the military for their treatment of the Jews, suggesting that the authorities were forcing them to live behind barbed wire with no other clothing than their "concentration camp garb." Harrison also asserted that they were "in concentration camps"—under military guard.

"One is led to wonder whether the German people, seeing this, are not supposing that we are following or at least condoning Nazi policy," his report asserted. In conclusion Harrison recommended resettlement of the Jews in Palestine.[6]

Truman had forwarded the accusations to General Eisenhower. In a September 14, 1945, letter, Eisenhower responded to the president, informing him that he had instituted his own investigation and had made trips to five DP camps himself. He had also asked for and received authorization for a Jewish adviser to travel among these camps and keep him personally briefed. Simon Rifkind, a federal in judge New York State, served in that capacity.[7]

Eisenhower asserted that any problematic conditions described in the Harrison Report were being "remedied," but that given the extraordinary needs of this population the only practical and logistical way to care for large numbers of people was to keep them together as a group while they were being fed, and especially while they were receiving medical attention. "I found no instances of displaced persons living in old 'horror' camps," wrote Eisenhower.

The general reported, too, that he did not see any instances where our troops hesitated in requisitioning German housing for the Jewish displaced persons. But the matter of guarding this population was a difficult one, Eisenhower told the president. Many Jewish leaders wanted the protection afforded by U.S troops for reasons of security—but recent experience still created powerful memories.[8]

Renee Goldenberg, a judge in Florida, was born in a DP camp after the war. She recalled that her parents, both Holocaust survivors, told her about the harrowing time before she was born. They had struggled their way across half of Europe so they could find their way into American hands. When they arrived at a camp—with memories of Nazi rule fresh in their minds—they were terrified when trucks rolled into the facility. Out of the trucks came Yiddish-speaking American soldiers, who brought with them U.S. telephone directories that enabled them to help Renee's parents make contact with their relatives in the United States. It was through what they thought of as Eisenhower's consideration that Renee, then six months old, came to the United States instead of resettling in Palestine, where her parents might have been sent.[9]

From the moment the war ended Eisenhower felt it imperative that we avoid adopting policies that might send the wrong signal, allowing those in Europe to believe that America condoned Nazi behavior. He issued orders to that effect. On November 4, 1945, he replied to a letter from Senator Alexander Wiley, a Republican from Wisconsin, on this topic. Wiley was concerned about preparation for the coming winter in DP camps—especially that there would be mass starvation, if press reports were to be believed. (Journalists had predicted that four million Germans would die that year because of "pestilence and famine."[10])

Eisenhower responded that his high command was spending considerable time on the matter and predicted that the winter, while "hard," would at least be "endurable." He went on to assure Senator Wiley that "the mass extinctions that you fear by reason of starvation, will not occur."

Also among these immediate worries was how to manage issues related to morale and advancing an understanding of what America stands for.

To Wiley, Eisenhower also wrote: "While I and my subordinates believe that stern justice should be meted out to war criminals by proper legal procedure, we could never condone inhuman and un-American practices upon the helpless, which is one of the crimes for which those war criminals must now stand trial."[11]

Part of assuring that credibility required the United States' own willingness to review the behavior of those in *our* ranks, and to determine if any had violated the rules of conduct in war.

In orders to his commanders two months after VE-day, Eisenhower wrote: "America's moral position will be undermined and her reputation for fair dealing debased, if criminal conduct of a like character by her own armed forces is condoned and unpunished by those of us responsible for defending her honor."

Reminding his subordinate commanders that the Germans had not lived up to their promises to purge their ranks of war criminals after the armistice of World War I, Eisenhower ordered a thorough investigation of U.S. conduct. He reminded them that "the plea that the accused acted under superior orders is not accepted as in itself a sufficient defense."

An investigation eventually yielded reports of some seventy-five war crimes that were allegedly committed by American forces, but only five had entailed serious incidents. Most of them related to stealing from prisoners of war.[12]

The general applied similar principles when he set up the framework for the American Zone of Occupation in postwar Germany. He must have felt gratification when in 1955, the president of the American Jewish Congress wrote him regarding a tenth-anniversary commemoration held in New York: "It is my high privilege to convey to you the profound gratitude which the meeting expressed for the deep, human understanding of the problems of liberated persons which you demonstrated in 1945 and for your magnificent contribution to their rehabilitation."[13]

Now as chief of staff of the army, Eisenhower had responsibility for such difficult issues not just in Europe but on a global basis. In addition to the sensitive issues of demobilization and the draft, the international situation was changing rapidly, and concerns about Soviet moves in Eastern Europe and tensions on the Korean Peninsula underscored the responsibilities the United States now had as the world's sole superpower.

Eisenhower's professional responsibilities were, as he described them, "maintaining the peace we had just won." And Ike was concerned by what he saw around him. "Washington," he observed, "seemed little bothered about the long-term future." In his words, the city was more consumed in rewriting the past by looking, for instance, for "a scapegoat for Pearl Harbor . . . But of the future, piled high with threats to our victory and to our continuing security, there seemed to be little thought."[14]

Far from the scene of battle, Americans could scarcely imagine the conditions that prevailed overseas. They thought only that the end of the war would mean the end of our obligations. Little had they anticipated that many troops would be called upon to go to or stay in Europe and Japan to provide stability to these and other countries left in ruins.

As a matter of fact, there was a continuing shortfall between the required numbers for overseas postings and the demobilization, which had become a political hot potato. Overseas postings had been given a bad name in the eyes of the public. And, Eisenhower thought that the underlying problem for those left abroad was the inequity of life in these postwar locations, the disparity of privileges between the enlisted personnel and the officer corps. He moved quickly to make overseas assignments more attractive. One of the reforms, for instance, was to create the opportunity for enlisted men to be given seventeen-day furloughs to travel around Europe, as many of the officers enjoyed doing. As time went on, overseas postings began to acquire some sense of glamour for enlisted men, but for the moment the problem was acute and the international situation unstable.[15]

A little more than a month after VE-day, Eisenhower had gone on a whirlwind trip around Europe—to show solidarity with both our Allies in the fight and those who had been occupied. He received every kind of decoration imaginable, including the lifetime use of a castle in Scotland, but he took this personal attention in stride.

"Humility," he said in his famous Guildhall Address on June 12, 1945, "must always be the portion of any man who receives acclaim earned in the blood of his followers and the sacrifices of his friends." He was touched when he received the coveted Citizenship of the City of London in front of millions of cheering Londoners.[16]

The trip afforded him the vital opportunity to gauge the mood of countries across Europe. The destruction and dislocation in the immediate postwar period was stunning. The European economies had been decimated, and while they had started on the road to recovery, it would be a long time before life returned to normal. In Britain alone the government was only able to terminate rationing in 1954, nine years after the end of the war.

Eisenhower's concerns, as he articulated them to himself, were rightly on the unstable situation overseas, but he was also worried about developments in the United States: "Although everyone believes in cooperation (the single key) as a principle, no one is ready to abandon immediate advantage or position in practicing cooperation." What was required was "moral regeneration, revival of patriotism, [and a] clear realization that progress in any great segment is not possible without progress for the whole."[17]

In this same period Ike expressed continuing concern about the fate of democracy, given considerable domestic upheaval. In the United States unrest was prevalent. During the railway strike in 1946, for instance, Ike complained in his diary that people worried too much about surface manifestations of something that is of life-and-death importance instead of the thing itself.[18]

What we failed to understand, he thought, was that our form of government was under persistent and constant attack. To mitigate this, he believed it was critical that the United States be a worthy example of democracy, and assume its responsibilities in the postwar world.

Eisenhower did not see a return to the old ways as any option for the United States. The use of the atomic bomb in Japan had changed warfare forever; and the United States' military systems in place from before the war also had to be reorganized to meet the new threats and opportunities of the times. It was vital that the War Department—and Congress—be receptive to the organizational lessons learned from the war, such as the critical importance of a unified command of the armed forces. Bureaucratic resistance within the Pentagon was heavy, which only added to Eisenhower's frustration.

While Ike, as former supreme Allied commander, was ideally suited to reshaping the military through unification of the forces and the functioning of a new Joint Chiefs of Staff, the hard part was resource allocation. The JCS was to present a unified military budget to Congress—in contrast to the former practice, where policy makers could easily pick winners and losers from among the services. After the war this old habit of debating the relative importance of the army, navy, and the army air corps—soon to be an independent air force—put Eisenhower at odds with many of his old comrades in arms. Perhaps not enough people in the military service could see what was so clear to him: Winning wars in the modern age would be about the coordinated and synchronized effort to defeat any future enemy. Interservice rivalry must be curtailed.

One salutary aspect of this was that Eisenhower knew many of these individuals intimately and could at least try to reason with them—but that did not necessarily win the day with the vast bureaucracies that had developed and grown during the war years.

With conditions looking shaky in Europe, issues like the selective service, demobilization, and the allocation of financial resources for this new set of circumstances were of vital importance and occupied all of Ike's tenure as chief of staff.

Differences of opinion raged over more than these issues, however. There were strongly divided views about China's "loss" to the Communists in 1948, the beginning of hostilities in Korea not long after that, and the constant pressure on the Allies in Europe from the Communist threat. An "iron curtain," as Winston Churchill had said in Fulton, Missouri, on March 25, 1946, had descended across Europe.

At the same time questions abounded as to how the country would pay for its security, given the demands of our own citizens as well as the clear and obvious needs of our Allies—especially those on the European front line of any conflagration with Moscow. Foreign aid, in this context, was crucial.

Not the least of these was the overriding estimate of how many troops we would need to retain overseas, to avert any provocations from the Communists. While military in nature, these issues brought with them a highly charged political dimension. And it was Eisenhower's job to manage this "process."

Ike was no stranger to politics—he had had his share during the war. But they were politics related to strategic considerations and military operations. This was different. In the minds of many Americans, the "emergency" had already been dispatched. The inevitable human response, from GIs' families to advocates for one branch of the services or another, was now to push hard, to be first in line to shape the new environment to their own advantage.

The difference for Eisenhower between what he had experienced during the war and what he was dealing with now was essentially straightforward. "A commander in a theater of war," he wrote in his diary on November 12, 1946, "has as his most difficult task the clarifying of his own convictions and conclusions. Once he has sorted out the conflicting promises and obstacles, he can pursue a simple line of action and devote himself and his organization to the one job of carrying on the execution of the decision. He runs into strange personalities, weird ideas, glory seeking, enemy reaction, and all the other incidents of war, but he has a clear-cut path to follow and he can carry on with a free mind and with his full energy. He has to wheedle, demand, cajole, order, follow up, inspect, urge, listen and talk; the job is always clearly outlined in his own mind, however, so the burdens are lightened."

He went on to say, "In Washington the job has not even started when self-conviction has been achieved. On every side are new and strange problems. Navy, state, chief executive, Congress are only a few of the points where a chief of staff has to argue and plead for considerations of his ideas, and in each of these places he encounters a different motivation. Votes, personal popularity, personal hatreds, political and partisan prejudices, ignorance, opposing ideologies . . ."[19]

Eisenhower, the perennial optimist, was nevertheless deeply concerned that the United States was in danger of thinking in old ways, of trying to re-create a prewar establishment. He believed that it was critical for this country to move beyond the narrow definition of national security. The unity of our country and the health of our economy would be key, and intertwined. With the enormous financial and industrial capability that the United States had been able to scale up during World War II, now, with a standing military force, our strength as a country should rest on a "combination" of four principles, he thought: "(1) complete devotion to democracy; . . . (2) industrial and economic strength; (3) moral probity in all dealings; (4) necessary military strength."[20]

These personal assessments about the future did not relieve the alarm he felt when many of his friends and acquaintances pressured him to run for president. He was annoyed that so many of them believed his "no" to be insincere.

Of a higher personal order for him, as he was prepared to leave the army after a thirty-three-year career, was how to think about the sum of these times he had been through and shaped, along with the broad questions that spurred them. For the next six years he would be constantly assessing, during this personal transition, where his duty now lay.

This personal drive persuaded him, eventually, to write his own wartime memoirs and to accept the job of president of Columbia University.

Corporate boards, consulting work, accepting speaking honorariums "I could decline out of hand," he wrote later. "I did not believe it fitting for me, a man who had been honored by his government with military responsibilities, to profit financially for no other reason than that my name was widely known."[21] Aside from writing, this was a policy he adopted in the immediate aftermath of victory in Europe and retained for the rest of his life.

But serving as president of an academic institution was another thing. And it would provide the newly retired general with intellectual stimulation and the opportunity to interact with students.

The rise of Hitler and the ideological challenge presented by socialists and Communists convinced him that democracy must be shored up through education. Our system, by virtue of its individual empowerment, must rely on personal responsibility and mature citizenship. He had seen again, this time as chief of staff, the weaknesses that were perhaps inevitable among even the most honorable of men and women.

Wasn't the desire to be reunited with your loved ones after long separations and anxiety quintessentially human? Wasn't the need to rest after the long fight to be expected? Wasn't it easy, perhaps even natural, for people to think only of themselves, rather than the great challenges of the future? And wasn't the impulse to remain in power and to avoid change not just predictable but perhaps also the norm?

Such questions, especially where deeply divergent viewpoints were concerned, could be answered most effectively when they were thought of as human problems, grounded in human needs. This would be the lens through which Eisenhower would view the challenges of his coming presidency. Whether domestic or international, psychological strategy would be central to the way he would continue to approach the pressing issues of the day.

Eisenhower addresses a large crowd in Jackson, Michigan, October 1, 1952. The campaign employed one of the most successful slogans ever: "I Like Ike." (Associated Press)

6

"I DON'T THINK HE HAS ANY POLITICS"

In 1952 New Hampshire governor Sherman Adams was eager to ensure that Dwight Eisenhower's name would appear on the state's primary ballot—New Hampshire was the earliest of the few states that held primaries in those days. Adams asked one of the state's officials to write to the town clerk in Abilene, Kansas, for confirmation of Eisenhower's political affiliation.

In a letter of inquiry to C. F. Moore in Abilene, New Hampshire's attorney general posed the question to the longtime official. Moore responded right away, carefully typing his response—complete with spelling and grammatical mistakes—on the bottom of the letter he had received from the state of New Hampshire, thus assuring no wastage of paper:

> *Mr. Eisenhower has never voted in this county as far as I know, the Primary laws were first put into operation in the year 1928 and he has never voted since then. I have been the county clerk since January 14th, 1927, Dwight has never been in the city as far as I know of until after war No. 2 at least he has never voted or I would have known it as the party filiation books are still here ever since the primary or branding law was passed in the spring of 1927 and never went in to effect until the Primary Election of 1928.*
>
> *Dwights father was a republican and always voted the republican ticket up until his death, however that has nothing to do with the son as many differ from their fathers of which I am sorry to see, the multitude beleives* (sic) *in going into debt and see how much they can spend, it has become a habit & will sink this nation into bankrupsy* (sic).
>
> *I don't think he has any politics.*[1]

As early as 1943, political activists approached General Eisenhower to run for president. This was a nonsensical idea given the critical imperative of defeating the Germans, and in light of Eisenhower's own view of his role in that regard. Desire to beat Franklin Roosevelt in the 1944 election for his fourth term motivated some, at least, to try even this political long shot. On October 4, 1943, *The Washington Post* offered the headline "Eisenhower Urged for President." The American Legion of New York was "determined to boost the candidacy of Gen. Dwight D. Eisenhower for President of the United States." The American Legion post had no idea of his political or religious beliefs, but the members wanted Ike to run because of his "outstanding leadership qualities."

George Allen, who had sent the clipping to his friend, added the line: "How does it feel to be a presidential candidate?" Eisenhower didn't think it was funny, writing back: "Baloney! Why can't a simple soldier be left alone to carry out his orders? And I furiously object to the word 'candidate'—I ain't and won't."[2]

Despite General Eisenhower's protestations that he had no interest in running, after the war and for the next six and a half years he was besieged with appeals to throw his hat into the presidential ring.

Many competent professionals—even leaders of great organizational enterprises—suffer from time to time from ambivalence, and Eisenhower was no exception to this phenomenon. His conflicting tugs, however, were multilayered, and each of them required time and considerable thought to assess. During the war Ike had been gone for three years, and there was much in life he and Mamie wanted to pursue, especially after the long, relentless demands on his physical and emotional energy.

At the same time, Ike had to weigh his principled desire to stay aloof from politics against his concerns about the deteriorating circumstances at home and abroad. He would continue to serve his country as an adviser to President Truman, but as a retired five-star general he clearly longed to find a meaningful way to advance American democracy and national security interests while leading a saner and more forgiving lifestyle. He wrote often about affiliating with a small rural college, where he and Mamie could buy a "ranch" and settle down. He wanted to play more golf, see friends from time to time, and even develop his emerging interest in oil painting. As things happened, however, Eisenhower was persuaded to become president of Columbia University, an institution, its board felt, that would benefit enormously from having a popular figure like Eisenhower serving as its chief fund-raiser and public face.

Eisenhower's decision to go into education only fanned the flames for people who thought the former supreme Allied commander might be a potential presidential candidate. While public perceptions might have suggested such a strategy, Ike was keenly aware of the fact that the military had always been separate from political life. In fact many officers, including Eisenhower and George Marshall, did not vote while they were in active service. It was not until 1948 that Ike cast his first electoral ballot.

For the general to enter the political arena would be to take the same step that George Washington and Ulysses S. Grant took after the Revolutionary and Civil Wars. He would never be so presumptuous to put himself in that category. Washington and Grant had entered the political fray because the country desperately needed stabilization and reconciliation. Nothing to date had indicated to Eisenhower that the circumstances demanded that his higher duty lay in assuming such a role.

On January 1, 1950, after years of managing this well-meaning onslaught, he confided in his secret diary: "I do not want a political career; I do not want to be associated with any political party. . . . My basic purpose is to try, however feebly, to return to the country some portion of the debt I owe her. My family, my brothers and I, are examples of what this country with its system of individual rights and freedom . . . can do for its citizens."[3]

Throughout his tenure as president of Columbia University and as first supreme commander of NATO, growing appeals continued to dog him. However, in reading the pages and pages of his correspondence, one can see an evolution in his thinking over the six years, and an attempt to delay any decision until the last feasible moment. By that time, he may have reasoned, he would be able to assess where his duty really lay.

Ike was not convinced that being a military man was any qualification for the presidency. But that is not what his supporters told him. Given the massive bureaucracy that had been assembled as part of the New Deal and the Fair Deal, as well as World War II and the Korean War, Eisenhower was told repeatedly by his followers that the nation desperately needed recalibration, and that only his candidacy could "save the country." Modest by nature, Eisenhower thought such arguments sounded "silly."[4] Yet both political parties, not just the Republicans who finally made him their standard bearer, were applying pressure.

First it was primarily the Republicans who wanted Ike to run—the only sure thing, they thought, to beat the New Deal Democrats. They feared Roosevelt's continued grip on power, even after his death. They wanted a winner, and it was Ike's victory in war—and his brand of leadership—that convinced them that he could bring them back to power. They worried sincerely and deeply about the future of the country and the possibility that our democracy would be imperiled by the continued domination of only one party. Perhaps they also admired Eisenhower's military credentials and saw in him an expert who could handle the increasingly hostile international environment. Yet had the GOP looked only for military credentials, they had Gen. Douglas MacArthur, the former supreme commander of forces in the Far East and commander in Korea, who demonstrably *wanted* to be president.

Then in 1948, not long after Ike became president of Columbia, the Democrats came calling. In the early part of 1948, some key leaders in the Democratic Party had reached the conclusion that President Harry Truman could not get reelected. Consequently they were hesitant to nominate him. Franklin Roosevelt's son James was among a considerable number of Democratic governors, senators, and other party leaders who spearheaded the effort to get Ike to agree.

"In this situation," Ike wrote to his wartime chief of staff, General Bedell Smith, "they are turning desperately to anyone who might give them a chance of winning, and they have the cockeyed notion that I might be tempted to make the effort."[5]

Around the same time, in a confidential exchange, Harry Truman offered to step aside so that Eisenhower could run for president in his place. Ike demurred.

Now at Columbia people camped outside his door. He was inundated with telephone calls. He was deluged with mail. And a steady stream of visitors came to visit him in New York. Such Democrats as Minneapolis mayor Hubert Humphrey, along with a bevy of other big-city mayors, endorsed him. Ike was even supported by the Americans for Democratic Action (ADA) and got the endorsements of the Textile Workers Union and other labor organizations.

That same year, former GOP presidential contender Alf Landon, who was defeated by FDR, and a raft of other Republicans also tried to persuade him to run. The polls indicated that "if only they could saddle him, Eisenhower would ride to the White House as either a donkey or an elephant."[6]

The situation was so out of hand that a Columbia professor had an idea on how to turn it into a virtue. Dr. Robert K. Merton and his team from Columbia's Bureau of Applied Social Research asked for permission to analyze what the twenty thousand letters Eisenhower had recently received actually said about Eisenhower's appeal.[7]

The vast majority of the letter writers saw Ike as a "healer or a symbol of national unity." They noted that he seemed "sincere," and that his "warmth" as well as his "competency" gave them "a sense of new found security were he to become president." Only 9 percent said that Ike should not run. Of that group the vast majority said that politics would "mar his otherwise unimpeachable position in the eyes of the American people." And 80 percent of the twenty thousand also "showed an indifference about which party should nominate him."[8]

The study revealed, surprisingly, that even though the group was self-selected, the letters did represent a fairly good demographic spread. All levels of education also seemed to be reflected.

Another study also looked at many of the same questions and noted that Eisenhower's supporters were "somewhat more conservative than the Democrats and more liberal than the Republicans."[9]

That winter, Leonard Finder, of the *Manchester Union-Leader,* wrote an editorial endorsing Eisenhower and sent a copy to Ike with a clipping and other evidence of New Hampshire's support. Ike didn't answer his letter for a week, writing on the top of it for his staff: "We'll have to answer, but I don't know what to say!"

In Ike's diary, he wrote on January 15, 1948:

> The tossing about of my name in the political whirlwind is becoming embarrassing. Much as I've hated to say more that "I don't want political office," I have decided I must. Too many people are taking the columnists' interpretation of my intentions as fact. How to say anything without

> violating my own sense of propriety—how to decline something that has not been offered to me, how to answer those, like Finder, who honestly believe I have a "duty"—all this cannot be done in the words of Sherman. What a mess![10] [11]

In a public letter in response to Finder, Eisenhower at last disavowed any interest in the presidency. He thought that would be the end of it. But after the 1948 election the Republicans resumed their courtship of Eisenhower, this time with even greater determination than before. The upset victory of Harry Truman over New York governor Thomas E. Dewey, who had been the odds-on favorite, stunned rank-and-file Republicans. With Dewey's defeat, the GOP feared oblivion.

On July 7, 1949, while Ike was still at Columbia University, Dewey came to visit Eisenhower at the university president's residence on Morningside Drive.

Dewey outlined the problem, as Ike understood it and paraphrased it in his diary: "The country was in danger of becoming a victim of paternalism, socialism and dictatorship. The GOP, he argued, had tried to raise that alarm in the past—but failed to be elected."

According to Ike's diary entry, Dewey went on to say that "what the GOP needed was someone of great popularity and who had not frittered away his political assets by taking positive stands against national planning etc etc."

The skeptical Ike noted Dewey's bottom line: "The governor says that I am a public possession, that such standing as I have in the affections or respect of our citizenry is likewise public property. All of this, though, must be carefully guarded to use in the service of all the people." And Ike added ruefully: "(Although I am merely repeating someone else's exposition, the mere writing of such things almost makes me dive under the table.)"[12]

Dewey ended his two-hour visit with a plan mapped out for the general's future political career—one that would assure that "I can save this country from going to hades in a hand basket," Ike joked paraphrasing Dewey—adding finally: "This reaffirms a conviction I have formed, which is that no denial of political ambition will ever be believed by a politician, unless the disclaimer is so old he is tottering rapidly to the grave. In this case the refusal would be not a denial of ambition, merely an expression of regret."[13]

Even though Eisenhower was now yet again the target of the Republicans, there were still noteworthy factions of Democrats who wanted him to run in 1952. Since no one knew which party he belonged to, both continued to write or visit him at Columbia or later at his NATO residence in Paris. Before Ike's disclosure of his party affiliation, Harry Truman made yet another offer to step down in Ike's favor, matching the one he had proposed in 1948.

"We have never had an example of an individual who had so little to gain by being president, including perhaps not even George Washington." Herbert Brownell, the first attorney general of the Eisenhower administration, later wrote: "Eisenhower enjoyed great fulfillment at this point in his life; a poor boy who was now well off, a popular hero in this country and abroad, [and a man with] a wide network of influential friends."[14]

Among the most persistent advocates for Ike's candidacy was Massachusetts senator Henry Cabot Lodge Jr. While Ike was at Columbia the senator sent him a pamphlet he had written: "Does the Republican Party Have a Future?"

In the article the senator argued that the party must reform and at the same time change its image. "The GOP has been presented to the public as a rich man's club and as a haven for reactionaries." While the senator took the position that this characterization was unfair in many ways, he did advocate that the party broaden its appeal and look to its progressive past: "There is no place in the Republican party—or in any American political organization—for reactionaries . . . who . . . refuse to accept changes which are here to stay."

Ike agreed with every word of Lodge's argument, he told the senator. Lodge also made another resonant point with Eisenhower when he said that "democracy required a two-party system and that depended on the revitalization of the Republican Party." The question was whether Eisenhower could or would run as a Republican if the party was unwilling to change its isolationist perspective.[15]

From the beginning Ike had confided to his diary something of his despair, and occasional irritation, at being the subject of so much interest in the presidential stakes. Yet people continued to approach him, outline their concerns, and draw Ike into a dialogue about the nation's problems.

Eisenhower's interest in education and young people was genuine, yet the size of the university made personal contacts with students rather rare. At a place like Columbia, however, the new president had considerable contact with the faculty, even if many were skeptical of the general's qualifications to lead a major Ivy League university.

While Eisenhower may have seemed to be an unlikely university president, he made innovations in some of the university programming. For instance, during his tenure he established the American Assembly, a consensus-building program on domestic and international issues, the Center for War and Peace, and the Conservation of Human Resources project. A Columbia professor of economics at the time, Dr. Eli Ginzberg, recalled its genesis at a lunch with Eisenhower and his personal physician, Howard Snyder, who had once been assistant inspector general of the army.

Over lunch Eisenhower had remarked on the fact that during the war, of the eighteen million men who were screened, selective service rejected five million. Eisenhower thought it was something that should be studied, so he contacted fifty people in public life for their advice and financial support. The Department of Defense (DOD) was especially interested in what the project could produce in terms of research and findings, and in the process they offered five hundred thousand dollars for its financing ($5.3 million in today's money).

Eisenhower wanted industry to fund the project instead, and sent Ginzberg to Washington to explain that Columbia would not accept the offer from DOD.

"I don't know of any other man who could turn down so easily a half a million dollars because of the principle that universities should get their own funds and not be dependent on government," Ginzberg later said.[16] Nevertheless Eisenhower raised the money privately, and the project was initiated under Ginzberg's leadership.

Eisenhower developed other close faculty relationships that he would carry with him into the White House, most notably the physicist and Nobel laureate Dr. Isidor I. Rabi, who would play a key role in the defense-scientific sector of the executive branch in his coming administration.

As much as Ike treasured the ability to work with young people and to foster opportunities for them, ongoing events began to engage more of his time. And the prospect of life at a "reasonable pace" attracted him, even if it still eluded him. He was often pulled to Washington at the behest of President Truman, to weigh in on unification of military command and other key matters. In fact, during Ike's Columbia tenure he also served as temporary chairman of the Joint Chiefs of Staff while the establishment of that institution was still in development.

Eisenhower and Secretary of Defense James Forrestal worked closely together as they began to put the pieces in place to reorder the Pentagon for the postwar world. This was a timely undertaking.

In Korea 25,000 servicemen had already died, and cease-fire talks were in deadlock. The United States also undertook, after much debate, the development of the hydrogen bomb—and the Soviet Union was quick to follow suit. The old world order of empires and colonialism was also giving way to independence movements throughout the world.

During this time Eisenhower was called to serve his country again as the first supreme Allied commander of NATO. He took a leave of absence from Columbia University to do so. It was a critical job. Given his reputation during the war, the Allies requested his appointment and because of it he had a unique capacity to bring the countries of Western Europe together to establish firmly a meaningful alliance and to build a strong military deterrent force. "In all of history," Eisenhower noted, "this is the first time that an allied headquarters has been set up in peace, to preserve the peace and not to wage war."[17] Eisenhower later said many times that he found the assignment in some ways more challenging than the war years as there was no consensus within Western Europe about the urgency of the threat.

With increased Soviet domination in Eastern Europe, our Western allies were concerned about the domestic pressures and Communist sympathies in their countries as well. On Ike's arrival in Paris, riots were staged by the French Communists in protest over NATO. Even in the rural countryside signs could be found that read "Ike Go Home." This was yet one more indication of the volatile political situation that existed in Europe less than ten years after the end of the war.[18]

Even though Eisenhower was in France while the U.S. party political drama was playing out, he was still subject to constant visitations from stateside luminaries, who called upon him to declare his willingness to run.

The evolution in Eisenhower's thinking about the presidency was influenced by a number of events. First, and perhaps most important, was a private meeting Eisenhower had with Senator Robert A. Taft in February 1951. Before Ike left to take up, officially, his post at NATO, he met with "Mr. Republican," the sure-fire GOP nominee in 1952. Eager to get Taft's support for NATO, he was disheartened by Taft's refusal to drop his isolationist position. It was ultimately this that would leave Ike with no option but to think seriously for the first time about running. Should the isolationists take the White House—and they might, given the unpopular war in Korea—everything Eisenhower had worked for could come to naught.

Herbert Brownell, later Ike's campaign manager, mused in his memoirs that everything would have been different if Taft had agreed to Eisenhower's request that he support NATO. Had he done so, Ike would most likely have given no more consideration to the idea of running for president.[19]

Eisenhower must also have been influenced, at least in some part, by the grassroots campaign that had been established to persuade him to run. Undertaken by Citizens for Eisenhower, its aims were to apply pressure on the reluctant candidate and to sign up others in the cause.

Citizens was the brainchild of Stanley M. Rumbough Jr., a veteran fighter pilot, businessman, and philanthropist (and member of the Colgate family—as in the Colgate-Palmolive Company), and Charles F. Willis Jr., also a former fighter pilot. They started the grassroots movement, although neither of the cofounders had had any political experience. Over time Citizens established itself in forty-two of the then forty-eight states, with hundreds of clubs and millions of volunteers. Despite this remarkable network, the organizers had never even met Dwight Eisenhower, and the reluctant general had given them no tangible indications of his interest.[20]

The groundswell of support was also being augmented by an executive group, comprised of heavy hitters including Sidney Weinberg, a Democrat who served as treasurer; Mary Pillsbury Lord, a Republican who became cochair with Walter Williams, chairman of the Council of Economic Development; Oveta Culp Hobby, who ran Democrats for Eisenhower; and Jock Whitney, a Republican, who was chairman of fund-raising. Crucial roles were played by Gen. Lucius Clay, Henry Cabot Lodge, aviatrix Jacqueline Cochran, Tex McCrary, Augusta National Golf Club cofounder Cliff Roberts, Bill Robinson, Sen. James Duff of Pennsylvania, and many others. In fact, some of them were deeply involved in putting on a massive public gathering at Madison Square Garden in support of Eisenhower's candidacy, a film of which was made and delivered by Jackie Cochran to Paris so that the general could see the overwhelming support that awaited him at home. The diversity of their activities, as well as the broad political perspective they represented, made their effort one for the history books.

The right wing of the Republican Party feared Eisenhower, perhaps precisely because he *didn't* have any politics. To the die-hard GOP establishment, Ike's election committee must have been a genuine reason to panic. Paul Hoffman, former administrator of the Marshall Plan and an Eisenhower supporter, expressed concern about a small cadre of GOP men who would "rather wreck the party than lose control."[21]

Taft's wing of the party, now in control, comprised mainly conservative and right-wing forces that wanted significant tax cuts and a retrenchment of our international commitments. Taft and his congressional colleagues voted against both the Marshall Plan and the establishment of NATO.[22]

Though stubborn, Taft was by no means the most doctrinaire of the Republican right wing. Not only did many of them agree with the outlandish claims of Sen. Joseph McCarthy regarding the scale of Communist infiltration of the United States government, but they were wary of international organizations and trade deals, and were determined to hold out for lower taxes despite the state of the budget. Furthermore, given the insular nature of some of these GOP stalwarts, they harbored deep suspicions of the popular general's worldview.

Leading in delegate count—estimated at 530–427—Taft had some big-name supporters as well. Before the GOP convention, former president Herbert Hoover supported Taft for the nomination, as did Ike's onetime mentor Douglas MacArthur, who did so after a failed attempt to get the nomination himself.[23]

As the 1952 election got closer, however, moderate Republicans feared that the party would lose again if Senator Taft got the nomination. This worry gave Eisenhower's supporters the arguments they needed to make a persuasive case that the popular Ike was the only figure who could save the Republican Party—and thus save the two-party system in the United States. Eisenhower had two mounting concerns: GOP isolationism and the Democrats' deficit spending. But the demise of the GOP risked one-party domination because the Republicans had not held the presidency since the Great Depression—twenty years before. Ike was convinced that one-party rule, which is what had in effect transpired, was a threat to our democracy.

The downside of this calculation was that Eisenhower was not going to get the GOP nomination without fighting for it. His closest friends and advisers—Brownell, Duff, and others—told him flatly that the forces arrayed against him would never offer a draft. He would have to come back to the United States and enter the race.

On May 28, 1952, Eisenhower wrote Secretary of Defense Robert Lovett tendering his resignation as supreme commander of NATO, effective May 31. He had made the decision once and for all to seek the Republican nomination for president of the United States.[24]

Despite Ike's public appeal, he would have an uphill battle for the nomination going into the convention. Taft was on the verge of sealing the nomination on the first ballot. And everything about the convention—its format, platform, and speakers—looked to be setting the stage for the coronation of Mr. Republican.

After a battle royal over the seating of delegates at the Chicago convention, Eisenhower forces exposed unfair convention procedures and managed, through something known as the "Fair Play Amendment," to seat contested delegates. With a noteworthy shift in support, Eisenhower won the nomination on the first ballot.

In an unprecedented move, Ike responded to his victory by crossing the street between the two Chicago hotels where he and his opponent were staying. In a gesture of goodwill, Ike paid a call on Robert Taft, a courtesy that opened the way for a close working relationship in the times to come.

Candidate Eisenhower and his running mate, Richard Nixon, were off on the campaign trail. After a rocky first outing in Abilene when Ike gave his opening speech in the pouring rain, he soon generated plenty of enthusiasm. His campaign mastered the art of short, pithy, and repetitive advertising, and the candidate himself displayed the stump style of a natural. Ike also demonstrated a ought to write the RNC and ask them: "How long has it been since you had a winner!?"

Ike then turned to Washburn and said: "Keep up the good work."[25]

The campaign broke new ground in other ways too, with its use of television, celebrity endorsements, and, for the first time, extensive air travel. In the months of active campaigning, Ike traveled 30,505 miles by plane and 20,871 by train. On those whistle-stop tours Mamie was always by Ike's side. An effective campaigner, she had a genuine interest in the voters and a breezy way of finding points of mutual interest. Having been an army wife, who'd been compelled to set up their household in various parts of the country, she had firsthand knowledge of many of the states they visited. Ike's "handlers" also thought her presence provided an effective subliminal way of reminding voters that Ike was a family man, unlike his opponent Adlai Stevenson, a divorcé.

The campaign knew about hoopla, too. In major cities confetti was distributed to supporters, with the idea that the flaky stuff would rain down on the candidate as he rode through town in his open convertible. In Los Angeles one man was so excited at the prospect of seeing Ike that he "almost brained" the general, when he absentmindedly threw his unopened package of confetti.[26]

On another campaign stop, in Boston, Ike's motorcade was "mobbed by students" as he passed Harvard University. The young people were so "enthusiastic that they brought [the cars] to a complete halt, plucking off Ike's buttons and pieces of his coat . . . as souvenirs."[27]

The historian Fred Greenstein noted that Ike made the effort to greet crowds at airports and utilize these open motorcades, even though he found them exhausting. Bryce Harlow, Ike's presidential political aide, understood their effectiveness and recalled Eisenhower giving a few of his political associates some tips on how to engage the public:

"Now here's what you do," Ike said. "Get out there. Don't look so serious. Smile. When people are waving at you wave your arms and move your lips, so you look like you're talking to them. It quality that he had shown during the war—his capacity to sincerely identify with the needs of others. Abbott Washburn, whom I knew well in the 1980s, served on Ike's campaign and later became director of the U.S. Information Agency. In a letter to me on April 20, 1998, Washburn recalled the 1952 campaign, and noted, for instance, Eisenhower's handling of the mail that poured in from around the country to his campaign headquarters. How would they deal with the many thousands of letters that were coming in each day? According to Washburn, Ike replied: "Well, throughout my public life, I've always tried to answer anyone who took the trouble to write me—except for the kooks and those who insulted me, so I don't think I should stop now."

Eisenhower wanted to compose and sign the letters directly. With his encouragement, Washburn and others put together a fully staffed office of volunteers to craft the responses, based on a variety of paragraphs that Ike himself had written, and when possible the candidate would sign the letters personally before they were dropped in the mail.

Washburn noted that they also had a special approved "baby letter" because so many proud parents sent in pictures of their babies that looked—well—a lot like Ike. They would say: "Our little Herman looks exactly like you!"

Washburn noted lightheartedly that on looking at the enclosed pictures of all the little "Hermans," they *did* bear an uncanny resemblance to the candidate—"with the round face and bald head."

It worked, Washburn remembered. "At whistle-stop rallies people would call out: 'General, we got your letter!' and hold up a battered letter that had been 'all over town'—to various clubs and churches so others could see the general's reply. "And [Ike] would grin, and wave and thank them for writing him."

After the nominating convention, the Republican National Committee wrote to the campaign to admonish them about the money that had been used for postage, saying they had never had a candidate who spent so much on mail. When Ike was shown the second RNC letter of complaint, he quipped that Washburn doesn't matter what you say. Let them know you are reacting to them."[28]

The campaign clearly demonstrated to the GOP establishment that a different political force had now emerged, but it was more than something new: It was *not* indebted to the Republican Party, or to any party. The bipartisan Citizens for Eisenhower had played a far greater role in mobilizing ordinary Americans to support Ike than had the Republican establishment. And the fact that Ike's victory was in part due to "outsiders"—independents and Democrats—only furthered the skepticism felt in some GOP circles.

New Hampshire governor Sherman Adams, who had played a key role in Eisenhower's campaign and later became his chief of staff, recalled: "The influential Republicans in Congress were, for the most part, conservatives who did nothing to help Eisenhower get the nomination nor did they accept the fact that he virtually saved their party from deepening oblivion . . . [even after his inauguration] they gave him only intermittent support and considerable opposition and personal aggravation."[29]

Eisenhower was determined to ride to Washington without making any deals. During the preconvention period, Adams remembered that in discussion with the candidate, he reiterated that he had made no promises to anyone on the way to his nomination. While it may have been assumed that certain people would take up positions in the new White House or elsewhere, according to Herbert Brownell and Sherman Adams: "He made it plain that if he was going to the White House, he would go there under no obligation to anyone." Later people would say that Ike had made a deal with California governor Earl Warren—for the chief justiceship of the Supreme Court—but Eisenhower himself never had such a conversation with Governor Warren, nor does the timeline bear that out.[30]

Given Ike's enormous popularity from the war years, it was apparent to many that the source of Ike's electability had not been confined to the moderate wing of either party. Eisenhower's popularity was based on a relationship of trust he had earned with the sixteen million Americans who had been engaged in the war effort. He developed a reputation as a warrior who hated war; a commander with compassion; a leader who prized fairness in the system; and a charismatic figure who had a natural affinity for the common man. Americans sensed that he would put the country first, and they had confidence that he, of all people, would know how to settle the Korean War and manage the turbulent international situation.

Ike's popularity was an asset, a force to be reckoned with. And since he did not have a political base in any conventional sense of that word, his popularity *was* his political base. His relationship with the public was one that he would have to nurture and preserve so that it could be deployed to bring about the change he was elected to achieve. Eisenhower had had a chance to see firsthand, however, that retail politics was a far different activity than he had experienced before, and the necessity to keep in the fold people whose attitudes and views were repugnant to him would be one of the greatest challenges facing him in the coming years.

Ike wanted broad American electoral support—large enough to give him a mandate to realign forces in Washington. Ike told Adams that he would rather be "licked" in the presidential election than "just squeak by." In some ways this attitude was reminiscent of his approach to D-day: He wanted the capacity to tackle his challenge with the use of overwhelming force.[31]

Candidate Eisenhower beat his Democratic opponent, Adlai Stevenson, in a landslide, winning the popular vote with 55 versus 44 percent. Ike carried the Electoral College with a whopping 442 electors to Stevenson's 89. Ike took every state in the Union except those of the Deep South, which was still a rock-solid base of Democratic power. Ike even took a number of former Confederate/Border states such as Texas, Florida, Missouri, Tennessee, Virginia, Maryland, and Delaware. The Republicans took Congress too, even if they were left with only a tiny leadership margin.

The last time the GOP had had a victorious presidential candidate was twenty-four years earlier, when Herbert Hoover became the thirty-first president. But it was not just the GOP that had put Ike over the top; it had been a coalition of GOP voters, as well as independents and moderate Democrats, that delivered this resounding victory for the newly identified Republican.

C. F. Moore, the county clerk in Abilene, had been right. Ike did not have "any politics"—only a determination to advance a middle way. The fight was not between the Democrats and the Republicans; the fight was for our way of life. Isolationism, and all its by-products, including pernicious McCarthyism, had to be addressed, directly or indirectly. Also the state of our democracy and social programs had to be readjusted, along with the endemic and immoral discrimination that kept America from fulfilling its promise to the country's racial and religious minorities. Technology, developing at exponential speed, assured that opportunities would have to be weighed against dislocation and national security threats.

Eisenhower wrote, and fervently believed: "The aggressive demands of various groups and special interests, callous or selfish, or even well-intentioned, contradicted that American tradition that no part of our country should prosper except as the whole of America prospered. Unless there were changes, I felt that eventually only the promises of the extreme right and the extreme left would be heard in public places."[32]

Eisenhower prepares to give an address to the nation on the budget, May 14, 1957. The broadcast originated from his White House office. James Hagerty is leaning over the desk talking with Eisenhower. (National Park Service)

7

SHAPING THE MIDDLE WAY

During Eisenhower's years at Columbia, before he even seriously considered running for president of the United States, he spoke openly to audiences across the United States about the dangers of the deep political divisions in the country. Now engaged in a Cold War with the Soviet Union, America needed internal cohesion and political and economic strength to withstand our adversary's desire to exploit our differences. He believed there was a middle way that could draw Americans into a moderate center that could serve as a gathering place for compromise and conciliation, a place to coalesce around a national unity of purpose.

Using a military analogy, he said, "The frightened, the defeated, the coward and the knave run to the flanks . . . under the cover of slogans, false formulas and appeals to passion—a welcome sight to an alert enemy," he said at an American Bar Association Labor

Day address in 1949. "When the center weakens piecemeal, disintegration and annihilation are only steps away, in a battle of arms or of political philosophies. The clear-sighted and the courageous, fortunately, keep fighting in the middle of the war."[1]

On January 20, 1953, Dwight Eisenhower was inaugurated as the thirty-fourth president of the United States. It would now be his moment to try and bring this vision into action—with help and support from the American public, which had given him a "mandate for change," and from his devoted family and friends.

At the inaugural ceremony that day Ike did two unprecedented things. The new president started his inaugural address with a prayer, and, after the swearing-in, he turned and kissed Mamie, his wife of thirty-seven years. She had stood by him for nearly four decades, and she would be there for him again, in her own indispensable way.

Friends and other family members saw Ike's rise to the presidency in differing ways. Many childhood friends, like Ike's pal from high school, Everett E. "Swede" Hazlett, were surprised and delighted that the new president continued to write, and respond to their letters. It was one way the president stayed in touch with the thinking outside Washington—and his correspondence with friends like Swede gave him a sounding board for his thoughts. At the same time, such old friends must have felt at least somewhat saddened by the distance that was a necessity imposed by the presidency.

For family members Ike's election was perhaps even more bittersweet. Many of those closest to him did not live long enough to see his achievement. By this time both of Ike's parents had died—those two devout Brethren who had been saddened by Ike's choice of the military profession. Mamie's father, John Doud, was also gone. He had warned his headstrong daughter during her courtship with Ike that the young soldier, given his profession, would "never make much of himself." Aside from Paul, who had died as an infant, and Roy, who died during the war years, Ike had four surviving brothers. And they were not indifferent to the pressures they now found themselves under, expected by many people to provide access to their famous brother, the president. While some aspects of public life were already known to intimate family members from the war years, all of us would live in Ike's long shadow—a legacy that now included the presidency.

Ike had come to equate the presidency with doing his duty. Once the supreme commander of Allied forces in Europe, he was now commander in chief. With regard to that duty, my grandfather shared a common language with my father, John. In 1953 my father was deployed in Korea. He was in a combat unit when Ike was elected president. As a West Point graduate (class of 1944), and as a soldier, he strained against any suggestion that he should be treated differently from his fellow officers by being denied the chance to remain in Korea. This was relevant because the new commander in chief was the decision maker on this matter.

Ike told John that he could return to his unit in Korea, but he must understand that his presence there would pose significant risk to him, as president, especially if the enemy captured him and held him hostage. To go back to his unit, Ike reiterated, John must promise that he would never be taken hostage. My father agreed, knowing that there might be a situation in which he would have to take his own life.

John was a young officer at the time, with three little kids—my two older siblings, David and Anne, and me. (Our youngest sister, Mary, would come along in 1955.) Dad shared this story with us long after the fact. But it was clear in his telling of it that this is what he and Ike knew to be "duty"—even if it would leave the president's grandchildren fatherless. Dad understood his orders and rejoined his fellow officers in combat, keeping, as he told us, his sidearm with him at all times, even as he slept.

If the Eisenhower family was somewhat of two minds about this new chapter Ike had embarked on, the public—especially long-discouraged GOP moderates—were euphoric that they had finally taken back the White House.

A humorous example of this can be found in a letter to the president on May 5, 1953. Ike's brother Edgar wrote that the local paper in Tacoma, Washington, had reported that someone had been trying to give the president a live elephant (the symbol of the Republican Party). This prompted one of Ed's acquaintances, a wartime sergeant, to offer the president a two-year-old Indian elephant, which he had somehow acquired. The elephant, Ed wrote dryly, "is pretty well trained; plays a mouth organ; plays with a Shetland pony; will get down on its knees and crawl etc. etc."

Apparently the sergeant was having a hard time meeting the elephant's needs, and decided *he* wanted to be the one to give the president an elephant, not the man who had appeared in the newspaper.

Edgar then got to the bottom line, writing: "Do you want the damn thing or not?"

The president returned his brother's letter with a startled response:

> *Dear Ed,*
> *For goodness sake, tell your friend, Mr. Irwin, that the last thing I need or could use would be a live elephant. I have enough problems without finding food and a caretaker for that kind of a pet.*
>
> *Thank him warmly in my name, but make sure your negative reply is very firm indeed!*
>
> *As for where he got his information, I can only say he seems to be another fellow who apparently believes everything he reads. As ever, DE*[2]

Ike had "enough problems" to be sure. At the time these letters were exchanged, there had been a brawl on April 30 between the new administration and the Republican leadership in Congress. During their weekly meeting that day, the topic had been cutting the budget. The Eisenhower administration had taken a razor to it, reducing proposed expenditures significantly, but refusing to cut the defense budget even more than what they had already proposed. In this regard, Eisenhower was in a bind. The Korean War and the Truman administration's policy to ramp up military spending to counter the Soviets, codified in a 1951 National Security Council policy known as NSC-68, had put the budget deeply in the red. In fact the result of these policies was that Truman had nearly quadrupled the defense budget.

On the matter of the military budget, aide Robert Bowie noted: "No one knew more about the defense budget than Dwight Eisenhower." And it was a message he had used during the presidential race: "I know better than any of you fellows about waste in the Pentagon and about how much fat there is to be cut," he said during the campaign.[3]

Nevertheless Senator Taft accused Eisenhower of merely adopting the Truman budget. He did this without acknowledging the enormous work the new administration had already done in identifying and making considerable cuts.

"Senator Taft," Ike noted in his diary, "broke out in violent objection to everything that had been done"—this despite the fact that the administration had inherited sizable contractual obligations from the Truman administration, which had passed along "frozen commitments and contracts made long ago."[4]

Taft asserted that should the GOP-controlled Congress accept this budget and fail to lower taxes, there would be a decisive defeat of the GOP in the 1954 midterm elections. That day, Taft declared he would refuse to support the president's budget and would have to take his grievances directly to the American public.

"I think everybody present was astonished by the demagogic nature of this tirade," Ike confided to his diary, "because not once did he [Taft] mention the security of the United States or the need for strength either at home or among our allies. He simply wanted expenditures reduced, regardless."[5]

But what may have gotten Ike's goat the most was Taft's failure to acknowledge the hard work that had been expended by Secretary of the Treasury George Humphrey and Budget Director Joe Dodge. They had literally gone through every expense and cut as much as they could. Taft's disregard made Ike's temper flare. Fortunately those in the room—who knew the president—managed to change the subject until he had cooled down. Ike was not angry for himself; he was offended that Taft had denigrated the work of his cabinet members, "particularly in view of the fact they had never failed to keep the [congressional] leaders well informed" on their progress.[6]

Ike was shocked by the vehemence of Taft's outburst, but perhaps not exactly surprised. Though the two men had developed a good working relationship after the convention, they were divided in their views about the necessity to cut the budget drastically and lower taxes right away.

While Ike agreed that the country could save "prodigious sums in the defense department without materially hurting our security," he did not believe that the cuts could be any greater for the moment. The administration had Truman-era obligations that still required funding and the president was convinced that the American public wanted security ahead of tax reductions.[7]

Eisenhower put this and other incidents like it down to the fact that "the Republican senators are having a hard time getting it through their heads that they now belong to a team that includes rather than opposes the White House."[8]

In fact, Eisenhower would point out more than once that no Republican then in Congress had ever served with a Republican president: "Therefore we must come at it on the basis of nurturing and carrying along these people until they understand that we . . . are their friends."[9]

The right wing of the Republican Party tended to be located in Western states, where the ethos of individualism was as deep as ever. The moderates were more broadly dispersed, but their power base, with Eisenhower's election, was the Northeast—though Eisenhower himself had no real geographic home except perhaps that of his boyhood in Kansas. These battle lines still followed, in significant measure, the ones drawn at the time of Abraham Lincoln's presidency, and continued through the progressive period of Theodore Roosevelt.

These divisions could be felt within Congress, and also within the White House among some of the president's inner circle. Eisenhower encouraged diversity of thought, and had staffed the

White House accordingly, to assure a lively private debate within his administration.

But it must have been of some amusement–or perhaps alarm—when the political divisions within the Eisenhower family were given headlines and colorful copy. In a way you could think of the Eisenhower family's political disagreements as a metaphor for what was under way in the Republican Party in general. And the president took the time to defend his positions in family correspondence—some of which became rather heated.

Of the five surviving Eisenhower boys—four of them, including the president, were politically active. It should be noted that there were no "shrinking violets" among them. All possessed a kind of raw animal energy, and except for Milton, the youngest, all had been highly competitive as kids. Arthur, the oldest, was the one outlier among them. He had left home before finishing high school and made a remarkable career for himself as a banker in Kansas City, eventually rising to the position of vice chairman of the board of the Commerce Trust Company. Edgar, the second oldest, and Ike, just two years his junior, were, however, the ones who joined the political fray with all the relish of boxing rivals about to enter the ring.

Edgar had deep ties to the Seattle area of Washington State, and to Arizona. He saw things as many Westerners did then and still do. He was a rugged individualist, distrustful of government and certain that America's sovereignty required vigilance in the face of "forces" determined to establish world government and federal domination over everything. Edgar was charming, disarming, and highly opinionated. I remember my father once telling me that there was a reason that family members had put their initials into the wet concrete after they'd poured a sizable cement slab at the Eisenhower family homestead in Abilene. "If we hadn't," my father said with a laugh, "Uncle Ed would have claimed credit for the whole project even though he had been nowhere on the scene when the work was done."

Ike shared Edgar's star quality, but his own nature, as well as his life experience, could not have been more different. As a military officer he was a disciplined, clear thinker, who did not allow himself to get pulled into emotional free-for-alls or make any consequential decisions in a noisy contentious room. Richard Nixon remembered, in fact, that Ike never made an important decision in front of others. He would go into his office alone and think about all he had heard. "[Eisenhower] was an emotional man," Nixon recalled, "but he never made emotional decisions. He did not let his emotions control him."[10]

Ike also knew international issues from deep personal experience. He and Mamie had lived not only in many places within the United States but also overseas. His first assignment abroad was in Panama in the early 1920s, then France in the late 1920s, then the Philippines in the mid-1930s, and again in Europe during World War II. In sum, Ike's grasp of the world was informed by years-long assignments in Latin America, Europe, and Asia. In the process he had learned from people overseas. He had observed their struggles and even their tragedies. He had helped shape their futures, and now as president he was determined to put that perspective to work.

While Earl, next in chronological line, was a quiet, private man, he showed an interest in politics, even if he tried to avoid getting into the political ring as his two older brothers duked it out. An electrical engineer, in 1965 Earl ran for and won a seat in the Illinois House of Representatives.

Finally, the youngest of the brothers, Milton, was perhaps the most "liberal" of the men. He was uncommonly close to his brother, the president. Remarkably Milton was unburdened by jealousy when it came to Ike, even though he had been the one who originally had the experience and connections in the nation's capital. Milton had been a regular in establishment circles in DC since the late 1920s, and he'd worked at the Department of Agriculture during the Roosevelt administration. Later he became the president of three major universities: Kansas State, Penn State, and Johns Hopkins, where he served in that role twice.

Once Milton described to me one of the incidents that contributed to his deep connection to Ike. As the smaller of the strapping

Eisenhower brothers, Milton had been sickly as a child and drawn to more studious pursuits. Milton recounted how Ike, his playground defender, had pulled him aside one day and said: "Milton there is no need for you to compete in athletics or join in this fight. It is *important* that you are an intellectual."

"In effect," Milton told me, "your grandfather gave me permission to be myself"—a noteworthy liberation from the intensity that characterized the alpha-male physical culture of the young Eisenhower clan.

Despite their differences, however, the Eisenhower boys grew out of one Republican tradition—that of the Kansas GOP. This progressive Republicanism was deeply ingrained in the culture. Ike, for instance, had been a youthful torchbearer during the campaign of William McKinley. And with respect to fiscal matters, their father, David, had known the desperation of falling into debt—an unfortunate experience he'd suffered as a first-time shopkeeper during the farm depression of the 1920s. Later, when the Great Depression ravaged the entire nation, David lost most of his retirement savings.

David Eisenhower worked on the Texas railroad and then became a laborer and engineer in a small creamery in Abilene, Kansas. These were the family experiences that shaped each of the boys—though inspiring very different political conclusions.

As Brethren pacifists, the generation before Ike's father did not fight in the Civil War. But as rock-ribbed progressives they still took a stand. The boys had their own "Uncle Abe." Their father, David's youngest brother—a farmer, a veterinarian, and later, with his wife, the founder of an orphanage—had been named Abraham Lincoln Eisenhower, in honor of the sixteenth president. Ironically, nearly one hundred years later Ike's nephew Earl Jr. would marry an aide to Barry Goldwater, and they would name their son Barry Goldwater Eisenhower. Not many families have displayed their political views in such a public way![11]

Still, it was Edgar who was by far the most outspoken of Ike's brothers. A Tacoma, Washington, trial lawyer, he must have worried privately that over the years Ike had become somewhat cosmopolitan in his thinking. This was a pejorative concept in the 1950s, one laden with the suggestion that anyone who fit that description was not tethered to the correct fundamentals, and was at the same time rootless—geographically and intellectually. This may have left Edgar with the feeling that he needed to "tutor" his brother on a continuing basis.

Less than three months after Ike's inauguration, Edgar wrote an apology to the president of the United States for an earlier missive: "I had no intention of making you feel that I was lecturing you or that you hadn't grown up. I am fully aware of the fact that you can look after yourself. . . . Maybe, after you have done your four-year term, you can settle down to being an ex-President, and then we can enjoy a game of golf together."[12]

Throughout his younger brother's presidency, Edgar peppered Ike with advice and admonitions, apologizing occasionally for the fact that people who wanted the president to change his views inundated him. Ed wanted Ike to know that he shared only a selection of such entreaties. Perhaps this revelation was a subtle way of suggesting that Ed's views reflected a groundswell of thinking in the GOP.

Once at a press conference when Eisenhower was asked about his brother Edgar's public remarks that he was becoming more liberal under the influence of Milton Eisenhower and Sherman Adams, the president quipped, with a broad grin: "Edgar has been criticizing me since I was five years old."[13]

Ike usually responded to Ed with a good-humored explanation for his administration's decisions. However, sometimes his annoyance was obvious, especially when his brother's condescending advice appeared not to be based in fact. I should add, however, that outside family circles Ike employed all the diplomacy he could muster in arguing each issue on its merits to an array of others, strangers and friends alike. Ike's exasperation was evident primarily with Ed.

The GOP had been full of expectations that the new president would start immediately to roll back the New Deal of the Roosevelt administration and the Fair Deal of the Truman presidency. Eisenhower's early-stated commitment to expand the Social Security net, however, left diehard GOP members desperate to figure out how to control their new party leader.

Factions within the Republican party were still clearly bitter at how Ike's election had unfolded. In the decades to come there would still be residual feelings within this strident element of the party that the reemergence of modern Republicanism had been hijacked by a popular war hero whose loyalties to the party were "suspect." Indeed, some GOP intellectuals, like William F. Buckley Jr., believed that the nomination had been stolen from Robert Taft.

"The fact that the public had chosen Eisenhower's Middle Way," wrote the historian Heather Cox Richardson, "proved" to Buckley that "people could not be trusted to choose what was right." He and others of similar views were determined to take back control of America from "the misguided masses" and orient the country toward fundamental religious adherence and free-market capitalism.[14] (In those years, it is interesting to note, Eisenhower and others referred to the economy not as "free-market capitalism" but as "free enterprise" or a "private enterprise" system.)

Buckley's philosophical approach was antithetical to Eisenhower's worldview. Ike was deeply spiritual, but he did not believe religion should be imposed or trumpeted. Like his adoption of a political party, Ike came to organized religion late, joining a denomination only *after* his election to the presidency in 1953.

Regarding what some called the "masses," Ike always reaffirmed his profound sense of respect for the American people, their fortitude, their capacity for sacrifice, and their valor on the battlefield. He deeply believed in their fundamental right to direct their own destinies. Elitist thinking repelled him, and he bridled when confronted by those who arrogantly suggested they might know better. Ike affirmed this even to his own brother: "Dear Ed, Thank you for your letter and advice, I am not, however, quite as jaundiced about the American people as you seem to imply you are; on the contrary my faith in them is one of my greatest strengths."[15]

In Dwight Eisenhower's first State of the Union message, he reaffirmed his belief in the importance of a balanced budget. On the ever-sensitive matter of tax reduction, however, he asserted that "the reduction of taxes will be justified only as we show we can succeed in bringing the budget under control. . . . Until we can determine the extent to which expenditures can be reduced, it would not be wise to reduce our revenues."

Getting to that tax reduction would not be at all easy. The country was still on a war footing, and many government controls over the economy were still in place.

Not long after Ike was elected, Herbert Hoover visited him in his office. The former president underscored the difficulty of Eisenhower's task, warning of a "great danger" that lay ahead. He told Eisenhower that the country could not continue on this road of increasing dependence on centralized government, which included economic and social programs. "You cannot go back." Hoover predicted, however, that Eisenhower's policies would be constrained in halting this trend.

"As a result," Hoover said, "the reactionaries will snarl at you, as well, of course, as the people that join the ADA and other so-called 'liberal' groups. Education of the entire people will be the task of the Party, and since so many people will misunderstand what is going on, that education will be a slow and laborious process."[16]

With the Great Depression and World War II behind us, the consolidation of federal government power was no longer critical for economic recovery or for victory. Eisenhower understood that a way had to be found to reempower the focus of our democracy: the people themselves. Furthermore, a strong economy and the building of a vibrant middle class were the bulwark against international aggression and the spread of ideas antithetical to American values.

This could be achieved only if the United States had economic prosperity, derived from fiscal responsibility, as well as a strategically oriented foreign policy based on our national interests. Ike's objectives were so intertwined and tightly articulated that he would view defense spending through the lens of what was truly *necessary*—in the context of a national strategy—rather than simply desirable. He was unmoved when the military brought him their wish lists.

Eisenhower's views, however, did not fit neatly into the orthodoxy of either party, and he understood the challenges inherent in what he would dub "the Middle Way."

While the moderate wing of the GOP may have embraced Ike's agenda, it was a source of enormous friction with the more conservative Republicans who still held sway over the vast majority of the GOP seats in Congress. They were convinced that Eisenhower was part of some dangerous conspiracy to assure America's continuing decline toward socialism. Edgar, as always the bellwether of that farther-right group, hounded his brother about failing to repudiate the New Deal.

Edgar's comments, while not so pithy, echoed those of Sen. Barry Goldwater, who later became a presidential candidate in 1964. The Arizona senator attacked Eisenhower by saying that the administration's budget policy was no better than a "Dime Store New Deal."

Expenditures were still being cut, but not apparently fast enough for Ike's GOP critics. It would take two years for the budget to come into balance, and Eisenhower would eventually produce three balanced budgets before his tenure was over, leaving his successor with a budget surplus. (In fact there has been no presidency since Eisenhower's that has brought about a decrease of any size in federal spending as a percentage of GDP.)[17] Later, based on this economic performance, Eisenhower was also able to lower taxes, in fact the largest tax cut in history up to that point.

At the same time Eisenhower regarded it as progress to extend the benefits of Social Security "to cover millions of citizens who have been left out of the social security system."

On September 1, 1954, Dwight Eisenhower signed into law an expansion of Social Security, adding ten million new enrollees. The expanded act also increased payments to future retirees by $4,200, or the equivalent of $31,500 in today's dollars.[18]

Passed when both houses of Congress were in Republican hands, the changes, the president declared, would "bolster the health and the economic security of the American people."[19]

At the same time other favorable technical details were changed, in effect enabling workers to earn more money without forfeiting their Social Security checks. The old and the disabled, who were vulnerable for long or indefinite periods, were also protected.[20]

Despite this progress, Edgar was not alone in being concerned about his brother's adherence to a social safety net. He would not let up on the president. Ike retaliated with strong words—at least for Edgar. He started by saying that it would be unwise and potentially dangerous to permit too much centralization of the federal government, but then he emphasized to Ed, revealing some irritation with his brother, that the government has responsibilities to the people as a whole:

> To attain any success it is quite clear that the Federal government cannot avoid or escape responsibilities which the mass of the people firmly *believe* should be undertaken by it. . . . This is what I mean by my constant insistence upon "moderation" in government. Should any political party attempt to abolish social security, unemployment insurance, and eliminate labor laws and farm programs, you would not hear of that party again in our political history. There is a tiny splinter group, of course that believes you can do these things . . . [but] their numbers are negligible and they are stupid.[21]

Another one of Ike's closest friends and supporters, Ellis Slater, confided in a diary that many of Ike's personal friends were worried that Ike did not appear to be inclined to scrap the New Deal/Fair Deal. Treasury Secretary George Humphrey told

Slater confidentially that he too was worried that the increased mail that was coming into his office seemed to be a "swing away from the Republicans."

Slater sympathized, and told Humphrey that his wife, Priscilla, had recently exclaimed: "Tell me where this administration differs from Truman and Roosevelt." Slater worried that "in the minds of countless loyal Ike supporters . . . there are many who dislike this new Republicanism they see."[22]

Ike got little or no credit from any of these factions for what he had done to unleash the potential of business. In another letter to Ed, the president rose to defend himself against his brother's criticisms:

"When we came into office there were Federal controls exercised over prices, wages, rents, as well as over the allocation and use of raw materials," Ike reminded Ed with evident frustration. "The first thing the administration did was to set about the elimination of those controls. This it did amid the most dire predictions of disaster, 'run away' inflation, and so on and so on. We were proved right, but I must say that if the people of the United States do not even remember what took place, one is almost tempted to regret the agony of study, analysis and decision that was our daily ration."[23]

Heather Cox Richardson observed: "Lincoln, [Theodore] Roosevelt, and Eisenhower each believed that government must not privilege any specific economic interest, neither stacking the deck for the rich nor redistributing wealth to the poor."[24]

The role of government, in Eisenhower's view, was to find measures that would foster conditions that would grow the middle class, and to provide a social safety net that would protect the elderly and those who suffered misfortunes such as an accident, illness, disability, or unemployment.[25] At the same time federal investments in infrastructure, such as the Eisenhower initiatives to build the Interstate Highway System and the St. Lawrence Seaway (with Canada), were vital for the growing economy. Ike worried greatly about our road network and our airports becoming outdated and unable to handle the requirements of the modern era.

He remembered well the 1919 Army Motor Corps convoy he was a part of that traveled from Washington, DC, to San Francisco. It took sixty-two days to cross the country—a "tortuous" journey punctuated by 230 road incidents that included getting stuck on muddy, unpaved roads and the repair of eighty-eight wooden bridges that gave way. Eisenhower also recalled the key role the German autobahn had played during the war. The United States would need to be connected more efficiently if it was to prosper economically and defend the entire country in case of attack.[26]

The federal government, he believed, must also help states build classrooms to accommodate the postwar baby boom—but only for states that could not afford to accommodate the students ready for school. In fact, the president pressed his cabinet members on this: "If we don't hurry and build schoolrooms our whole level of education is going down," he told them.[27]

Ed, no doubt, worried out loud about this policy. In a reply Ike explained his views:

> There is a vast difference between Federal domination and Federal performance of a job that needs to be done . . . inadequate education of our youth could, and would unless greater facilities were provided, become a *national* calamity. Consequently, the Federal government, without trying to take any control of education to assume any dominant position with respect to it, still has to view with the deepest concern the failure of the states to move promptly and adequately in this regard.[28]

Education was at the heart of commerce and progress, Eisenhower believed. But so, too, were equity and conciliation between workers and management, according to Heather Cox Richardson. Given his deeply embedded empathy for working men (and also veterans) he did not "see disaffected workers as a threat. . . . Protesters," he thought, "identified important inequalities that the government must address."[29]

At the same time, Ike observed before and during the war

that "economically dispossessed people were natural targets for political and religious extremism."[30] His wartime experience no doubt led him to conclude that business and labor need not be on opposite sides of the barricades. He had seen firsthand how the synchronization of America's industrial might, along with the commitment, courage, and tenacity of ordinary Americans, had produced not just results—but victory. In the United States, however, in the immediate postwar period, America had experienced long-forgotten labor disruptions. This trend had to be addressed. It seems almost like science fiction today to note that on being elected president in 1953, this Republican president's first secretary of labor was the former president of the nation's most important trade union—the AFL-CIO.

Eisenhower had been thinking about labor and management for many years. In 1947 he told an audience that class interests were not irreconcilable; rather, labor and management were interdependent: "In our tightly knit economy, all professions and callings . . . have points of contact and areas of common interest, banker or housewife, farmer, carpenter, soldier—no one of us can live and act without effect on all others."[31]

And, finally, one other group that needed to find its place back at the table was what the historian Robert Ferrell called "the controllers of the enterprise"—the business community, who were still largely blamed for the Great Depression. Eisenhower had had a different experience with the captains of industry during the war. These industrialists were behind the "Arsenal of Democracy"—which produced vitally important equipment and armaments for the United States and our Allies in the struggle against the Nazis.

During the 1950s, wealthy businessmen would pay tax rates unheard of today, at a top rate of 91 percent, and they would be tapped to modernize our country's industrial base and infrastructure as the United States prepared to provide the necessary leadership at home and abroad.[32] At the same time millions of veterans took advantage of the 1944 GI Bill, which offered free higher education to those who had served. They entered the work force educated and prepared to build a strong middle class, a bulwark against subversion—and the platform on which the Middle Way could be built and sustained.

However, throughout Ike's two terms in office, the president's brother Edgar never tired of expressing his views. Ed, and many like him, wanted a mythical America, a laissez-faire society in which freedom is, in essence, freedom from obligation. Edgar, and the others who espoused this view, never gave up—but neither did Ike.

On May 2, 1956, the president defended his "middle-of-the-road policies" in a letter to his brother. Edgar—who surely knew that among the things that Ike disliked most was the practice of using labels to describe people and their political views—had apparently sent Ike a newspaper clipping for his response.

Ike wrote: "I am a little amused about this word 'real' that in your clipping modifies the word 'Republican.' I assume that Lincoln was a *real* Republican—in fact, I think we should have to assume that every President, being the elected leader of the Party, is a *real* Republican. Therefore, the President's branch of the Party requires, for its description no adjective whatsoever. I should think that the splinter groups, which oppose the leader, would be the ones requiring the descriptive adjectives. In any event, please look up sometime what Lincoln had to say about the proper *functions* of government."[33]

The Republicans were flailing and divided on what kind of party they wanted to be—the Republican Party that existed before the Great Depression or a modern one, ready to embrace the postwar reality that had inescapably changed.[34]

Matters became more complex as the economy in 1953 looked likely to fall into recession. This was a challenge for the administration, given the GOP's long association with the origins of the Depression in 1929. Eisenhower ordered that the government plan for "remedial" action should an economic "emergency" arise, but he was loath to take preemptive stimulating actions—as satisfying and as politically useful as they might be. He also held firm to his assertion that there would be no tax cuts until the budget was in surplus. The administration was making progress in that direction: The Truman estimate of the budget deficit for June of fiscal 1954 had been $9.9 billion—and under the Eisenhower policies the actual budget deficit was just $5.5 billion.[35]

All the recession-fighting measures that the administration had kept at the ready were never necessary. The recession, in the administration's assessment, never became severe enough to warrant them. However, the economic downturn did have some effect on the 1954 midterm elections. Without Eisenhower's coattails, the GOP lost their slim majority—and their control of Congress—though the shift was relatively small, indicating that the voters had not given a mandate to the Democrats either.

The GOP "blamed the 1954 defeat on the administration," recalled Sherman Adams, "for not giving people the change from policies of the New Deal that they voted for in 1952."[36]

Aside from the alarm and pessimism that a faction of the GOP felt about their party's president, "1954 turned out to be the most prosperous year that the United States ever had under a peacetime economy up to that point," Adams later wrote. "[It demonstrated that] free enterprise could hold its own under pressure with no government intervention other than indirect money control to discourage deflation and inflation."[37]

Despite these achievements, Edgar saw nothing but dangers on the horizon, and he harassed the president about what he should do. Ike snapped back on November 8, 1954: "You also talk about the 'bad political advice' I am getting. I always assumed that lawyers attempted accuracy in their statements. How do you know I am getting *any* political advice?"[38]

Ike continued with exasperation: "Next, if I do get political advice, how do you know that it is not weighed in the direction you seem to think it should be—although I am tempted at times to believe you are just thrashing around rather than thinking anything through to a definite conclusion? . . . But the mere repetition of aphorisms and political slogans and newspaper headlines leaves me cold."[39]

Ike was justifiably proud that within only a short time his administration had begun the necessary re-centering and political renewal, after years of emergency improvisation due to the Depression, World War II, the Korean War, and one-party rule.

His first term had produced some landmark accomplishments. At the top of the list was inspiring new confidence in the country's governmental institutions. This had required "cleaning up" Washington after Truman-era corruption scandals that had ensnared the IRS and the so-called five percenters, people who traded in government influence.

Next was the necessity to redefine and recalibrate the country's economy after two decades of price controls and wartime defense budgets. And finally, presidential leadership had to address the rising fears of ordinary Americans, as the United States was engaged in its third year of war in Asia.

Eisenhower worked hard to mitigate the pessimistic messages of his party's right wing, so that they would not overwhelm ordinary Americans who were weary of war and eager to find prosperity and calm. At the same time, he focused on convincing the nation that the United States had new leadership responsibilities in the world.

In addition to the economic reforms, Ike's first term in office would entail securing the end of McCarthyism, orchestrating an armistice in Korea, and recalibrating U.S. security policy after the death of the Soviet Union's absolute dictator, Joseph Stalin, on March 5, 1953.

The president believed that a strong bulwark had to be built against Communism. This required domestic harmony, a strong two-party system, financial solvency, which demanded a sound tax and Social Security policy, and the imperative to make our system work for *everyone.*

The administration's progress, and Ike's cool head, would strengthen our democracy in many ways, not least of which would be a commitment to assure that civility was a mainstream value in our political life. But for democracy to prosper, he thought, we would have to guard against the influence of "pressure groups" and "the inability of men to forego immediate gain for a long-time good."[40]

As he had said that day in 1949 in St. Louis, before he was even a presidential contender:

> [The Middle Way is] progress down the center, even though there the contest is hottest, the progress sometimes discouraging slow . . . Extremists hope that we will lack the stubborn courage, the stamina, and the intelligent faith required to sustain this position. By appeals to immediate and selfish advantage. . . . [They recommit us to the proposition that] no part of our society may prosper permanently except as the whole of America shall prosper.[41]

Cabinet meeting, May 10, 1957. Left to right: Wilton Persons, Henry Cabot Lodge, Fred Seaton, George Humphrey, Richard Nixon, Herbert Brownell, Sinclair Weeks, Marion Folsom, Val Peterson, Percival Brundage, Gordon Gray, James Mitchell, Arthur Summerfield, John Foster Dulles, Dwight Eisenhower, Charles Wilson, Ezra Taft Benson, Maxwell Rabb, and Sherman Adams. (National Park Service)

8

IKE'S RULES FOR GOOD GOVERNANCE

Not long after Eisenhower was elected president, his brother Milton asked him to come to Penn State University to give the convocation address. The university planned for guests to assemble in the outdoor stadium to hear the president's speech. That morning over breakfast Milton noted that the weather was unpredictable: Intermittent showers were forecast. He asked Ike whether they should take a chance and hold the event outside or move it indoors to a smaller venue, thus drastically reducing the number of people who could hear the president speak.

Ike looked up from his eggs and said nonchalantly: "You decide. I haven't worried about the weather since June 6, 1944!"[1]

To the consternation of his brother, this true story tells a lot about Eisenhower as a strategic thinker: "Don't sweat the small stuff" to avoid being drawn into second- or third-order issues that should be properly handled at a lower level. The president believed it was imperative to organize the executive branch in the right way, consistent with the special roles and responsibilities of the president of the United States, while addressing the rapidly changing geopolitical and technological environment.

Eisenhower understood perhaps better than most presidents that the job brings with it special challenges, the most significant of which is a strategic/constitutional one. The responsibilities placed on the president by our Constitution demand that this public servant be head of state, head of the executive branch, and head of his or her political party simultaneously. In most other Western countries, these responsibilities are handled separately by monarch and prime minister or president and prime minister. Our Constitution has thus given our president contradictory roles, prompting most presidents to focus on serving as the head of the executive branch and/or the leader of his or her political party.

Eisenhower understood that the key role of a head of state is to unify the country. Since national unity was arguably his highest priority, it was from this point of view that he tackled his job for eight years. This did not mean, however, that he did not address his other roles. He was deeply engaged in them, but he tried to keep the messy political jostling and wrangling out of view, while behind the scenes he was chairing the debates, directing the maneuvers, and making the crucial final decisions. He was adept at working through others to achieve his objectives.

Fred Greenstein, who was one of the first prominent Eisenhower revisionist historians, asserted that he was an "activist" president, but of a "distinctive kind."

"It was [his] activist style that resolved [the] contradiction inherent in the job specifications of the American presidency," Greenstein wrote. This was one reason why Eisenhower had for so long been "misunderstood."[2]

Herbert Brownell, the nation's top lawyer, observed Eisenhower in this context and once told me that the president was sensitive to these differing goals and worked hard to find ways to reconcile them.

As president of the United States, Eisenhower took an oath to defend the Constitution. He understood the depths of this profoundly important pledge (one that he had first made as a young cadet at West Point), and he was utterly dedicated to its precepts. He was a constitutionalist. There is no greater evidence for this than his approach, as president, to the courts.

Eisenhower did not believe that the political process should taint the courts, as an independent branch of government. He also wanted to see a balance on the Supreme Court between Democrats and Republicans. During his two-term presidency, Eisenhower appointed five judges to the Supreme Court.

Herbert Brownell wrote: "The President believed and acted upon the belief that the Supreme Court's membership should represent diverse ideological points of view." This would, in turn, foster public confidence in the court, which is an "unelected body."

"If the Senate should confirm only nominees with an ideology that conforms to the Senate's prevailing ideology," the former attorney general asserted, "it would be a signal that the Senate wanted the Court to decide constitutional issues not on an independent judicial basis but on a political ideological basis."[3]

When a Supreme Court vacancy occurred in 1956, Eisenhower told Brownell to search for a Democrat to be nominated for that position. "The president said the Supreme Court belonged to all the people and that a Democrat ought to know he has a friend on [the Court]." Justice William J. Brennan Jr., a New Jersey Democrat, was selected. He later went on to become one of the longest-serving—and most progressive—justices on the bench. It is noteworthy that his selection took place *during* the 1956 campaign year.[4]

Eisenhower told Brownell that except for the position of chief justice, the administration would confine its Supreme Court selections to individuals who had served minor federal benches or on state supreme courts.[5]

Ike also had very strong views on the professionalism of federal judges, insisting that they must also be endorsed by the American Bar Association and other distinguished bodies. This, however, did not stop his brother Edgar, a trial lawyer, from offering more unsolicited advice.

Ed's personal recommendations, or those of his colleagues, regarding federal bench nominees, infuriated the president. He was so irked by a letter from his brother that he responded with the verbal equivalent of a good Abilene punch in the nose. In a terse reply on March 23, 1956, Ike wrote:

> *Dear Ed,*
> *Nothing gives me such a great sense of frustration as to realize that even the lawyers of this country have not come to understand that I do not consider federal judgeships as included in the list of appointments subject to "patronage." In any event, when my own brother and, from my viewpoint, my best political friend in the entire Northwest, begins to get at odds on such things, I had better be especially careful. As ever*[6]

With regard to Congress, the Constitution's other coequal branch, the president was ever mindful of that body's solemn responsibilities.[7] Over the course of his eight-year presidency a number of critical issues would emerge that required a thoughtful approach to the respective authorities granted each branch of government by the Constitution. His efforts included, among other things, intensified outreach to members of both parties.

For carrying out his complex mixture of duties, Eisenhower built a White House organization that worked not only for his own management style but also to ensure the proper study and consideration of proposed policies, not to mention examining contingencies that might be required for any critical domestic or international situation.

The president deeply believed that any major endeavor had to be organized for success. Eisenhower was said by his associates to have a healthy dose of self-awareness and self-knowledge in understanding his own default assumptions and convictions. That's why he embraced the idea of surrounding himself with people who were smart, confident, and accomplished—with strong opinions of their own. During the war he had been enormously effective at managing diverse viewpoints and über-type-A personalities. As much as that job may have worn on the supreme commander, he gained something invaluable from it too. It forced him to question his own thinking constantly, and he encouraged this push-back from officers and aides, an interaction he found useful to replicate in his presidency.

In the White House, Eisenhower would elicit the views of his subordinates, referee their debates, listen for new perspectives, and then make his own decision. He was the supreme decider: the strategic leader.

Ike believed in a cabinet-oriented executive branch, and he delegated significant authority to cabinet members, under the framework of his policies.

Many in the president's cabinet came from American industry, but most of them were previously personally unknown to the president. After the election, Ike set up a small transition team to identify possible candidates, along with a systematic process to ensure that each of them was properly vetted. There was one exception to the rule, Brownell recalled: "Eisenhower generally instructed us not to leave Taft's people out of the cabinet, telling us he wanted all points of view represented, but beyond those . . . [Lucius] Clay and I had a remarkably free hand in the process."[8] This would be a way to unify the party after the bruising nomination fight.

Indeed, Eisenhower made it clear from the outset that he was more intent on getting good people to join the administration than he was concerned about a possible appointee's political orientation—as long as they could be counted on to join the president's Middle Way. (This approach extended to the East Wing. When planning receptions and dinner gatherings, the First Lady would tell her staff that she was *not* interested in knowing what political party her guests were associated with. "When they come to the White House," Mamie would say, "they come as guests of the American people.")

After cabinet nominees had been selected and the president made his choices, he would leave it to others to propose to them the idea of joining the administration. The transition team would establish a candidate's interest, and was there to help avoid embarrassment for the potential recruit should he or she decline to join the administration. However, very few, if any, turned down the opportunity to serve.[9]

Eisenhower wanted the cabinet to be well versed in *all* administration policy, even areas outside any particular secretary's authority. Before each weekly cabinet meeting, the agenda and a background paper would be sent to each member and other invited participants, and they would be expected to participate in a discussion on far-ranging subjects, even those outside a member's expertise.[10]

Arthur Larson, as director of the United States Information Agency, which promoted America's story overseas, had occasion to attend cabinet meetings. If not for the system, he said, he would have never had the opportunity to weigh in on matters such as Social Security, for instance.[11]

At the same time Eisenhower sought the views of liberals, conservatives, and everyone in between, including his family members—even Ed!—as well as high school classmates, leaders from many sectors, and anyone else who could offer a different perspective. Many of those with divergent views were right there in the White House. Among the conservatives: Secretary of Commerce Sinclair Weeks; Secretary of Agriculture Ezra Taft Benson; "Cold War conservative" Lewis Strauss, chairman of the Atomic Energy Commission; and Secretary of State John Foster Dulles. He also listened to the "liberals"—his own brother Milton Eisenhower, who was given intermittent advisory assignments; Herbert Brownell, attorney general and civil rights advocate; and Secretary of Health, Education, and Welfare Oveta Culp Hobby, the second female cabinet member; and long-serving Secretary of Labor James P. Mitchell, who advocated for migrant workers, opposed employment discrimination, and supported labor's right to organize.

J. Ernest Wilkins Sr., who was appointed assistant secretary of labor for international affairs in 1954, also periodically attended cabinet meetings—the first African American in such a high-ranking position and the first to attend presidential cabinet meetings.[12]

Eisenhower's associates were clear on this point: The president did not like yes-men, and he wanted to know his advisers' real convictions: "Prove your case to me" was his approach.[13]

When the president challenged or prodded an adviser during these discussions, "[he] was not being hostile," recalled Gen. Lucius Clay, who had known Eisenhower since the 1930s. "He was merely trying to test the man's strength of belief and his logic."[14]

Eisenhower was also committed to empowering others and earning their buy-in. His diverse cabinet, and their interaction on all issues before the president, created a de facto integration of domestic and foreign policy. Treasury Secretary George Humphrey came to the administration determined to cut government spending and taxes. But being part of this coherent organizational structure gave him a deeper appreciation of the nation's requirements as a whole, including national security issues.

When Colorado senator Eugene Millikin was lobbying the secretary for an immediate tax cut, Humphrey "indignantly" reminded the senator of the "atomic Pearl Harbor that is hanging over our heads"—making clear reference to the extreme dangers of a surprise attack on the United States, and the military requirements necessary for deterring it.[15]

The president relied on Attorney General Brownell on legal matters, as well as on other cabinet secretaries whose fields were outside Eisenhower's experience. But when it came to national security, the president had "mastery" over the most crucial role a chief executive plays—in the national security of our country. "[The president] may not have learned too much from us," Brownell recalled. "In the two-thirds of his job dealing with foreign and military affairs he knew more than all of us put together." Despite this, Eisenhower was always open to constructive advice and opinions from his cabinet members—indeed, he relied on vibrant discussions.[16]

As the strategic leader the president had to balance and integrate the overall goals and policies of his administration. Ultimately he would be the one to ensure policy coherence and keep his administration and the country on a steady course. At the same time, he had to avoid allowing himself to get too far into the details, relying on an able corps of administrators, such as his chief of staff Sherman Adams, a gruff, no-nonsense guy, much like Gen. Walter Bedell Smith, his wartime staff chief.

Ike, adept at this approach from his earlier experience, watched, listened, and tested his subordinates—eventually learning how much autonomy he could give each one to get the maximum results.

General Goodpaster recounted that he once said to President Eisenhower: "It must take guts to delegate." Eisenhower's reply was to quote the nineteenth-century German general Helmuth von Moltke, who said: "Centralization is the refuge of fear."[17]

This systematic approach to structuring the policy-making process was a key way to hold his associates and himself accountable. The delegation aspect was critical. General Goodpaster recalled that the key was to get the "straightforward" and "routine" matters out of the White House and handled by the relevant departments and agencies. Policy guidelines were imposed so that decisions made at that level were consistent with the administration's overall policy.[18]

To ensure that administration policy was followed and that there was a clear accountability loop, Eisenhower instituted a highly effective internal process.

Not only did the cabinet meet once a week, but so did the National Security Council (NSC) as well as a Planning Board and an Operations Coordinating Board that supported it. The NSC, chaired by the president, met 366 times over the course of eight years. Eisenhower himself chaired 329 of those meetings—a remarkable record when one considers the health problems he endured and the enormous amount of overseas travel he undertook.[19] This is in contrast with the Kennedy administration, for instance, which disbanded this system. Kennedy held only two cabinet meetings before the Bay of Pigs fiasco on April 19, 1961.[20]

The Eisenhower system involved considerable work, but its structure was rather simple. The NSC was a small body of eight. Aside from such key people as the president, the vice president, the secretaries of state and defense, and the director of the CIA, the secretary of the treasury, and the director of the Bureau of the Budget also sat on this body. Eisenhower wanted to ensure that every foreign policy decision he made would be informed by what we call today a cost-benefit analysis—or an economic impact statement.

In preparation for the weekly NSC meeting, the Planning Board, a small group of undersecretary-level officials of the departments involved, would resolve interagency disputes, produce memorandums, and brief their principal before the meeting convened.

At the NSC a vigorous debate would ensue. After the two-hour meeting a rapporteur would assemble the minutes, which he would then share with the president and others for their accuracy.[21] The president's decisions would be directed to a coordinator assigned to follow up on them. Through the Operations Coordinating Board this small group would see to it that the president's decisions were implemented. A special assistant to the president for national security, a position held for many years by the New England banker Gen. Robert "Bobby" Cutler, supervised the whole process.[22]

Other innovations were fashioned for the times. One was the establishment of a congessional liaison office. First occupied by retired general Wilton "Jerry" Persons, its purpose was to assure steady, ongoing communications with members of the House and Senate, making members of Congress, including Democrats, partners in some of the critical issues that needed to be addressed.

Eisenhower started by making it clear to his staff that if a congressman or senator, Republican and Democrat alike, called to talk to the president, he or she should be put straight through.

Another important effort in the field of national security was Eisenhower's attempt to bring some kind of accountability to the Central Intelligence Agency (CIA). Over his eight years he was behind a "steady effort to tighten control" over the agency—and its independent-minded director, Allen Dulles, brother of John Foster Dulles. When Eisenhower became president the agency had the authority to conceive of and launch covert actions. The presidential apparatus could offer advice but had no final authority.

On March 12, 1955 (in NSC 5412/1), authority for CIA activity was moved to the Operations Coordinating Board, under the president himself. Later that year a "Special Group," eventually known as the Forty Committee—with representatives from State, Defense, and the president's office—assumed this oversight. The struggle to rein in the CIA was never wholly successful. The agency was so freewheeling in its mentality that there were those who actually thought that it was an independent entity, like the Federal Reserve Board.[23]

The job of the presidency, Eisenhower thought, was too big for any one individual. He needed the full picture and diverse input, and as a man trained in military matters he insisted on robust contingency planning.

The *New York Times* columnist Arthur Krock once asked President Lyndon Johnson what he thought of President Eisenhower. Johnson praised Eisenhower for his "sharp" mind and recounted that when he conferred with Eisenhower, Ike would say: "Have you taken steps against these contingencies and plugged these holes?" And Johnson added: "They were always acute points overlooked by most whiz kids."[24]

Ike was determined that the White House inner workings be organized in a way to ensure that the chain of command enhanced cooperation and coordination. Key to the consideration of any issue was a commitment to establish the facts and then follow them no matter where they led.

As Bill Ewald later observed, Eisenhower set up an organization that "in the end served him, not he it." And Ike understood that all wisdom *cannot* reside within the mind of one man.[25]

For all this structure, nobody knew better than the former supreme commander of Allied forces that personal relationships are central to everything—with other policy makers and with the public at large.

Once a week the president hosted a breakfast for rotating members of Congress so that he could get to know them and learn more about what was on their minds. He also met once a week for a meal with the congressional leadership. Ike's friend Ellis Slater noted with surprise that even at state dinners, Ike invited all his adversaries.[26]

Ike would also engage them in a good game of golf, as a way to build trust and mend fences. When pundits once predicted that Gov. Frank Lausche of Ohio would be the Democratic candidate to run against Eisenhower in 1956, the governor came to see Eisenhower in the Oval Office, to assure the president that he had no such intentions. At the conclusion of the meeting Ike invited Lausche to play golf with him at Augusta National, joking that they could set tongues a-wagging. "Let's do it," the president said, "We'll confound all the political experts. They will think we're trying to make up a combination [presidential] ticket."[27] (Later some of his advisers reported that Eisenhower actually considered putting Lausche on the 1956 ticket as his running mate.[28])

The only way to make progress, Eisenhower asserted, is "compromise, conciliation and persuasion." This approach produced results, especially during the six years that Congress was in the hands of the Democrats. As president he managed to get 80 percent of his legislative agenda through Congress.[29] The record on Ike's vetoes is also noteworthy. For seven years—through one

Republican and two Democratic Congresses—Eisenhower did not have one veto overturned, until 1959 on a "typical pork-barrel bill."[30]

While the president was a believer in team building, he was not what Herbert Brownell thought of as a personal friend. Eisenhower did not, by and large, make friends—in a social sense—with his cabinet and subcabinet team. The only possible exception was Treasury Secretary George Humphrey.[31] This no doubt had to do with the fact that he and Humphrey had mutual friends. This desire to stay aloof socially from his "subordinates" made it easier for Ike to take a firm stand if he had to relieve anyone on his team.

"We were comrades in arms, but not cronies," Brownell recalled.[32]

Nevertheless Ike had enormous regard for the people who were part of his team. He gave them a lot of latitude, and did not much care if they, not he, got the credit for their accomplishments. He also backed them up to the hilt—even when he did not necessarily agree with the ways they sometimes solved their department's problems.

Ike wanted good reviews for his administration, and cabinet members were expected to take some of the political heat. But Eisenhower did not demand that he be the person to take the bows. Herbert Brownell later marveled at Ike's lack of concern over bragging rights.[33]

The respect the president afforded his colleagues could be discerned in the way he would respond to an issue. Ike did not say at press conferences, "I have directed the Secretary," but rather, "I have approved the Secretary's proposal."[34]

As Eisenhower once said: "It is better to have one person working *with* you than three working *for* you."[35] (Emphasis added.)

In dealing with the public, Eisenhower had a key rule that would guide his entire team: Be transparent and accountable. This was quite an important charge, given the amount of personal autonomy Ike afforded his cabinet colleagues. The insistence on transparency was important for public confidence and trust, and it ensured that cabinet members would be held responsible for the proper workings of their departments.

Jim Hagerty, Ike's press secretary, recalled that he was one of the first presidents to institute weekly press conferences where he would face reporters and answer their questions. Eisenhower had "two fundamental rules he used in the Army that always worked well," Hagerty noted. The president shared his thoughts on them not long after the start of the administration. Hagerty was told:

"[One], if an error [is] made, admit it in detail and spell it out so that it [tells] the complete story of the error, and two, . . . show a plan for preventing the recurrence of any such error. Then stand your ground. Be dignified but tough. Say it was an error. Say it won't happen again and don't say anything else. [And three,] Don't try to be cute or cover up. If you do, you will get so entangled you won't know what you're doing."[36]

He was also insistent that it is good policy to "get the facts out."

As events would show, however, some circumstances impeded even the president's most deeply held views. Where national security and classified programs were concerned, during the U-2 incident and the missile gap controversy for instance, he would find himself constrained in his public pronouncements by the necessity to deprive the enemy of our intelligence findings and our intentions.

As his presidency progressed, the president would also refuse to counter his critics, and would not criticize them publicly.

Hagerty remembered that once Ike watched the Republican majority leader, California senator William Knowland, an opponent of the United Nations, as he "popped off" on the subject. The president told his press secretary, as he was walking into a press conference, that rather than say something critical of Knowland, he would simply find an analogy for why the United States should work harder to make the UN successful: "If I am asked a question [about Knowland's remarks], I am going to say that we do not give up on our research laboratories here at home just because we have a few failures in research. Instead we should double our efforts to make them work."[37]

In a letter on March 9, 1954, Eisenhower wrote a California friend, Paul Helms, on this refusal to attack individual personalities. During the past thirteen years of being in the public eye, he began:

> I developed a practice which, so far as I know, I have never violated. The practice is to avoid public mention of any name unless *it can be done with favorable intent and connotation*; reserve all criticism for the private conference; speak only good in public.
>
> This is not namby-pamby. It is certainly not Pollyanna-ish. It is just sheer common sense. A leader's job is to get others to go along with him in the promotion of something. To do this he needs their good will. To destroy goodwill, it is only necessary to criticize publicly. This creates in the criticized one a subconscious desire to "get even." Such effects can last for a very long period.[38]

Eisenhower simply would not talk personalities, nor would he use the "bully pulpit" if he thought the broader objective could be undermined by moralizing.

Jim Hagerty and speechwriters like Arthur Larson soon learned that along with this iron will, Eisenhower had his own ideas on how to communicate. No speech draft was safe from the president. As a former speechwriter himself, Ike was intimately involved in crafting what he would say publicly. He would provide penetrating analysis privately, but did not want to talk above the public in a way that would make them feel like they were being lectured to or patronized. Regarding the president's manner of speech, Larson recalled: "I quickly learned that [he] would practically never use comparables and was death on superlatives."

Eisenhower also had a "distaste" for "flamboyant and ostentatious" language, not to mention public pronouncements that were "imprecise" and "unprovable." "After all, if you claim to be the leader of the greatest political movement of your time, for instance, you might arouse in others defensiveness, and—who knows?—you may at some later date need their help in pursuing your policies." The president, according to Larson, had developed this philosophy having watched his old boss, Gen. Douglas MacArthur, "who was always tossing off such grandiose statements."[39]

If Eisenhower had a number of rules for his administration, he had just as many for himself. Three illustrate the point:

As Ike tried to bring America's spending habits under control, he was the first to order such savings in his own household. Mamie never got the chance to decorate the White House as she had hoped, not even their second-floor living quarters. Ike and Mamie kept their own personal car that she would use for long drives to visit family. And the Gettysburg vegetable garden, at their personal farm, often yielded produce that Ike and Mamie sent to the White House, at no cost to the taxpayer, for state dinners as well as family meals. Mamie clipped coupons for the White House shopper and could often be heard to say: "Don't run it on the eagle"—which meant not to waste taxpayers' money.

My great-uncle Milton, who was often on assignment for the government, stayed at the White House when he was in town. He stopped this practice when he discovered that the president and First Lady were paying a nightly room rate for him to stay overnight in the executive mansion. "Even though I was there on official business Ike thought that a brother should be regarded as a guest," he recalled.[40]

Eisenhower insisted that no special consideration should be given any of his friends, either for a job or in the pursuit of policy. According to associates, this was nearly an obsession with the president: "He delivered a strong warning against such favor seekers at his first cabinet meeting," Sherman Adams recalled. The president said: "If anybody says he wants a job because he is a friend of mine, throw him out of your office." And at a cabinet meeting on July 29, 1955, he reminded his colleagues of his strong views on this: "May I remind you once again if anybody seeks a favor out of alleged friendship with me, let this please fall on stony ears." Indeed, Adams recalled: "The patronage pickings were so lean under Eisenhower that they became a subject of grim humor among the Republican politicians in Washington."[41]

For himself, Ike's political and foreign policy principles were advanced with a kind of optimistic fatalism about his own standing. His responsibility was to make the strategic decisions, have a strong group of associates to execute those decisions, and then let the cards fall where they may. On countless occasions I heard him say: "You've got to play the hand you've been dealt."

This came with an apparent indifference to his political future, a seemingly odd attitude today.

Throughout his presidency Ike's sense of duty, and the philosophy that came with it, prompted the same kind of fatalism that he had demonstrated during the war. He was determined to do what he had to do, take responsibility for his decisions, and put aside his own personal fortunes.

For decades after the Eisenhower presidency, his critics wrote vociferous critiques about the cumbersome White House bureaucracy, Eisenhower's "inept" and "lazy leadership," and many other assessments that did not reflect the real situation. Perhaps there was one principle the president employed that was never understood by his greatest critics: a strategic leader's responsibility to avoid impulsiveness and short-term thinking.

After the war's end, when the luxury of a longer lead time for decision making became possible, Ike recounted how important it was in this new environment to avoid jumping to conclusions. He learned that in the political world, where goals might differ and special interests might dominate, what he might read or what he could glean from others might not be the full picture of what was really going on.

Over the years "I grew increasingly cautious about making

judgments based solely on reports," he wrote. "Behind every human action, the truth may be hidden. But the truth may also lie behind some other action or arrangement, far off in time and place. Unless circumstances and responsibility demanded an instant judgment I learned to reserve mine until the last proper moment. This was not always popular."[42]

Eisenhower and members of his staff work on the annual budget in his office at Key West Naval Station, January 3, 1956. (U.S. Navy Photographical Center)

9

THE INTERCONNECTIONS BETWEEN WAR AND PEACE

Gen. Andrew Goodpaster and other associates of the president used to tell me that one of the great assets Dwight Eisenhower had in any negotiation was his honesty and trustworthiness. Our allies and adversaries did not question his credibility or his word. Like Eisenhower's relationship with the public, his integrity abroad—even in the Soviet bloc—would be beneficial for the president on many occasions to come. With respect to peace, Ike understood that saying that it was desirable would never be enough. He was determined that America, under his leadership, would clearly demonstrate our peaceful aspirations.

"It is essential in the [geopolitical] struggle that the world know something about our good intentions, latent strength, respect for the rights of others," Ike once wrote. "Since our opponent has to depend on lies, and we can tell the truth, the advantage would seem to be with us. But the truth must be nailed, banner-like to a staff, and we must do that by convincing the whole world that our announced intentions of peace are the truth."[1]

The year 1953 was a time for such bold reminders. Concurrent with budget fights, Republican intraparty strain over foreign aid and the United Nations—as well as issues related to managing Sen. Joseph McCarthy's toxic anti-Communist crusade—there were even more urgent items of business around just such issues. These included the Korean War, which was still being fought; the unexpected death of Soviet dictator Joseph Stalin; and recalibrating America's thinking on the Cold War and our defensive posture in meeting the continuing Soviet threat.

In the last weeks of the campaign, candidate Eisenhower had declared: "I will go to Korea." In December, after his victory, the president-elect made a secret visit to Korea to assess the situation. He had a schedule jammed full of meetings during his seventy-two-hour trip. Among the most important things he did was ride in a helicopter over the front lines to assess the situation personally. He did not need more time to come away with a very clear conclusion: "We could not stand forever on a static front and continue to accept casualties without any visible results. Small attacks on small hills would not end wars."[2]

To President Truman's consternation, on Eisenhower's return he contacted his old boss, Gen. Douglas MacArthur, who had been fired the year before as commander in Korea, and they compared notes. Eisenhower, like MacArthur, had concluded that the status quo in Korea was unacceptable, and that even a demarcation between North Korea and South Korea would be preferable to a stalemate—though they both might have had a different way of concluding the standoff.[3]

Intelligence suggested that the North Koreans might be ready for an end to the fighting. But there were factual misconceptions, a complex geopolitical situation with the Chinese and Russians involved, and difficulties in effecting concerted action among the other UN forces. Perhaps the greatest challenge to reaching an armistice was the attitude of the South Korean president, Syngman

Rhee, who refused bring an end to the war without total victory. In this Rhee's views aligned with those of many GOP hard-liners.

It has been suggested that the administration let it be known through nonpublic channels that it was prepared to use nuclear weapons to bring about the end of the war. This is disputed by some of Eisenhower's associates and scholars. But certainly the administration was studying the prospects for scaling up the war with the aim of achieving a conclusive victory. Given the president's credibility as the successful supreme Allied commander in Europe, the enemy may have had good reason to believe that the choice was a stark one.[4]

By the late spring of 1953, the Chinese and the Russians, along with the North Koreans, were ready to make major concessions in the armistice talks.[5] The confluence of these factors led to an end to the war.

On July 27, 1953, six months after Eisenhower came into office, the armistice was signed and is still in effect today.

Americans were split about the United States' ascension as the world's sole superpower—but that was only part of the reason Ike was able to bring the Korean War to an end. He saw little prospect of complete victory, short of resorting to extreme measures. The president did not think that the military should be involved in stalemates. Wars without a clear path to victory would either bleed dry our forces and resources, or threaten to get bigger, possibly even leading to an existential confrontation. The United States was already in danger of violating maxims that Eisenhower had absorbed from Gen. Fox Conner: "Never fight unless you have to"; "Never fight alone"; and "Never fight for long." Ike had made this thinking his own.

The other legacy that had been left to the new president was the management of what might be called the "nuclear dilemma." In the public mind anything "nuclear" spelled unparalleled destruction and danger—the world had seen its capacities in Japan at the end of World War II. If the United States could bring such destruction on Japan, why couldn't our Cold War enemy do such a thing to us? The terrifying scenario that consumed policy makers and the public at large revolved around the prospect of a "surprise attack." With no way to monitor Soviet preparations for war, and no way to really get a handle on the Kremlin's thinking, the nation felt a sense of vulnerability that would become starkly evident during specific early chapters of the Cold War.

Dr. Isidor I. Rabi, who had known and worked with Eisenhower at Columbia, described the period as one of "intense emotionalism."[6]

"Fear, anxiety, uncertainty and suspicion colored the discourse and established the mood," wrote Rabi's biographer, John S. Rigden.[7] Despite Eisenhower's determination, dispelling the sense of pessimism and fear that had gripped Americans would be one of his biggest challenges.

The building of the hydrogen bomb had been a controversial Truman decision, and not just among the scientific community. At the heart of the issue were two basic facts: In making the decision, Truman had signaled to the world that we would be pursuing this weapon, even though at that time the United States did not yet know how to build one. Many believed that this statement of intention provoked the Russians to begin a crash program to develop the same technology.[8]

Second, the debate also swirled around what would constitute an adequate nuclear deterrent that would assure our security. Because of its exponentially greater capacity for destruction—from twenty thousand tons of TNT to one hundred million (which could vaporize its targets and beyond), there appeared to be a disconnect between those who thought that this weapon could be rationalized in current thinking and those who assured their colleagues, as well as policy makers, that "The power of this bomb is beyond the reach of our imagination."[9]

Indeed, Maj. Gen. James Burns, chairman of the Munitions Assignments Board, testified in favor of an accelerated program to produce the hydrogen bomb: "It is a fundamental law of defense that you always have to use the most powerful weapon you can produce."[10]

In the view of critics, however, what Burns and others failed to understand was that nuclear weapons of this destructive power broke all precedents and traditions. These weapons made "novices" of everyone. The developers of the weapons systems themselves, they asserted, were most qualified to help shape the debate because they understood the science behind the devices and they could envision their terrible potential.

On November 1, 1952, the United States tested its first fusion bomb, or hydrogen bomb, at Eniwetok in the Marshall Islands. It was one thousand times more powerful than the bombs that obliterated Hiroshima and Nagasaki. Three days later Dwight Eisenhower was elected for his first term as president of the United States.

Less than nine months after the U.S. test, on August 8, 1953, the Soviet Union detonated a hydrogen bomb of their own. Though only a prototype, it was shockingly clear that unless the United States and the USSR could find some way toward a "just and lasting peace," the two powers might, in Eisenhower's words, "confirm the hopeless finality of . . . two atomic colossi . . . doomed malevolently to eye each other indefinitely across a trembling world."[11]

To add to these urgent matters, Eisenhower confronted another big foreign policy challenge only months after his first inauguration. On March 5, 1953, Soviet dictator Joseph Stalin died. Stalin had transformed the Soviet Union, assuring literacy for all and building a scientific establishment capable of competing on many levels with its number one rival, the United States. The Soviet premier, however, left a very dark legacy for his own country and the world. He had been a butcher, a murderer—a man who had ruled his country with a fist of steel.[12] The number of people who perished under his rule is nearly incomprehensible. Some estimate that forty million Soviet people died under his brutal regime, in addition to the USSR's war losses. People were executed because they were rivals for power, but most were killed or left to starve for their political dissent or resistance to the Sovietization of the economy. Many also perished on Stalin's simple whim and that of his henchmen. This unrelenting terror was an end in itself and a guarantor of unlimited power.

On Stalin's death, Eisenhower expressed his simple hope that the Soviet people need not "continue the ways of a dead man." With his team, he laid out five precepts that the United States wished to advance. He clearly had the Soviet Union in mind when he compiled it, hoping its constructive tone would spur some cooperation on a range of security issues. It also encompassed America's strong view that the Soviet satellite countries had rights of their own:

> First: No people on earth can be held, as a people, to be an enemy, for all humanity shares the common hunger for peace and fellowship and justice.
>
> Second: No nation's security and well-being can be lastingly achieved in isolation but only in effective cooperation with fellow nations.
>
> Third: Any nation's right to a form of government and an economic system of its own choosing is inalienable.
>
> Fourth: Any nation's attempt to dictate to other nations their form of government is indefensible.
>
> And fifth: A nation's hope of lasting peace cannot be firmly based upon any race in armaments but rather upon just relations and honest understanding with all other nations.[13]

Stalin's death offered, in the best case, an opening with the USSR; in the worst, a continuation of his barbaric rule. The new Soviet leadership, however, was untested, and it was not clear which of the Soviet dictator's associates would rise to ultimate power.

Inside the administration there was a great debate about how to respond to what might be an "opening" for improving relations. Georgy Malenkov, the presumed heir to the Soviet strongman, suggested a four-power summit. One group within the administration thought agreeing to such a meeting would be premature without some clear signal that the new triumvirate ruling the USSR truly wanted to change its country's course. Others felt that a speech might serve to feel the Soviets out. Gauging their response to such a public presentation might yield valuable clues.

Eisenhower took control of the debate and decided to give a speech, introducing his five precepts and outlining the clear choice that now faced the USSR. If they would live by the precepts he set out, our countries could avert the lost potential for human betterment necessitated by the diversion of resources for armaments. If not, the cost of the continuing arms race would be high. The president worked closely with one of his speechwriters, Emmett Hughes. After one of the drafting sessions, Ike looked at Hughes and said casually after hearing an aircraft overhead: "[That] jet plane that roars over your head costs three-quarters of a million dollars. That is more money than a man making ten thousand dollars every year is going to make in his lifetime. What world can afford this kind of thing?"[14]

The president's observation would end up being one of the major themes of his address, which he eventually called "A Chance for Peace."

On April 16, 1953, a little over a month after Stalin's death, Eisenhower declared before the American Society of Newspaper Editors that if left unaddressed, the current situation offered two unacceptable outcomes. "What could the world or any nation in it hope for if no turning were found on this dread road? The worst is atomic war," he said:

> The best would be this: a life of perpetual fear and tension; a burden of arms draining the wealth and labor of all peoples. . . .
>
> Every gun that is made, every warship launched, every rocket fired, signifies, in the final sense, a theft from those

who hunger and are not fed, those who are cold and are not clothed. This world in arms is not spending money alone.

It is spending the sweat of its laborers, the genius of its scientists, the hopes of its children.

The cost of one modern heavy bomber is this: a modern brick school in more than 30 cities.

It is two electric power plants, each serving a town of 60,000 population.

It is two fine, fully equipped hospitals. It is some 50 miles of concrete highways.

We pay for a single fighter plane with a half million bushels of wheat.

We pay for a single destroyer with new homes that could have housed more than 8,000 people.

This, I repeat, is the best way of life to be found on the road the world has been taking.

This is not a way of life at all, in any true sense. Under the cloud of threatening war, it is humanity hanging from a cross of iron.

These plain and cruel truths define the peril and point to the hope that comes with this spring of 1953.

The speech, translated into forty-five languages, appeared on the front pages of *Pravda*, the USSR's main newspaper. Nevertheless it brought a muted response from Moscow. Several days later Secretary of State John Foster Dulles gave a speech himself that advanced a much tougher line—demonstrating a "good cop, bad cop" approach to the message the Kremlin received. The choices the Soviets faced were laid out clearly by these speeches.

The implications of Stalin's death were global. Understanding that, upon taking office Eisenhower asked for the Truman administration's contingency plans in the case of Stalin's death. There were none.

There were, however, Truman policies in place that continued to impact budgetary matters and the U.S. military posture. Under NSC 68, the administration had called for significant investments in the military budget—a hard-line approach designed to counter the Soviet Union largely through military means.

"National Security Council document NSC 68, a legacy of the Truman administration, would not be sustainable on a long-term basis, as the foundation for American security and military planning," General Goodpaster later recalled. "As a result Eisenhower devoted himself as a top priority to the development of policy and doctrine for dealing with the realities of security that *would* be sustainable."[15]

To Eisenhower the options currently on the table were "overly simplistic"—and experts within the government itself were deeply divided.

The secretary of state, John Foster Dulles, was in favor of "rollback," a hard-line notion that the United States should attempt, just short of war, to take back territory that had fallen to the Communists. Another group favored a more modest approach, "accepting communist expansion or risking a major war."[16]

Still others recognized that the costs associated with Korean War spending and the continuation of a hard-line approach to the Soviet Union were not "sustainable" for a country at peace. These three divergent views prompted Eisenhower to call for an internal assessment of the U.S. options for a cohesive strategy. It would take the form of a structured study that would give all viewpoints an opportunity to be examined, articulated, and weighed.

The process was called the Solarium Project. The exercise got its name from a sunroom/lounge on the third floor of the White House—the Solarium—that overlooks the Washington Monument. It is a highly informal space that was, in this case, conducive to real brainstorming sessions. Eisenhower assembled Robert "Bobby" Cutler, his special assistant for national security affairs, Secretary of State Dulles, and C. D. Jackson, his special assistant. He also included Treasury Secretary George Humphrey. They devised a three-team approach, using the best strategic thinkers in the government. The goal of the study was to produce a coherent strategy design that would "contribute to the demise of the communist states."

Team A was assembled to argue for "containment"—a policy that had been advanced during the Truman years. George F. Kennan, author of the concept—adopted in NSC 153—served on that study module.

Team B, or the "Drawing Line Team" was brought together to argue for prescribing a line around the Soviet bloc–controlled areas, which if crossed could trigger general war.

And Team C came together to make the case for "rollback." Eisenhower made sure that General Goodpaster was on that specific team to bring rigor to the deliberations, knowing that this group might be swayed by rollback's emotionally and politically satisfying appeal, without thinking through the costs and consequences of it.

There were twenty-one study participants, seven on each team. To facilitate their work the three groups were given full access to the intelligence files and assessments and any other government records that might be useful. They were also given cost estimates of military expenditures.

The groups were to address twenty key questions, as Goodpaster recalled years later. They were broad strategic questions, incorporating both the likely response of our adversaries and the cost of this policy. Some of the questions included: "What general results were expected over what time frame? What specific actions should be undertaken by the United States to implement the policy? . . . What would be the estimated cost? What features should be made public, and what should be kept secret? What would be the likely effects on relations with others?"[17]

Goodpaster remembered the enormous value of the exercise. As each team met and discussed the questions in the context of the constraints, strategic clarity began to emerge.

On July 16, 1953, the three teams presented their best arguments to more than sixty people, including all the key leaders in the administration, including the NSC cabinet principals, the vice president, the Joint Chiefs of Staff, and the CIA director.

That day, after each of the teams made their presentations, the president rose and for forty-five minutes—without notes—"summarized each argument."

When George Kennan later told Goodpaster that Eisenhower had demonstrated "his intellectual ascendancy over every man in the room," Goodpaster laughingly replied, "George, that includes you."

"That's right," Kennan responded, "because Eisenhower knew the military side of it, which I did not."[18]

The president concluded with his support of an idea that might be called "Containment Plus"—a hybrid of the policy options. Its objective would be "a sustainable balance of political and military power for long-term competition with the Soviet Union." Eisenhower would, in addition to a "robust" deterrent, establish psychological operations, support for some covert activities, and programs aimed at reaching citizens behind the Iron Curtain. This objective resulted in the founding of the United States Information Agency (USIA) in August 1953. Its mission was "to understand, inform and influence foreign publics in promotion of the national interest, and to broaden the dialogue between Americans and U.S. Institutions, and their counterparts abroad."[19]

However, the president rejected the notion of military rollback and buried the argument, in his administration, once and for all.[20]

While the exercise provided an important policy review in the wake of Stalin's death, it also served as a way to give everyone involved a voice. In cruder terms, it effectively co-opted all the principals who participated.

In sum, through the Solarium Project, Eisenhower rejected ideas associated with trying to defend the United States everywhere at once—and paying the costs associated with a failure to prioritize. He believed that preemptive interventionism was a concept outside American values, and that a society no longer at war should not expend resources equivalent to those at current Korean War levels.

In other words, Eisenhower's decision aimed to be "desirable in terms of policy objectives, but also feasible in terms of costs." Finally, a sustainable policy would end the "cut and crash" defense programs that resulted in wasted resources, difficulty in planning, and dangerously reduced efficiency. The Defense Department would be able to count on expenditures by virtue of the fact that they were associated with a sustainable strategy.[21]

Eisenhower had observed over his years of experience, in Goodpaster's words, that operations tend to absorb all the attention of government staff. Operations tend to "eat up policy." The Solarium Project gave policy the primacy it required over operations that were, after all, tactical in nature.[22]

Just as the Solarium Project had its final meeting, another study was producing recommendations on the nuclear deterrent. This would eventually be adopted and become a policy called the "New Look," a strategy that, according to General Goodpaster, "shaped our nuclear deterrent and our commitment to a strong economy."[23] This policy, as noted by Richard Nelson, retired army officer and Goodpaster biographer, was adopted when the U.S. had an overwhelming advantage over the Soviet Union in nuclear weapons.

While on the face of it this strategy would make the United States more dependent on deterring Soviet expansionism with our nuclear arsenal, the role of nuclear weapons in this context would be accompanied, in Eisenhower's mind, by a refusal to be drawn into small regional wars. It was also based on his strong feeling that the leaders of the new Soviet state had one objective: to survive and retain their power. In fact, when I once asked my father what the most important Eisenhower assumption had been about the USSR, he replied: "The Soviet elite are not early Christian martyrs." In other words, they were not likely to engage in a first strike, a threat they, too, feared. They knew full well the power of these weapons and did not want to risk annihilation and the loss of their own power in the process. However, this assessment was distinct from what the USSR might do if a war was already under way and they were losing.

The New Look strategy generated considerable controversy, especially in military circles, where many officers and planners were opposed to the notion that small wars were to be avoided where absolutely possible, and to the organizational and resource reductions and realignments such a policy would inevitably require.

Atomic weapons made it unnecessary and potentially impossible to move large conventional forces, so the advent of the nuclear age would require recalibrating World War II and Korean War force structures. While nuclear weapons would not make conventional forces obsolete, a greater emphasis on bombers and then rockets was inevitable. This put the U.S. Army at heated odds with the president.

The New Look may have effectively produced a policy of "Mutual Assured Destruction" (MAD), a key element of America's military power, but in the president's view the USSR was unlikely to undertake a first strike. So small wars, therefore, had to be avoided. Eisenhower knew that in conventional wars, before accepting defeat, commanders will try everything they have in their arsenal. "Any tempering of this tendency by moral, religious or chivalric limitations on violence" ended with World War II, he thought. He had seen firsthand the brutality and unbridled violence that accompanied the Nazis' behavior and their denial of impending defeat. Even the United States, a civilized democracy, had dropped the atomic bomb on Japan.

Despite this reasoning, Gen. Maxwell Taylor, later chairman of the Joint Chiefs of Staff under Kennedy, opposed the president's policy on the basis that the Soviet Union was unlikely to use nuclear weapons in *any* confrontation, perhaps even small wars. Eisenhower rejected this view on the basis that Taylor "failed to grasp the natural dynamic of war" and felt strongly that Taylor had not factored in human nature.

Goodpaster later wrote that General Taylor made some big assumptions about the nature of our adversary. Given their record during World War II, the president was skeptical that the Soviets would be able to resist the pressure to use nuclear weapons under a range of circumstances.[24]

The power of deterrence, however—Eisenhower's favored approach—relied on its credible use. He knew well that this required that he never give a hint as to what he might do under provocation. By remaining inscrutable, even during the internal debates at the White House, he left many of his aides then—and years later—to speculate on whether he would ever have used nuclear weapons. This is what author Evan Thomas meant by "Ike's Bluff."

During international tensions and crises, "I do know that on a number of occasions [Eisenhower] received advice from Admiral Arthur Radford on the possible use of nuclear weapons; Eisenhower never came close to entertaining the notion," Herbert Brownell asserted. Goodpaster later similarly affirmed to me that he doubted Eisenhower would ever have used the weapons.[25]

Eisenhower had, after all, opposed the use of the atomic bomb on Japan at the conclusion of World War II, when he and other military leaders believed that the Japanese were on the verge of surrender, and the bomb was unnecessary for their capitulation.[26]

The advent of the hydrogen bomb, however, given its destructive power, was incomprehensible by any human standard. "Eisenhower was increasingly of the view that fusion weapons truly changed the nature of warfare." He believed that nuclear war would be "insanity, mutual suicide rather than a means of conducting any other kind of rational military action."[27]

So strongly did Eisenhower believe that nuclear war, under these new circumstances, was unwinnable, that he even refused advice to build a bomb shelter at his home in Pennsylvania. (On our adjacent property, my mother was squirreling away canned goods and other essentials in our windowless basement, just in case.)

Ned Beach, Eisenhower's naval aide, not only served as a liaison between the White House and the navy but was also responsible for White House civil defense, which included continuity of government under attack. Beach was expected to provide an alternative location to which the president and his advisers would repair in case of enemy attacks. After considerable work, Beach brought two architectural plans to the president for his consideration. Eisenhower selected the more modest of the designs but "hesitated." He knew that the shelter would represent a refuge for many more people than just White House personnel, but he was sure in the public mind that it would be seen as "just a White House shelter."

"As President," Beach recalled, "he said he could not build himself a shelter when other Americans did not have them. He could not, as President, expend public funds for his personal protection against the type of attack we were talking about." Despite his aides' assertions that continuity of government demanded that such a facility be built, the president said that if Washington were under attack, he would not leave the city. Beach, in writing this added wryly that when Ike made that final declaration, it was not the president speaking, but "the General."

Eisenhower was finally persuaded that the facility must be built, and that the president must be prepared to go. But he left it—firmly—that he would only agree as part of "a much larger plan; to have the entire population of Washington evacuated . . . until then," he said firmly, "he would not go."[28]

The imperative, then, with the potential for nuclear nightmare, was to find a path toward peace. Eisenhower was determined to make clear our country's good intentions and sincere desire for it.

The president was also deeply concerned about the dangers of nuclear proliferation in the world. With nuclear-arms reductions with the Soviet Union stalled, and large swaths of the colonial world emerging as sovereign states, Eisenhower wanted to find a way to reverse the incentives to build nuclear weapons. It was clear, given the destruction that the USSR had sustained during World War II, that no country needed significant resources to acquire an atomic bomb: They needed only the political will. Both the Eisenhower and later the Kennedy administrations understood well that soon some countries, possibly all, would be capable of acquiring nuclear weapons.

It was Eisenhower's own desire to address the dual nature of the atom that opened the way for the peaceful uses of the atom for the generation of electricity, as well as for medicine and agriculture. From his time at Columbia University, physicists had told him about the miraculous things that could be done with atomic energy. Nuclear power even held out the promise of desalinization of salt water—a vital step not just for our country but also for the developing world.

With Eisenhower scheduled to address the UN General Assembly that winter of 1953, Special Assistant to the President C. D. Jackson was given the job of coming up with some ideas of how the administration could promote the development of peaceful uses of atomic energy. Jackson convened a small group, holding regular breakfast meetings at the Metropolitan Club to discuss proposals. Known as the "Wheaties Group" (for a favorite breakfast item), they worked hard to find themes for the president's upcoming speech. The group was struggling to find the right tone, but every draft the president read left him with a sense of discouragement. He wanted a proposal that would offer the world hope and underscore the United States' sincere desire to find a just peace.

The president himself brought up the idea of establishing an international bank of fissile materials, which would come out of what was then a limited stockpile among the nuclear powers. This material would be donated to an international atomic energy agency to be set up under UN auspices, to research the peaceful uses of nuclear energy.

Like all great strategies, this effort aimed at tackling a number of interdependent problems at once. The American people, Ike believed, had a right to know that their tax dollars, invested lavishly on the development of nuclear weapons, could also benefit them in their peaceful lives. At the same time the initiative had the potential to entice the Soviet Union to the bargaining table for arms-control discussions. And—unconnected but also of great importance—Eisenhower wanted to flag to Third World nations that the United States had a practical interest in developing their economic futures.

On December 8, 1953, the president's plane circled New York numerous times as he put the finishing touches on his groundbreaking "Atoms for Peace" speech. When he arrived at the United Nations, 3,500 people, from sixty countries, were in attendance. In an unprecedented move the president of the United States challenged the international community to regard the atom as neither inherently good nor bad: "[The atom] is neither moral or immoral. Only man's choice can make it good or evil."

That day, in the second major address of Eisenhower's presidency, he declared that the United States wanted to be identified with the "book of history" rather than just its "chapters": "My country wants to be constructive, not destructive. It wants agreement, not wars among nations. . . . The United States pledges before you—and therefore before the world—its determination to help solve the fearful atomic dilemma—to devote its entire heart and mind to find a way by which the miraculous inventiveness of man shall not be dedicated to his death, but consecrated to his life."

Lewis Strauss, head of the U.S. Atomic Energy Commission, recalled the response in the hall of the General Assembly when the president of the United States had finished his proposal: "There was a sound of indrawn breaths, followed by a gigantic, collective sigh—then wave after wave of applause. . . . [Even] the Soviet Union delegation was caught up in the general enthusiasm."[29]

Among the first initiatives of the plan was Isidor Rabi's proposal for a series of Atoms for Peace conferences, an idea Eisenhower wholeheartedly endorsed. But when the international scientific community received a "call for papers," the uncertainty and anxiety elicited by this subject brought forth only a tepid response. Rabi worried aloud to the president that there was still hesitation to take part. But Eisenhower, committed to this scientific endeavor, phoned UN Secretary General Dag

Hammarskjöld and asked him to help advance the international conferences, which he did.

From August 8 to August 20, 1955, the first Atoms for Peace conference was held in Geneva, Switzerland. More than 3,600 scientists and technologists attended from seventy-three countries, and 1,132 papers were presented: "It changed the whole direction of things," Rabi said. In order to put forward an international agenda on the peaceful uses of atomic energy, the United States and the Soviet Union agreed to declassify a "whole field of nuclear physics and technology."[30]

UN Secretary General Hammarskjöld concurred that the conference was "one of the most important events of the postwar world." Even the Soviet scientific community was enthusiastic, calling it "unique in history."[31]

On September 23, 1954, less than a year after "Atoms for Peace" was unveiled at the UN, the Eisenhower administration called for the founding of an International Atomic Energy Agency. On December 4, 1954, the General Assembly voted unanimously to establish such a body. By design this would open the way for a grand bargain. In 1957 the International Atomic Energy Agency was given safeguard responsibilities for verifying that signatories to the agreement were not using their nuclear know-how to build weapons. In return for compliance they would be given the opportunity to use atomic energy and nuclear technologies for agriculture, medicine, and to generate electricity.

It was not enough for Eisenhower to end the Korean War and refashion the administration's national security strategy. What he longed for most was to initiate programs that would eventually produce results in lessening tensions between the two major nuclear powers, thus contributing to what he called a "just and lasting peace." This would require not just a robust diplomatic agenda but meaningful steps toward disarmament; slowing the headlong race for armaments; and favoring and working diligently toward a partial test-ban treaty, which was later achieved during the Kennedy administration.

Eisenhower also looked for areas of potential flashpoints that, if not managed properly, could one day become grounds for a new East-West confrontation. To meet these goals required managing the political forces that sought a grip on the American imagination. It was already clear that fear would become a potent political weapon.

Eisenhower a moment before giving the commencement address, "Don't Join the Book Burners," at Dartmouth College, 1953.

10

A STRATEGIST TAKES ON A DEMAGOGUE

Today airstrikes, interventions, sanctions, and cyberattacks are so commonplace that we have forgotten the range of other means at our disposal for prevailing over those who threaten us. Eisenhower understood from World War II that a smart strategist must do all he can to deny an adversary the ability to choose the timing, the battlefield, and the weapons of the fight.

This approach could be seen in the way Eisenhower applied it in a nonmilitary context; not with a foreign adversary but with a domestic demagogue. Eisenhower would deprive Sen. Joseph McCarthy of the opportunity to choose the conditions in which their battle would take place—and it would be Eisenhower, not McCarthy, who chose the weapons.

The challenge came early in Eisenhower's administration, with his appointment of foreign service officer Charles "Chip" Bohlen as his ambassador to the Soviet Union. Joseph R. McCarthy, the Republican senator from Wisconsin, opposed Bohlen's appointment. Eisenhower would refuse, then and throughout this period, to use measures that seemed on the face of it appropriate—indeed satisfying. Eisenhower would resist all temptation to attack his adversary publicly. He was determined to deny McCarthy the one thing he wanted, and then without the senator's knowledge find another way to weaken his adversary's strength and dismantle his hold on the public imagination.

Chip Bohlen was debonair, a charming well-spoken diplomat. He had been schooled in the 1920s as a Soviet expert—just one of a handful to provide badly needed expertise on the USSR. Such credentials were urgently required when the United States granted diplomatic recognition to the Soviet Union in 1933, the last of the world's major nations to do so.

Over time Bohlen became one of the most influential experts on that part of the world. Fluent in Russian, he served as translator and assistant secretary of state during the Roosevelt administration, and was the first to hear of and report on the Molotov-Ribbentrop agreement between the Soviet Union and Germany, a pact that paved the way for the German invasion of Poland and the start of the war in Europe in 1939. Bohlen also served as an interpreter at the wartime Tehran and Yalta Conferences. He was a competent, informed anti-Communist.

Eisenhower had known Bohlen since the latter days of the war, and saw him episodically in Paris while Ike was at NATO and Bohlen served as U.S. minister to France. In keeping with the president's desire to get the best-qualified people available to fill key administration spots, he was quite certain that Bohlen was his man. Eisenhower spoke to Senate Majority Leader Robert Taft and was assured that Bohlen would be confirmed.

As events would unfold, this nomination proved to be one of the first battles between the new GOP president and the isolationist wing of his own party. To them Bohlen represented all the things they hated. He was Harvard educated, urbane, and well-traveled—and a symbol of what they thought of as FDR's "Yalta appeasement." The right wing of the Republican Party was convinced that FDR had sold out Eastern Europe and part of the Far East to the Communists, by allowing the division of the world into zones of influence in the last days of the war.

"Bohlen had no illusions about the Soviet Union," according to historian H. W. Brands, but neither did he have patience with people who wanted to blame the cold war on Yalta. During the late 1940s, Bohlen became increasingly irritated at the exaggerations, omissions, and downright falsifications that obscured what actually happened at the conference, and enthusiastically seconded attempts to correct the erroneous allegations.[1]

Just hours before Bohlen was to speak at his confirmation hearings before the Senate Foreign Relations Committee, word was beginning to filter out that Soviet dictator Joseph Stalin had had a stroke in Moscow. Not surprisingly, the Eisenhower administration wanted to send Bohlen to Moscow right away, but the committee decided to postpone the hearings for a week. By that time Stalin was dead.

In the intervening time opposition to Bohlen's nomination seemed to strengthen, and on March 13 Sen. Joseph McCarthy declared his opposition to the appointment. His accusations revolved around Bohlen's associations with the convicted perjurer Alger Hiss, a man accused of Communist sympathies and spying. The nomination was also imperiled when it was discovered that the State Department's security officer Scott McLeod had opposed it.

The administration could not allow the situation to spiral out of control in Congress and dutifully conducted a short investigation, negotiating with the Senate to allow Senators Robert Taft for the Republicans and John Sparkman for the Democrats to "look at but not copy" a summary of the Bohlen file. Taft found nothing that could be construed as disloyalty, and Bohlen was confirmed.[2]

Eventually the Bohlen hearing was held by the Senate Foreign Relations Committee, with the unanimous approval of his appointment in a 15–0 vote: Taft had delivered.

The Bohlen vote in the full Senate, however, did not go as smoothly. All but two Democrats voted to confirm him, but as many as eleven Republicans voted against both Taft's recommendation and their president's nominee. Joseph McCarthy's crusade against Bohlen was having its effect.

This surprised and perplexed Eisenhower. If he could not count on the support of the Republican Party on such crucial votes, he confided to his diary, perhaps he should reconsider an idea proposed to him only days before the vote: to look, quietly, into the formation of a new political party. The "method" for establishing such a new entity would entail appealing to every member of the House and Senate, to every governor, and to every national committee member whose general political philosophy and purpose seemed to belong to that school of thought known as the Middle Way. Ike acknowledged that such a proposal had possibilities, but that success in establishing a new political party would be a "vast" endeavor.

Realizing that undertaking such a radical step might be "forced upon us," however, Eisenhower fervently hoped that he would be able to commit the GOP "more deeply . . . to teamwork and party responsibility."[3]

To reduce and eventually nullify McCarthy's power, the president had to find a behind-the-scenes way to embolden McCarthy's fellow senators to censure their own renegade colleague. But McCarthy did not act alone. He was in essence the stalking horse for the isolationists in his own party, and a threat to international engagement.

Many of Ike's most vociferous exchanges with his brother Ed revolved around just this topic of international engagement. Ed had nothing good to say about foreign aid, and he employed all the predictable slogans to make his point. Ike resisted labeling, and frowned on his brother's use of such phrases as "give away programs." "[Those who oppose this foreign aid] have not the slightest idea as to what has been the effect of these programs in sustaining American security and prosperity," Ike wrote Ed.[4]

Ed also supported the so-called Bricker Amendment, which sought to limit constitutionally the powers of the presidency in making agreements with foreign powers. Reintroduced on January 7, 1953, the proposed amendment to the Constitution had considerable support in Congress. Named for the Republican senator from Ohio, John Bricker, the measure was a direct challenge to the presidency itself, and the fight over it was later regarded as the zenith of American isolationism.[5]

Eisenhower and his team worked hard to find a compromise to the measure, until an even more restrictive amendment, the "Which" clause, was proposed. It would require any treaty or agreement with a foreign power to be ratified by each of the forty-eight state legislatures then in the Union.

This gross encroachment on presidential powers animated Eisenhower, and he was committed to ensuring its defeat. Not only was the measure unconstitutional, the president believed, but it would also tie the hands of the federal government in concluding relatively minor measures such as status-of-forces agreements—bilateral pacts related to the stationing of U.S. forces overseas and other such transactional measures.

Ed, in contrast, was an ardent supporter of the amendment, as were the American Bar Association and many other reputable institutions. When Ed sent the president yet another fulminating letter on the Bricker Amendment, asserting that the measure was not in conflict with the Constitution, the president shot back: "You keep harping on the Constitution; I should like to point out that the meaning of the Constitution is what the Supreme Court says it is."[6]

Given the Eisenhower administration's strong opposition to this amendment, and an all-out effort by the president to kill the "Which" clause, the measure was finally defeated—largely with support from the Democrats and with no help from many within the president's own party.

The fight had been so time-consuming and so aggravating that by February 2 the president was telling his press secretary, Jim Hagerty, "To hell with him." Then he added: "If it's true that when you die the things that bothered you most are engraved on your skull, I am sure I will have there the mud and dirt of France during [the] invasion and the name of Senator Bricker."[7]

Ed's skepticism about the United Nations also made Ike's temper flare. Even in the 1950s complaining about the UN was often code for deeper and darker views of any governing and regulating bodies. Ed, like others who were adamantly opposed to the UN, saw the international institution as a threat to U.S. sovereignty. Many in the South also worried that the UN Declaration on Human Rights might be invoked at some point to address segregation in the South. Furthermore, isolationists were also skeptical of the United Nations since it had been under its authorization, not that of Congress, that President Harry Truman had sent troops to Korea. Fear of the UN and the Bricker Amendment were closely linked.

While this vocal minority opposed the international body, others still regretted the failure of the League of Nations, established at the end of World War I, and believed that the withdrawal from this global institution had contributed to the catastrophe of World War II. They argued that two world wars—in less than twenty-five years—gave such institutions an important role to play in helping to keep such cataclysms from ever happening again.

In countries where decolonization had begun, like India and other parts of the British, French, and Belgian Empires—not to mention outposts in Latin America—the UN provided a valuable outlet for such countries to find their voices. The tenuous condition of these newly emerging nations cried out for such a body. Other institutions, like the World Bank and the International Monetary Fund, both formed in 1945, were also established to offer help to emerging economies with trade and foreign investment.

Mindful that a stable international environment was crucial to American democracy and way of life, Eisenhower also supported free trade, voicing little concern about our allies' trading with Red China or countries in the East European bloc. He did not believe that we could dictate to our allies on such matters. More important, Eisenhower ardently believed that trade created interdependencies that could reduce the risk of war.

The biggest roadblock to unifying this country and ushering in a new era of engaged internationalism was Joe McCarthy and his ilk. The senator was determined to lay waste to the internationalists who had, in his view, "lost China" to the Communists in 1948 and given away Eastern Europe to Stalin. At home, he ranted that we had Communists in our ranks, "fellow travelers," and other conspirators trying to bring an end to American greatness.

McCarthy's appeal resonated with many people. But he also tapped into the grievances of many small but outspoken groups like the John Birch Society and other reactionary organizations. He also sparked the interest and support of the *National Review*, run by William F. Buckley Jr.

McCarthy's support went far deeper than just the isolationists in Congress. He also had a devoted following among Roman Catholic voters. In fact, in his home state of Wisconsin, his most fervent supporters were among the Poles and the Catholics. On the East Coast other Catholic ethnic groups also supported McCarthy passionately.[8]

The Wisconsin senator was an unlikely crusader, with little charm and no particular gifts as a speaker. He was described by a Washington power broker as "an ill-mannered and unpredictable outsider" in the Senate "club."[9]

Elected to the Senate in 1946, McCarthy had a lackluster career, and by 1950 he was worried about his reelection prospects going into 1952. He was ambitious and tired of sitting in a Congress that had been dominated by Democrats.

He was said to be looking for "a dramatic issue" when it was suggested to him that he take up the cause of driving the Communists out of the U.S. government. McCarthy knew little on the subject—he did not even serve on the Foreign Relations Committee—but his instincts told him that just such an issue might catapult him into the presidency.[10]

In the immediate aftermath of the war, it was revealed that a Soviet spy, Klaus Fuchs, had worked on the U.S. nuclear weapons program and had passed sensitive secrets to the USSR. To address these concerns, in 1947 the Truman administration put in place, by executive order, the federal Loyalty-Security Program, a measure later supported and amplified by the Eisenhower administration. This measure would mandate screening for federal employees who had associations with "Totalitarian, Fascist, Communist or subversive" organizations—or were advocating the alteration or overthrow of the U.S. government. In 1951, with the passage of the Internal Security Act of 1950, McCarthy recognized that exploiting America's fear of Communists and subversives was a winner.

In 1950, at a Lincoln Day dinner in Wheeling, West Virginia, McCarthy declared that he had the names of 205 then-current State Department employees who were Communists—and presumably spies. While this number was already known to the State Department, a Senate committee was established to investigate the allegations, and at once the obscure young senator was an overnight sensation, a media phenomenon, and a thorn in the side of the Truman administration.

After the Wheeling speech, Dean Acheson, Truman's secretary of state, took on McCarthy directly in the hopes of discrediting the man and putting an end to the hysteria that the senator had created around the State Department. President Truman also took many occasions to denounce the senator. This attention only served to make McCarthy into a bigger figure.

As we now know from the Venona Project, an American undertaking to decode classified Soviet cables, a couple of hundred Americans actually played some role in espionage for the Soviet Union or had passed along sensitive information to their Soviet interlocutors. And the Soviet Union allocated millions of dollars over the years to the American Communist Party (CPUSA). But many, perhaps thousands, were innocently caught up in this red scare.

For all the power McCarthy accrued over the years, it is ironic that his investigations never produced any hard evidence, nor did any convictions for spying arise as a result.[11] Yet, even before Eisenhower's election, McCarthy had already gone far in his accusations, fingering government employees at the State Department and the Government Printing Office, as well as many others. Eventually a range of distinguished public servants would be tarred with McCarthy's brush.[12]

During the 1952 campaign candidate Eisenhower had a few uncomfortable encounters with McCarthy. He did not want to see the man during the campaign, but Wisconsin could not be written off. Inevitably Eisenhower was subjected to campaigning in the same state with a man whose views he abhorred.

On October 3, Governor Walter Kohler boarded Ike's whistle-stop train before it reached Wisconsin. He knew of Eisenhower's views and was concerned that it might appear that Ike did not support the local Republican Party. He persuaded Sherman Adams to join him in urging Eisenhower to remove an out-of-context paragraph in the candidate's forthcoming speech, in which he planned to make yet another defense of Gen. George C. Marshall, who had been accused of disloyalty. Regrettably one of Eisenhower's aides hinted to a *New York Times* reporter that Eisenhower would be including praise for Marshall in his speech.

Without knowledge of this leak, Eisenhower was talked into removing the paragraph for the sake of party unity. He was reluctant to do so, but naïvely thought that his many other past pronouncements in defense of his former boss would suffice. The inexperienced candidate was not ready for the ruckus that ensued in the press. Ike was angered and humiliated by the whole incident.

Eisenhower reflected on this miserable episode: "If I could have foreseen this distortion of the facts, a distortion that even led to some question of my loyalty to General Marshall, I would have never acceded to the staff's arguments, logical as they sounded at the time."[13]

After Eisenhower's inauguration, the president opted for a different strategy—what the historian Fred Greenstein called "containment without confrontation."[14]

Ike knew that McCarthy, whom he despised, had poisoned the atmosphere not only in the country but among members of his own party. The senator and his methods jeopardized everything the president was trying to accomplish. Yet Eisenhower also understood one fundamental fact: In a system of three equal branches of government, the president had no authority to discipline the behavior of a member of another government branch. The president might engage in a rhetorical battle, but he could do nothing to actually stop what was under way on Capitol Hill. In his view, he could win this battle only by other means.

A formula for dealing with McCarthy was of vital importance, especially since the loss of his supporters could threaten the GOP's leadership in the Senate. The GOP's slim majority was an asset that Eisenhower needed for the passage of key legislation during his first term. The GOP had only a one-vote margin.

Several factors were clear from the start. First, Senator McCarthy's Committee on Government Investigations was out of control. It would be incumbent on the president and his team to assure the American people that a responsible force—the executive branch—was protecting the country's internal safety, thus implying that McCarthy's tactics were superfluous. The administration had an internal security program, under the auspices of the attorney general.

Second it would be vital to deny the publicity-seeking senator the very thing he wanted most—more attention.

Third, Eisenhower would work behind the scenes to create a dialogue with the Republican leadership in the Senate—an interaction that would eventually have an impact.[15]

And fourth, the president would exercise patience, and give the senator and his team enough rope to hang themselves. Ike was confident that this approach would finally pay off. McCarthy had a very odd team of people working for him and their methods were unorthodox and unethical. Roy Cohn, the senator's legal assistant, a singularly unattractive man with many hidden agendas, would eventually be caught in a controversy he himself had initiated. McCarthy's methods were damaging and painful, but ultimately unsustainable.

McCarthy routinely brought suspected individuals before closed congressional interrogation, where he served as the sole examiner. This was followed by an account of the proceedings that came only from the committee itself. People's reputations were being sullied without due process or transparency.

Eisenhower was not inured to the trials that McCarthy, literally and figuratively, imposed on people. When the president heard that Ralph Bunche, a distinguished African American diplomat serving the United States at the United Nations, was under investigation he privately feared that the innuendo created by an FBI report that was being compiled might "kill [Bunche's] public career."

The president spoke in glowing terms about Bunche's public service. "I am not going to be party to this, I am willing to bet he is no more Communist than I am," he told Max Rabb. Eisenhower wanted Bunche to know that he would support him however he could, so he sent Rabb, his cabinet secretary and adviser on minority groups, to visit the UN official. Rabb told the 1950 Nobel Peace Prize winner that the president was deeply upset about the suggestions of his disloyalty. Bunche, however, decided to fight the problem alone. But later, while the hearings on Bunche's case were under way, one day's session was brought to an early end. Bunche was excused so he could be on time for dinner with Eisenhower at the White House. While Bunche may have wanted to handle the false accusations in his own way, the invitation to dinner with the president made it plain what Eisenhower's views were.

The allegations against Bunche were eventually dropped.[16]

Ike's public restraint was born of discipline, not indifference. "President Eisenhower had a sense of loathing and contempt [for Senator McCarthy] that had to be seen to be believed," recalled aide Arthur Larson. "At the peak of McCarthy's power, a Labor Department official was "explaining to the Cabinet a new kind of insurance being provided to government employees, called a 'sudden death policy.' Eisenhower immediately cracked: 'I know one fellow I'd like to take that policy out for.'"[17]

The president's apparent public silence on the subject, however, was deeply frustrating for people who were alarmed by these events. Eisenhower refused to mention the senator's name—ever. This inspired outpourings of criticism from newspaper columnists (some of whom called him a "coward"), academics, Democrats, and even a number of people working in the White House. Eisenhower simply refused to engage the senator directly—as much as he might have been tempted to do so. As McCarthy's antics became bolder and bolder, the president resolutely declined to rise to the bait.

In the year and a half that the president had to deal with

McCarthy he managed never—not once—to utter the senator's name publicly. Ike was convinced that if he took on McCarthy it would give the senator the headlines he so badly craved. It would also raise the junior senator from Wisconsin to the level of the president. Eisenhower was convinced that publicity was McCarthy's oxygen, and the source of his power and influence.

"McCarthyism was a much bigger issue than McCarthy," Eisenhower wrote in his memoirs. "This was the truth that I constantly held before me as I listened to the many exhortations that I should 'demolish' the senator himself." Eisenhower feared that for every personal jab he might take at McCarthy, the senator would gain new followers among the public, but also potentially in Congress. It was what Ike called "the underdog syndrome."[18]

While Eisenhower was roundly criticized for stubbornly refusing take on the senator directly, there might have been more to this approach than a simple refusal to get back at this despicable man. Whenever the senator received a rebuke from anyone, he would demand equal time. And equal time would assure him further headlines. Given McCarthy's probable interest in a future run for the presidency, it was imperative, in his mind, that he stay in the headlines. His instincts for drama, and his skillful use of innuendo and what is now called "fake news," strengthened the senator's power and influence.[19]

On October 9, 1953, the president, under increasing pressure to attack Senator McCarthy for his toxic methods, wrote his brother Milton:

> Only a shortsighted or completely inexperienced individual would urge the use of the office of the Presidency to give an opponent the publicity he so avidly desires . . . Frankly in a day when we see journalism far more concerned in the so-called human interest, dramatic incidents, and bitter quarrels, than it is in promoting constructive understanding of the days' problems, I have no intention whatsoever of helping promote the publicity value of anyone who disagrees with me—demagogue or not![20]

Instead of publicly attacking McCarthy, Eisenhower confronted the issues raised by McCarthyism, but he did so as a matter of principle. With any demagogue, the issue he or she exploits is laced with falsehoods and extravagant conspiracy theories, but there is usually some element of truth or some fear that appears to justify such claims, and ultimately their power. Instead of highlighting the falsehoods, the president used his position to tell the American people about the dangers the current atmosphere posed to our democracy.

With McCarthy's failure to stop the appointment of Chip Bohlen as ambassador to the Soviet Union, McCarthy's "junketeering gumshoes"—Roy Cohn and a close personal friend and committee consultant, David Schine—went on a European boondoggle to "dig up dirt" on the subversive activities of the USIA's Voice of America. They also toured American overseas libraries to investigate their holdings.[21] A list of "subversive" Communist authors had been issued, and the suggestion that the libraries might be stocking these "dangerous" works led many librarians to take the books down from their shelves. In some cases it was even said that these questionable books had been burned.

The president's response to the latest uproar came during a commencement speech at Dartmouth on June 14, 1953, in the midst of these unfolding events. Hearing about the torching of books overseas, Eisenhower abandoned his text just before he was to give his remarks, and spoke extemporaneously.

Ike started on a lighter note, speaking to the graduating seniors about "just fun in life." He also spoke about the courage to look at yourself with clear eyes and be honest about who you are.

"There will be tough problems to solve," he told the graduates:

> You've heard about them. You can't solve them with long faces, they don't solve problems—not when they deal with humans. Humans have to have confidence; you've got to help give it to them.
>
> This brings me up to my second little topic, which is

> courage. You must have courage to look all about you with honest eyes . . . have you actually measured up? If you have, it's that courage to look at yourself and say, "Well, I failed miserably there, I hurt someone's feelings needlessly, I lost my temper."

And then he got to the topic of the day that was bothering him most:

> Don't join the book burners. Don't think you're going to conceal faults by concealing evidence that they ever existed. Don't be afraid to go in your library and read every book as long as any document does not offend any of our own ideas of decency. That should be the only censorship. How will we defeat Communism unless we know what it is? What it teaches, and why [it has] such an appeal for men? Why are so many people swearing allegiance to it? It's almost a religion . . . And we've got to fight it with something better, not [by] trying to conceal the thinking of our own people. They are part of America and even if they [have] ideas that are contrary to ours, their right to say them, their right to record them, and their right to have them in places where they are accessible to others is unquestioned or it's not America.[22]

The "Don't join the book burners" speech did nothing to quell criticism of the president. His critics exploded with accusations of "appeasement"—strong language directed against a man who'd beaten Hitler. The president's response frustrated and angered those who were convinced that the only way to finish McCarthy was through direct confrontation led by the president himself. Eisenhower stood firm.

Ellis Slater noted in his diary the evening of July 30, when a number of friends had gathered for a barbecue at the president's invitation, that the topic seemed to be mostly McCarthy and his tactics.

"Ike believes the newspapers made McCarthy," Slater noted, "and that he would fade out of the picture quickly if they would ignore most of the furor he creates which is certainly not entitled to front page play any more than is the work of other congressional committees."[23]

Then on August 31, 1953, McCarthy began a set of hearings into Communist infiltration in the United States Army. Sure to get a rise from the president, this attack on the army would, eventually, be the senator's undoing.

The hearings into the army had already been going on for months when, on November 24, Senator McCarthy spoke on a nationally televised news program. In his remarks, he went from lambasting the Truman State Department, to taking aim instead at the Eisenhower administration for retaining people who were still deemed to be security risks, especially John Paton Davies, a China hand considered by McCarthy to be one of those guilty of losing China to Communism. The newspapers asserted that McCarthy's was "an assault on the Eisenhower presidency itself." Some members of the president's staff were determined to get Ike to respond to some of his most ardent critics. Hagerty reported in his diary that the president refused, saying that all these people want is for him to "get down in [the] gutter" with Joe."[24]

As the meeting progressed, Ike began to put his pen to the draft, and at his next press conference, he read his prepared remarks—again speaking at the level of principle, without engaging the senator. The president responded to a number of attacks made by McCarthy related to Britain's trade with China and on the perennial subject of Communists in government. Regarding McCarthy's attacks on free trade, the president said: "The most powerful of free nations must not permit itself to grow weary of the process of negotiation . . . If it should turn impatiently to coercion of other free nations, our brand of coercion . . . would be the mark of the imperialist rather than of the leader."[25]

When asked, Eisenhower reassured the public that given the "effectiveness" of the administration's internal security efforts it would not be an issue in the 1954 election. Then he tried to move the conversation back to the importance of his Middle Way, noting that, "unless the Republican Party can develop and enact . . . a [progressive legislative] program for the American people, it does not deserve to remain in power."[26]

Ike was deeply concerned about the impact the corrosive political atmosphere in the country was having on its political culture. But he understood that Americans could not blame any outside force for what we were doing to ourselves. Our capacity to engage in civil debate was something we ourselves controlled. "Only Americans can hurt America," he once said during the 1952 campaign.[27] "[We] can't defeat Communism by destroying America."[28]

McCarthyism and its rancor continued unabated. The president himself had been viciously accused by right-wing groups of being a Communist sympathizer, and some of Eisenhower's most important appointments were threatened by unfounded accusations from McCarthy and other extremists. But McCarthy extended his rampage. On March 16, as the drama was reaching its crescendo, the senator began to go after the president's family, accusing Milton Eisenhower of being "a New Deal member of the [Eisenhower] palace guard."[29]

"New Deal" to McCarthy and others was synonymous with treason.

McCarthy again failed to provoke the president publicly.

What finally created the shift in the president's strategy was McCarthy's escalating attacks on the U.S. Army. Ever since November 1953, when the army drafted David Schine, the friend of McCarthy's wingman Roy Cohn, the senator and Cohn were none too happy. They were angry that Schine might be given typical army assignments. Behind the scenes Cohn was using the threat of further official inquiries into the army to demand easier assignments for Schine—no KP (Kitchen Police or Kitchen Patrol), no overseas travel, and no work on Sundays.

When Schine's assignments became a source of private frustration for Cohn, in apparent retaliation, McCarthy demanded answers from the army about one Maj. Irving Peress, a one-year draftee who served as a base dentist at Camp Kilmer, New Jersey. He accused the dentist of Communist sympathies and demanded answers from the army.

Gen. Ralph Zwicker, a hero of D-day and commander of the

camp, refused to relinquish any information. McCarthy snapped back by declaring that Zwicker must have the "brains of a five-year-old child." And that he was "not fit to wear that uniform"[30]

At least two Eisenhower administration figures tried to reason with McCarthy: Secretary of Defense Charles E. Wilson and Secretary of the Army Robert Stevens, but both got trapped by the senator in ways that made them look cowed and weak. The president was infuriated.

But perhaps most pivotal was a revelation by Army Counsel John Adams. In congressional testimony he revealed that on January 21, 1954, he attended a private meeting at the White House of key administration figures, including Herbert Brownell, Sherman Adams, and Henry Cabot Lodge—at which time he was instructed to keep track of McCarthy and Cohn's efforts on behalf of David Schine. Investigators wanted to know more.[31]

On March 11, under orders some scholars believe came from President Eisenhower himself, the Pentagon released the Adams report. When the army released this chronology of McCarthy and Cohn's interventions on behalf of Schine it became obvious that something had to be done about McCarthy's possible overreach. The release of the report placed before members of McCarthy's committee assertions of scandal, making it impossible for them to close their eyes to what may have transpired. In April they convened what are known today as the Army-McCarthy hearings. Since McCarthy's methods were under investigation, he was not, this time, the interrogator, but subject himself to cross-examination.

Behind the scenes Ike and Brownell worked hard to make sure the hearings were televised, and the president helped select the Boston lawyer Joseph Welch, to represent the army. When the hearings finally began—as General Goodpaster once put it to me—McCarthy was "a dead man walking and he didn't even know it."

Over the coming months McCarthy would demand information from the army and later the Eisenhower White House, insisting on private memorandums and other material supposedly pertinent to his investigations. Eisenhower made it clear behind the scenes that he saw no reason why the army should not provide the information for the senator on the basis that transparency, where feasible from an administrative and national security perspective, was always the best policy. Army Chief of Staff Matthew Ridgway, however, "violently objected," fearing that it would subject officers to "virtual persecution by congressional committees."[32]

On May 14 Eisenhower evoked executive privilege, bowing to Ridgway's concerns. The executive branch would refuse to relinquish any information on the matter, a measure in their view that was necessary to protect the confidential counsel Eisenhower was getting from his advisers. Despite the novel declaration, the Senate did not challenge the president.

Executive privilege was a measure that went back all the way to the presidency of George Washington. Yet the Eisenhower administration and the president himself understood that it was also limited. Years later Herbert Brownell and William Rogers, both attorneys general during the Eisenhower administration, agreed that the president would never have attempted to withhold evidence necessary for an investigation of a crime.[33]

According to Herbert Brownell, after the imposition of executive privilege, Eisenhower met with Senate Majority Leader Everett Dirksen and other congressional leaders and urged them to make efforts to restrain the renegade senator.[34]

Despite these developments, the televised hearings went on for nearly three months. In the meantime, Eisenhower made sure to show support for his team by having his photograph taken with army secretary Stevens, who had been under fire from McCarthy.

On May 28, McCarthy, by this time growing desperate, went over the president's head during the hearings and appealed to federal workers, including those in the executive branch, to "disregard Presidential orders and laws and report directly to him on graft, corruption, Communism and treason."[35]

That same day Jim Hagerty wrote a diary entry chronicling the president's reaction to McCarthy's appeal to federal employees, saying that the president was really angry at what he termed "the complete arrogance of McCarthy." Walking up and down behind his desk and speaking in rapid-fire order, Eisenhower said:

> This amounts to nothing but the wholesale subversion of public service. McCarthy is making exactly the same plea of loyalty . . . that Hitler made to the German people. Both tried to set up personal loyalty within the government while both were using the pretense of fighting Communism. McCarthy is trying deliberately to subvert the people we have in government, people who are sworn to obey the law, the Constitution and their superior officers. I think this is the most disloyal act we have ever had by anyone in the government of the United States.[36]

On May 31, 1954, the two hundredth anniversary of Columbia University's founding, in a speech to the campus community, Eisenhower alluded to the accusations hurled at people who were sometimes deemed "guilty" simply by association:

> Amid . . . alarms and uncertainties, [citizens] begin to fear other people's ideas—every new idea. They begin to talk about censoring the sources and the communications of ideas. . . . We know that when censorship goes beyond the observance of common decency . . . it quickly becomes for us, a deadly danger.
>
> Without exhaustive debate—even heated debate—of ideas and programs, free government would weaken and wither . . .
>
> Effective support of principles, like success in battle, requires calm and clear judgment, courage, faith, fortitude. Our dedication to truth and freedom . . . does not require—and cannot tolerate—fear, threat, hysteria, and intimidation.
>
> As we preach freedom to others, so we should practice it among ourselves.[37]

. . .

The hearings ground on. As the days rolled by McCarthy increasingly wilted under the bright hearing-room lights, and the public watched as the curtain was torn away from this Wizard of Oz. He had been accustomed to being the accuser; he was now in the witness chair as the accused.

When McCarthy denounced one of the lawyers in Joseph Welch's law firm as having been associated with a Communist-affiliated organization, Welch dramatically addressed the senator by rebuking him for tarnishing the name of a man who was not even on the case: "Have you no sense of decency, sir?"—an expression that continues to resonate in history.

During the hearings the tide had turned. It became apparent at one point that McCarthy and his team had doctored a photograph and an unprecedented viewing audience made their own conclusions about McCarthy demeanor throughout the hearings. And the Senate, now mindful of the growing public hostility to McCarthy, prompted Republican senators Ralph Flanders and Arthur Watkins to open another investigation to determine if McCarthy had been in violation of Senate rules. This and public opinion compelled the Senate eventually to censure the Wisconsin senator—a reassuring outcome, if not for the fact that the Republican leadership did not vote in favor of the measure. Nevertheless the Army-McCarthy hearings marked the end of McCarthy's influence as a political force.

Years later Ambassador Bohlen spoke about his nemesis and this strain of thinking in the country: "McCarthy was a product of sixteen years of being out of office," he told a State Department interviewer. "Eisenhower had not been alone in thinking that McCarthy's crusade against Communists in the government was a tactic he used for getting the attention he craved after ten years of serving in obscurity in a Democrat-controlled Congress. The Senator, in fact, apparently had help in crafting his first speech on the subject in Wheeling, West Virginia in 1950. His charges were resonant with the times, though not everyone saw the Communist threat as a force that [was likely] to distort our own institutions."[38]

Conscious of the grave injustice done to those who had been falsely accused, Eisenhower no doubt realized it must have been cold comfort to them that the national nightmare had taken this long to end. Discrediting McCarthy had taken time, while the majority party in Congress still supported the senator. There had been little choice on how to resolve this matter.

At the same time the president understood that damage from McCarthy's populism had not been wholly a domestic issue. While Ike had, behind the scenes, gone into battle to destroy McCarthy's influence, our allies abroad, countries that only less than ten years earlier were still under the Nazi yoke, were repelled by the developments inside the United States.

Ike noted this concern and specifically referred to it in his diary. The transcript of a German radio program caught his attention: "McCarthy makes it so easy to hate Americans," the German broadcaster had said, "that it is necessary that all of us who understand America's decent motives and basic friendliness should speak up on behalf of the things she is doing in our own countries."[39]

Eisenhower never accepted credit for the senator's political demise, yet it is hard to imagine any other presidential strategy that might have worked as effectively, noted Fred Greenstein. Ike was bitterly criticized for failing to take McCarthy on directly, but Eisenhower's refusal to do so in this case was based on his belief that it would have produced counterproductive results.[40]

The president knew he had been the one holding the cards. He had the power over the thing McCarthy had most deeply desired—to engage Eisenhower in this circus, thus legitimizing his own status as an important leader while raising himself and his shameful shenanigans to the level of a coequal branch of government. Eisenhower's approach eventually ended McCarthy's power, and in that process, avoided the senator tarnishing and belittling the very office of the presidency itself.

President Eisenhower (second from left) and British prime minister Harold Macmillan talk with Foreign Secretary Selwyn Lloyd (left) and Secretary of State John Foster Dulles (right) during the Anglo-American conference at the Mid-Ocean Club, Tucker's Town, Bermuda, March 21, 1957. The president and prime minister discussed immediate and long-range problems in the Middle East at the start of their talks. (United Press–*New York Herald Tribune*)

11

PRINCIPLES AND TENACITY IN TIMES OF CRISIS

The United States was fortunate to have a man in the White House with decades of experience in both military and geopolitical affairs—an individual who had built the NATO alliance and other treaty arrangements with countries around the world. Eisenhower had had countless years to think long and hard about the cultures of other nations, the meaning of nationalism, and America's own vital national security interests. Most of all, the catastrophic breakdown of legality and order during World War II left him with clear-minded thinking and intuitive responses—well-honed by his role in those events.

The country was also fortunate that Eisenhower valued intelligence gathering, including the acquisition of tools to avert surprise military strikes. He vigorously sponsored a newly developed U-2 aerial reconnaissance plane that could photograph developments on the ground. This capability added critical information to his complex calculations. In short, it is hard to know how the events during the fall of 1956 might have ended had there been a less experienced person at the nation's helm.

Two crises arose in 1956. Both involved the Soviet Union, both threatened wider war, and both would come to a head just as American voters were going to the polls in the presidential election that November. Also noteworthy, both entailed controversial decisions by Eisenhower that hit at the heart of key American ethnic sympathies.

Despite the precepts Eisenhower had laid out in his "Chance for Peace" speech, delivered just after Joseph Stalin's death, the United States would be confronted with flagrant violations of international law, and events would prove to be a test of his leadership and stamina. With two illnesses behind him, Eisenhower, the candidate, would rise to these crises and demonstrate to our allies and adversaries that he was in no way distracted or diminished by his circumstances.

Going into 1956, as tensions were developing in the Middle East and in Eastern Europe, Eisenhower had had a difficult twelve months from a health perspective.

The previous year—in the wee hours of September 24, 1955—Ike had had a heart attack. He had been in Colorado on vacation with Mamie, and they were staying at the Doud house at 750 Lafayette Street in Denver. Dr. Howard Snyder, who had cared for Ike since the war years, was called at once, and after administering some medication, he took no further action for as many as eight unconscionable hours. A tall, brittle man—ten years older than his patient—Snyder took a risk in downplaying the incident. With Mamie's soothing care, however, the president lived through the night and was finally sent to Fitzsimons Army Hospital later that morning. Increasingly on the mend, seven weeks later Ike went with Mamie to their Gettysburg farm to continue his recuperation.

By early winter a team of doctors gave the president a thumbs-up, telling him he was fit to run for reelection should he choose to do so.

Eisenhower had hoped by 1956 that he'd have developed a cadre of young leaders to take over, but given growing tensions at home and abroad, he wondered if they were ready. The Republican Party was still split, and the president's standing with the public was still second to none. With his continuation as chief executive, his approval ratings would force the Republican Party to continue along a more moderate path, with the prospect of cementing a Middle Way. By 1956 Eisenhower had submitted a balanced budget, and the real incomes of ordinary Americans had gone up 20 percent.[1] The policies that brought about these economic milestones required stewardship and, where necessary, a fierce determination to continue on this economic path.

Despite these arguments, those closest to the president—his brother Milton and his son, John—argued that he should retire. On January 16, 1956, Milton acknowledged the loneliness of Ike's decision. He wrote his brother: "If you decline to run, you will clearly go down in history as one of our greatest military and political leaders, with no major domestic or international difficulty to mar your record. If you go on, you might enhance your standing, contribute mightily to peace and to sound principles at home; or you might face serious economic setbacks at home and upheavals abroad." But, he cautioned Ike: "You might jeopardize your health and your ability to carry the burden of your office."

After Ike read the letter he drew a long line on the page. "Of no great moment," he wrote, "even though history might condemn a failure it cannot weigh the demands of conscience."[2]

After considerable family debate and consultations with his associates—one was even held in secret at the White House—his colleagues unanimously urged the president to run. Mamie, however, might have been one of the most important deciding voices. Of all the family members, she thought Ike should run again. Deep down, she felt that Ike's work was not yet complete. She also believed that her husband's health might actually suffer if he were simply sitting on the sidelines when there was still so much more to do.

On February 29—five months after his coronary thrombosis—Ike declared himself a candidate for his second term in office.

Despite the president's decision, he would constantly monitor his capabilities for the next four months, always alert to the prospect of a dutiful resignation. Then, in early June, the president had an attack of ileitis, an inflammation of the ileum in the small intestine. The attack was so serious that emergency surgery was required, and the doctors feared for his life.

This condition had flared up episodically since Ike's tropical postings in the 1920s and 1930s. After surgery on June 8, an infection at the incision site proved stubborn. Nevertheless Ike rested, recuperated, and after a few weeks resumed his regular schedule.

Despite this setback, Eisenhower decided to accept an invitation to visit Panama only a little more than a month later. A meeting of heads of government was scheduled, which would give him the opportunity of interacting with many Latin American leaders in one place. At the same time such a trip would also give him the chance to test both his stamina and his performance.

Before departing, Ike was not only back in the office; he was signing legislation, including the bill he championed to establish the Interstate Highway System. That day, he gave one of the signing pens to Sen. Albert Gore Sr., a Democrat from Tennessee, for his important commitment to the project on Capitol Hill. Then the president readied himself to take what would no doubt prove to be an exhausting three-day trip to meet Latin American leaders.

In fact the trip turned out to be grueling. During long hours in a motorcade, the presidential limousine was nearly overwhelmed by tens of thousands of well-wishers. The brief trip also included official talks, meetings with many heads of state, and long dinners, one of which lasted nearly four hours. At the president's request, the only concession to his recent surgery was a nap after the midday banquets.

Ike's naval aide, Ned Beach, was on the trip. One day after lunch he was asked to come to the president's room as he was preparing to rest. As Eisenhower discussed some logistical arrangements for the trip, Beach was "stunned" to see him nonchalantly changing the dressing on his still-weeping incision: He had not yet healed from his abdominal surgery but carried on, according to Beach, without any change of schedule or request to shorten the lengthy public appearances.[3]

Jerry Persons, the White House congressional liaison, remarked on Eisenhower's nearly heroic stamina in the face of this trip: "That Friday before [the president] left he was a sorry sight," Persons told presidential speechwriter Emmett Hughes. "And he said to me privately 'If I don't get better than this pretty soon, I am going to pull out of this whole thing [the 1956 presidential campaign]. So he goes down to Panama, almost gets crushed by the mobs, meets God-knows how many Latin American diplomats, suffers through all the damned receptions—and Tuesday, *Tuesday* mind you, three days later, he comes waltzing back [into the White House] looking like a new man."[4]

The race between Eisenhower and Adlai Stevenson was already under way, and Eisenhower pushed forward even though he made it clear he would not be staging a campaign like the one in 1952. There was too much going on, and the president would opt to use television much more and to make some key speeches at well-selected locations around the country instead.

Only months after his return from Panama, two crises in Egypt and then Hungary were coming to a head that would be a test not just of his vigor but also of his leadership capability and his commitment to the rule of law.

The first was in the Middle East, one of the most vitally important regions during the Cold War. For centuries it had been a cauldron of tribal and religious rivalries, and now it was breaking free of colonial rule. This left the region vulnerable to divergent U.S. and Soviet interests, especially given its geostrategic location and the vast Arab oil reserves that fueled Western economies.

Andrew Goodpaster underscored that what had been needed was a "balanced strategy to promote peace between Israel and the Arab states and block Soviet inroads" into the area.[5]

At the heart of the drama was the swashbuckling figure of Egypt's Lt. Col. Gamal Abdel Nasser. He had emerged as the galvanizing figure in the Middle East, "a uniting leader who sought for decades to ally Arab nations in a struggle against foreign domination."[6] For at least a decade he had worked tirelessly to oust the British from his homeland.

Like many other jurisdictions in transition, the past served as a troublesome backdrop to stability. As tensions were rising, a number of factors from recent history were to have a significant impact on the crisis:

First, the armistice after Israel had been recognized as a state in 1948 had not been codified with a peace treaty.

Second, on May 25, 1950, during the Truman presidency, the United States, Britain, and France signed the Tripartite Agreement, pledging to enforce the existing borders between Israel and its neighbors, and stipulating that there should be a balance of forces in the region, including no arms sales for offensive purposes, and a commitment to coordinate military assistance programs. These allies also pledged to go to the aid of any victim of aggression.[7]

Third, Nasser and his colonels had overthrown Egypt's British client, King Farouk, in July 1952—changing not only his country's relationship with Great Britain, but also with others in the region. Nasser, who came to power in 1954, undertook major land reforms, and did little to stop Arab guerrillas from making raids into Israel from the Gaza Strip.[8]

And finally, Nasser, a nationalist and a strong proponent of neutrality in the Cold War, also repudiated the Anglo-Egyptian Treaty of 1936 and ordered British forces out. In 1954 Eisenhower used his considerable influence to encourage Britain to pass control of the Suez Canal to the Egyptians and to withdraw their troops—some eighty thousand of them—by June 18, 1956.

As General Goodpaster reflected on these events, he asserted that Eisenhower had deftly sorted out the difference between *ownership* of the canal, which was Egyptian by virtue of its status as a sovereign nation, and *operation* of the canal, which in this case would be managed by an international consortium of users.[9] This was vitally important as two-thirds of Western Europe's oil came through the Suez Canal, a factor of overriding significance as the crisis unfolded.[10]

Britain and France—reluctant to leave the region—saw Israel as a useful hedge against the "rising tide" of Arab nationalism—so they sold arms to the Israelis. Only the United States continued to adhere to the arms embargo stipulated in the Tripartite Agreement.[11]

Eisenhower believed that he must be an honest broker in the region. He did not want to take sides in this situation for fear of losing U.S. influence over his larger strategic objective: to checkmate the USSR's growing designs on the region.

At the same time, Nasser had ambitions that extended beyond the boundaries of his own country. He wanted to be the leader of a pan-Arab world. To solidify his base at home and raise his prestige regionally, Nasser proposed a massive infrastructure project, the building of the Aswan Dam in southern Egypt. Not only would it create a 350-mile-long reservoir that would irrigate 1.3 million acres of farmland—a boon for the country's agricultural sector, but it would also generate half of Egypt's electricity. This pivotal project would transform the living conditions of ordinary Egyptians. Life expectancy in that impoverished country was only thirty-five years, and per capita income ranged around sixty dollars a year.

The Soviet Union, since Nasser's ascension to power, was working overtime to cement its relationship with the charismatic Egyptian leader. The USSR saw an opportunity when Nasser made clear that he wanted to buy weapons and President Eisenhower, per the Tripartite Agreement, declined to arm either Egypt or Israel, in the hopes of avoiding an arms race in the Middle East. Nasser now sought to buy Soviet arms, via Czechoslovakia. In addition, Nasser was looking for foreign investment for his Aswan Dam project, and hoped to have it financed by the West. But this was not to be.

On May 16, 1956, Nasser recognized mainland China. Other countries, like Britain and Israel, had already taken that step, but their recognition was not an issue. Nasser's action, however, caused an outcry in the United States.

Two days later, Eisenhower suffered his ileitis attack. While Ike was recovering, Secretary of State Dulles withdrew U.S. financial support for the building of the dam. He had been one of those incensed by Egypt's recent recognition of Communist China. Eisenhower gave nominal approval for Dulles to withdraw support, as Egypt was not willing to abide by our conditions. But later when Eisenhower was informed that the State Department had actually withdrawn U.S.–World Bank support for the Egyptian infrastructure project, Ike deemed it a mistake, recognizing that this new element would make it harder for the United States to build and leverage its influence in the Middle East.

In Dulles's own defense he told the president that there had not been the needed support in Congress for financing the Aswan Dam—as apparently key members of Congress saw this transformational project as bad for Israel, unjustified in the face of Nasser's arms deal with the USSR and its recognition of China, not to mention the increased competition that U.S. farmers would face once Egypt could utilize the thousands of acres of new arable land that would result from the dam project. Still others objected on the grounds that it would help Nasser himself—a man who refused actively to join our side in the Cold War.

Eisenhower had some sympathy with the notion of neutrality. "We were a young country once," Ike observed at a press conference, "and our whole policy for the first 150 years was [one of neutrality]."[12]

One week after Dulles cancelled Western financing of the Aswan Dam, Nasser seized and nationalized the Suez Canal.

Eisenhower immediately called in the attorney general, Herbert Brownell, for an assessment of the legal underpinnings of Nasser's move. Brownell told the president that "the entire length of the canal lay within Egyptian territory."[13]

"Egypt was within its right," Eisenhower told Dulles, "and until its operation of the Canal proves incompetent, there is nothing to do."[14]

The president's concern turned to what our allies' position would be. Eisenhower had heard through a trusted source that the British and others were considering a military response. "Dear Anthony," he wrote British prime minister Eden on July 31, proposing an international conference to exert pressure on Egypt rather than use a "precipitous resort to force."[15]

The British and their comrades agreed to negotiation, but despite this appeal, Britain and France continued to work behind the scenes on plans for an intervention and the ultimate overthrow of Nasser. Dulles, the Joint Chiefs, and even Senate Majority Leader Lyndon Johnson and his colleagues voiced support for Britain and France and declared that they deserved our backing and financial assistance. Talk among the Washington policy elite centered around Nasser's audacity and arrogance, and there were calls to take him out, to overthrow the regime. Adm. Arleigh Burke, chief of naval operations, took the position that "Nasser must be broken."[16]

Eisenhower refused to support such an approach. "Unless we are careful," the president told them, from "Dakaar to Philippines," the Muslim world, in solidarity, "could be arrayed against us."[17]

The prospect of a conference and other negotiations made it appear that Britain and France had stood down—at least for the time being. Eisenhower was convinced that war—possibly one that would draw in the USSR—had been averted.

British prime minister Eden kept assuring the president that the British and the French were eager to negotiate a settlement over the issue of the canal. However, despite his assurances to Eisenhower, in reality Britain, France, and Israel were using this time to plan a military operation designed to retake the canal by force. The historian Robert Ferrell summarized their motivations: "The British were irritated because of President Nasser's confiscation of the Suez Canal Company. The French wanted to have a go at Nasser because he had been harboring Algerian revolutionaries. The Israelis saw a chance to enlarge their territory by taking the Gaza strip and the Sinai Peninsula."[18]

The United States noted the buildup of British and French forces in the area, but assumed that they would not be used unless negotiations broke down. Ike could not imagine that he would be double-crossed by our wartime Allies.

By mid-October, however, the size of this buildup was well beyond anything that was required as a bargaining chip in negotiations.

Little did the president know that on October 24, 1956, a secret protocol was signed by Israeli prime minister David Ben-Gurion, British prime minister Anthony Eden, and French premier Guy Mollet. The idea was for Israel to send forces to invade the Sinai Peninsula, thus creating a pretext for the British and the French eventually to attack. Presuming that the Egyptians would respond by meeting the challenge, the British and the French would issue an ultimatum to the two sides to stand down. The Israelis would refuse, thus giving France and Britain the "justification" they needed to intervene militarily—recapturing the Suez Canal and overthrowing Nasser in the process.

However, the British and the French had made two major miscalculations. They thought the United States would have to support them because of our long-standing alliance. They also believed that Eisenhower, only a week away from the presidential election, would not make any unfavorable move before the balloting, and by that time they would have secured their objectives.

In others words, they did not know Dwight Eisenhower as well as they thought they did.

Throughout the crisis, made more difficult by the distractions of the campaign, Eisenhower was, in the words of the historian Jim Newton, "determined and stalwart, patient and clearheaded." And Ellis Slater noted: "Here were . . . the ten most frustrating days of his life, and yet there is no evidence at all of pressure, of indecision or of the frustration he mentioned. Actually he seemed completely composed."[19]

Then, on October 29 the Israelis struck. Ike was furious. American intelligence had missed the impending attack, and Eisenhower felt he had been left flat-footed. He convened an emergency meeting of his advisers.

Eisenhower reminded his top people of the Tripartite Agreement. Dulles saw Eisenhower's temper flare when he informed the president that the British and the French were of the view that we had to support them.

"What would they think if we were to go in to aid Egypt to fulfill our pledge?" Eisenhower fumed. "Nothing justifies double-crossing us. I don't care whether I am re-elected or not. We must make good on our word, otherwise we are a nation without honor."[20]

The next day Eisenhower contacted UN ambassador Henry Cabot Lodge and asked him to introduce a motion in the Security Council calling for an immediate cease-fire and withdrawal of Israeli troops. Later that afternoon the vote was taken, and the British and the French vetoed the measure, the first such vetoes in the history of the United Nations.

This further infuriated the president. What a public display!

Then, on October 30, the Israelis, British, and French, by design, demanded that Israel and Egypt stop fighting and allow an Anglo-French occupation of the Canal Zone to ensure that commercial traffic could continue uninterrupted. Failure to agree to this would give Britain and France no other option than to take the Canal Zone by force, they said.

Just as anticipated, Egypt ignored the ultimatum, thus falling into the trap. Less than twenty-four hours later, Britain and France started bombing targets in Cairo, Alexandria, and Port Said. In retaliation Nasser sank a 350-foot ship in the narrowing part of the canal to block shipping—eventually sinking as many as forty ships, thus immobilizing any transport vehicles.[21] It looked like all-out war. *The New York Times* noted that not since World War II had there been a concentration of naval forces of this size in the eastern Mediterranean.[22]

Having failed in the Security Council, Eisenhower instructed Lodge to propose the measure for a vote in the General Assembly. The tally was 64–5. Those who voted against the withdrawal measure were, not surprisingly, the three protagonists as well as Australia and New Zealand.

Britain and France, however, continued their assault. They deployed as many as two hundred ships, five aircraft carriers, six battleships, a dozen cruisers, and other, lighter craft.

Then, as Eisenhower had feared, things began to escalate as the Soviet Union threatened to intervene. In response, Eisenhower ordered that the U-2, the new high-altitude military reconnaissance plane, be sent to overfly Syria and Israel to determine whether there was a Soviet military buildup in the region. At the same time he ordered the readiness of all American forces, which included putting the Sixth Fleet in the Mediterranean on alert. This move was enough to check the Soviets, at least for a while.[23]

General Goodpaster, who had been working intimately with the president during the crisis, recalled that Eisenhower, ever the contingency planner, had anticipated that the situation might become a crisis, and earlier that summer had the government set up plans for American citizens in the Canal Zone to be evacuated. Three thousand Americans were withdrawn from the conflict zone.[24]

The British, French, and Israelis refused to back off. Eisenhower was determined that they do so. Understanding that calls for withdrawal would not be enough, he instructed Secretary of the Treasury George Humphrey to send the British a few lessons in economics. The United States blocked their access to their dollar accounts held in Washington, and refused to give them a loan.

International shipping that went through the canal—the lifeblood of many European economies—was now jeopardized. The president issued instructions to Arthur Flemming, director of defense mobilization, to deny them U.S. oil assistance.[25]

On November 6, Election Day, Eisenhower got the good news that the U-2 had detected no Soviet buildup in the area, and at twelve thirty that afternoon, Anthony Eden indicated that they were willing to accept a cease-fire. Having declared the end of military action, Eden hedged, however, by proposing a range of ways that Britain might stay in Egypt, for instance as peacekeepers.

Eisenhower would have none of it. The Soviets, too, wanted to have just such a status. To the president's mind, none of the Security Council members should provide peacekeeping in this volatile area. The United Nations created an emergency force and would serve as peacekeepers instead.

According to many accounts, Eisenhower told Eden that he planned to keep the heat on their economy, the effects of which were already being felt.[26] Eisenhower was convinced that all forms of leverage had to be used.

The British and the French ultimately withdrew, but not for military reasons. Both countries faced significant opposition from their political foes and their public at home. Oil shortages were beginning to bite, and in Britain there was a run on the pound.[27]

No doubt behind Ike's anger was sadness that our great country, which had intervened on behalf of Britain during the war, liberated France, and opened the Nazi concentration camps, had been betrayed. But he also believed that our allies, had to be brought back into the fold. Eisenhower understood their concerns and skepticism about Nasser, and their fears, which he did not "quarrel" with. However, as he wrote in a letter to his childhood friend Swede Hazlett on November 2: "I have insisted long and earnestly that you cannot resort to force in international relationships because of your fear of what might happen in the future. In short, I think the British and French seized upon a very poor vehicle to use in bringing Nasser to terms."

He added further that when the United States "demanded" that Ben-Gurion "keep the peace" they suspected that the Israeli leader, like the British and the French, might be trying to take advantage of the fact that the United States was on the verge of a presidential election—knowing that the Jewish vote might play a role in the election outcome. Eisenhower had given the State Department "strict orders" to make it clear that the "welfare and best interests of our own country were to be the sole criteria on which we operated."[28]

What bothered Eisenhower most was our allies' failure to think things through. Didn't they understand how this would have looked had they been successful? It would have been seen as the imposition of something that smacked of neocolonialism, and it would have exacerbated tensions in the region, giving the USSR fertile ground on which to seed more influence. Furthermore, the way the attack had been planned ran the risk of fanning crazy thinking that invariably led to unhinged conspiracy theories about some "Jewish plot." Had our allies worked on a strategy together, taking into account the new era in which we lived, this sorry chapter might have been averted. The standoff lasted forty-eight days, but the cleanup of the canal would be a long, arduous task. When the British and the French started to withdraw, it would not be long before U.S. aid to our allies began.

The Suez crisis exemplified Eisenhower's deep belief in the very nature of the allies' relationship and the emerging world. He respected the fact that all countries have their own vital interests, but in the pursuit of peace there could not be second-class global citizens.

Suez did not end the mounting pressure of that election period.

Just as the United States was confronted with a crisis in the Middle East, weeks before the 1956 presidential election, the Soviet Union chose—those very days—to put down an uprising in Hungary, restoring Soviet Communist control over reform-minded Hungarians. The brutal tactics used by the Soviet military in crushing the reformers resulted in the deaths of at least 2,500 protesters. Given the timing of these events, Eisenhower was prompted to admit that this was "the most . . . demanding three weeks of my entire Presidency."[29]

Eisenhower understood the limitations of military action to assist Hungary, but he nevertheless ordered an assessment of the role the United States may or may not have played in stirring the uprising. Again General Goodpaster was tasked with getting the president that information. His inquiry revealed that "some government officials" might have implied in their outreach to Hungarian reformers that the United States might intervene militarily. Goodpaster believed that the CIA "went beyond policy guidance in promising support."

"Our policy," Goodpaster recalled, "was to encourage [Hungarians] . . . to keep their hope of liberty alive." That was a far cry from implying military assistance.[30]

Like all freedom-loving Americans, the president's sympathies resided with the Hungarian reformers, but as a military man, he was angered by the apparent overreach of some U.S. officials. Sherman Adams asserted that Eisenhower had said many times that the liberation of Eastern Europe would have to be advanced by "peaceful instruments." Yet, Dulles had also sent ambiguous signals, leaving out the word "peaceful"—which prompted the president to "call Dulles to task for this difference in their words."[31]

The sad truth is that Hungary was surrounded by Soviet-bloc

and neutral countries—"as inaccessible as Tibet" from a military perspective, Eisenhower later wrote.[32]

His calculation had to be one, regrettably, of realism. Ike understood that Hungary was not the Middle East for the Soviets, but an area of vital interest that, less than four years after Stalin's death, could well become a battleground, maybe even a nuclear one.

After the Soviet crackdown, Eisenhower pushed hard to achieve special status for Hungarian refugees who wanted to come to the United States—bringing in twenty thousand to the U.S. not long after the Soviet intervention. Ultimately, Eisenhower's refusal to intervene militarily on behalf of the Hungarian reformers, though a controversial and frustrating call, underscored the importance he placed on knowing his adversary and understanding the limitations, even of a great power.

The campaign had provided a demanding backdrop to the critical events that had been unfolding. Eisenhower had been persuaded that he needed to make a limited number of campaign stops before the voters went to the polls. Yet Stevenson had gone on the attack in the last week of the campaign. When things in both the Middle East and in Hungary were at a critical point, the Democratic candidate crossed a threshold that, until this time, had not been breached. Adlai Stevenson declared to an audience in Chicago: "The Chief Executive has never had the inclination and now lacks the energy for full-time work." The president's "age, his health and the fact that he cannot succeed himself make it inevitable that the dominant figure in the Republican Party under a second Eisenhower term would be Richard Nixon."[33]

This was the first time, but not the last, that the Democrats would weaponize Eisenhower's health problems, or make inaccurate assessments of what was really going on behind the scenes. Ike shrugged off such attacks as signs of desperation.

The president's decision to force our allies to stand down over the Suez Canal and America's refusal, or inability, to intervene in

Hungary left many of Ike's supporters, including family members, concerned that the twin crises would cost the president his second term. "If I lose the election," he told my father the night the vote was being tallied, "then so be it."

The president was reelected for a second term with a massive landslide. Eisenhower improved on his popular vote and swept the Electoral College, winning 457 electoral votes to Stevenson's 73—giving Eisenhower a personal mandate. The Republican Party did not share correspondingly in this overwhelming indication of approval—signaling to Democrats that even though the popular Eisenhower could not run for a third term, he would still be the man to beat in 1960.

Despite a rising tide of media criticism going into the 1958 midterm elections and the 1960 presidential race, during his second term Eisenhower worked hard to mend relations with U.S. allies, and to further contain the USSR's influence, while looking for ways to reduce nuclear dangers.

Nevertheless this chapter of international relations had a far-reaching impact. The historian Michael Korda has noted that the Suez crisis "brought the end of Britain's remaining pretension to independent imperial power . . . and it speeded the end of Britain and France as colonial powers." Britain, he pointed out "shortly abandoned Malaya, Kenya, Uganda and Tanganyika . . . France would shortly lose Morocco, Algeria and most of its African colonies."[34]

But the Suez crisis also assured that henceforth the allies would work as one.

With the departure of Anthony Eden as British prime minister, Harold Macmillan became prime minister—again Eisenhower had the benefit of a long association with Macmillan dating back to the war. In 1958, when the United States intervened in Lebanon, the British were with the United States in this short operation. Unlike the Suez/Egypt crisis, the democratically elected president of Lebanon, Camille Chamoun, invited the allies to intervene. An overwhelming display of power was used, and it was planned that allied forces would stay in Beirut, the capital city, for a specific period of time while the elected president tried to stabilize the country. We had an exit strategy ready if he proved unsuccessful. There were no combat casualties as a result: The operation and its outcome were successful.

In France it would not be long before Eisenhower's friend and comrade in arms, Charles de Gaulle, would come to power as president—thus assuring better lines of communication.

In Israel, as elsewhere, mixed feelings no doubt existed. However, asserted Israeli author Isaac Alteras, "Neither Eisenhower nor Dulles ever tried to impose any solutions that would endanger Israel, despite cold war calculations and Arab pressures to do so. The administration continually upheld the commitment to resist any attempt to alter by force the territorial and political status quo as well as the integrity and independence of all states in the Middle East . . . economic aid and grants [to Israel] actually increased during the Eisenhower years."

The Suez crisis, Alteras went on to note, should be seen as "part and parcel" of the administration's view that the "attack on Egypt was both morally and legally unjustifiable . . . [The] difficult period of strain and confrontation during Eisenhower's first term in office gave way to cooperation and even coordination."[35]

The United States delivered on a range of things, including the adoption of the Eisenhower Doctrine, which afforded Middle East countries the ability to seek U.S. aid or military assistance if being threatened by armed aggression. Its aim was to curb Soviet inroads into the Middle East and to contain rising Arab nationalism.

Nevertheless, Eisenhower had made his point: In a campaign stop just before the 1956 election, he had set out his beliefs and policies in clear terms: "We cannot and will not condone armed aggression—no matter who the attacker, and no matter who the victim. We cannot—in the world any more than in our own nation—subscribe to one law for the weak, another one for the strong; one law for those opposing us, another for those allied with us. There can only be one law or there will be no peace."

The president's swift and decisive action in 1956 was the by-product of decades of making tough strategic choices. Trade-offs abounded, but in the end he had kept the peace in the Middle East and in Europe, restored relations among our allies, checked the expansion of Soviet influence, and averted a nuclear show-down.

Eisenhower paints his grandchildren and daughter-in-law Barbara at his studio at Camp David, August 1954. (U.S. Navy Photographical Center)

12

THE LONELINESS OF POWER

Not long after the war, while Eisenhower was president of Columbia University, he was encouraged to take up painting by his own portrait painter, Thomas Stephens. Perhaps also inspired by his friend Winston Churchill, who took the hobby seriously, Ike painted mostly for relaxation and time to think. He called them his "daubs" and made no pretensions that they were great art.

Richard Cohen, a columnist for *The Washington Post,* learned something about this. He once recalled meeting Eisenhower for the first time. Cohen had pretty fixed ideas of what to expect. He had come from a long line of liberal Democrats who believed the president's critics who thought Ike was a "dullard," a "good-natured dolt" who had failed to stand up to Sen. Joseph McCarthy and been "inexcusably tardy" in confronting Arkansas governor

Orval Faubus over civil rights. The press, noted Cohen, was relentless in its attacks on Eisenhower, and the cartoonists in those days, especially Herbert "Herblock" Block, were "tough on Ike and his meandering ways"—constantly depicting Ike with golf clubs while other cartoon characters were also satirically projected, but at least with some significance.

That evening Eisenhower and Cohen were both late to an exhibition at the Huntington Hartford Museum in New York (now the Museum of Arts and Design), where Ike's paintings were on display for a charity fund-raiser. The former president invited Cohen to walk through the exhibition with him. When they got to one particular farm scene, Cohen asked—in what he later admitted was a rather "patronizing" way: "What is the symbolism in this one, General?"

"Ike knew what I was saying but did not take umbrage. 'Let's get something straight here, Cohen. They would have burned this [expletive] a long time ago if I weren't the president of the United States.'"

In a split second Cohen realized that Eisenhower had been "miscast" as a naïve farm boy. "This was the suffer-no-fools, down-to-earth warrior-cum-politician who knew many things, not the least of which is that a museum show did not make him a painter. He could not be flattered."[1]

Ike knew exactly what painting did for him. He used to tell me that it helped him see the world in another way, through color and light. He usually painted from photographs. Though not as rich as painting on-site, the interplay of color and texture could still be discerned. Color, in particular, fascinated him.

Ann Whitman, his personal secretary, also remembered how he would point out the different shades of the same color in the gardens of the White House. "All amateurs . . . should go back to using only three primary colors, or at most 6 or 7, and blend them as the early artists did" he once told her.[2]

Former prime minister Winston Churchill once gave Ike a painting with a white-water stream at the center of it. After the PM had gone I found myself back in Granddad's closet-size studio.

"I wonder how Winston gets his water to look that way," he murmured as he examined the painting. I always remembered that comment, and I've noted over time that Ike was better at painting portraits than he was at rendering landscapes, with some very notable exceptions. I have always thought that this was where his true interests resided—in people.

Eisenhower had some very good paintings and also some real duds—which he would instruct his valet, Sgt. John Moaney, to discard. Moaney never did. Instead he squirreled away these half-done rejects in a secret place, from which they miraculously reappeared after Ike's death.[3] As great as the relaxation painting may have afforded the president, the pastime gave Eisenhower something else that was related but different: the opportunity to rest his mind, while his brain had a chance to absorb and sort through the complex questions he was grappling with. Perhaps smoking had played some of that role for Ike during the war, but since quitting—cold turkey—on his return from Europe, he got his mental breaks by making quick stops at his White House studio for fifteen minutes, sometimes longer. They were a vital part of how his decision-making process worked.

William D. Snyder of the Eisenhower Presidential Library and Museum in Abilene once remarked that "[Eisenhower] . . . did not want to be churned up or full of unchecked emotion. The paintings were vital to him not as artwork, but as a way to fill himself with calm as he carried out his presidential duties.[4]

The president, however, also used his paintings for purposes beyond meditation or relaxation. He often painted portraits of his friends that he would later present to them as gifts. Ike painted, for instance, many of his wartime colleagues, including Prime Minister Winston Churchill, Field Marshal Bernard Law Montgomery, Gen. Walter Bedell Smith, Col. James "Jimmy" Gault, Ike's British WWII aide, and many others. He even painted a young Prince Charles and Princess Anne for Queen Elizabeth II—a gesture I am sure the British monarch appreciated. One can think of no more flattering surprise than to receive such physical proof that you or your loved ones had been the focus of so much of the president's attention. One of my most valued possessions is a small painting, rendered on the message side of a postcard, created for me when my grandfather received the news of my birth. Painted while he was serving as the first supreme commander of NATO, the lovely little impressionist daub is called "A French Garden," perhaps the view from his studio window at his residence outside Paris. Despite the demands on his time, he had painted what my grandparents regarded as his best, on a postcard that said on the other side: "Bon Anniversaire"—or Happy Birthday in French.

Sherman Adams recalled that the president phoned him one day with a surprising question. After covering a number of administrative items, the president asked his chief of staff a personal question: "Are your eyes blue?" He wanted to know because he was painting a portrait of Adams from a photograph, and the color of his eyes was indistinct. He wanted to be sure he had it just right.[5]

Eisenhower's painting studio in the White House was a tiny room, located to the right of the family elevator on the second floor in the private quarters of the executive mansion, overlooking Lafayette Square. On those occasions when I was invited into this sanctuary, I would stand behind him as he worked on a canvas. On at least two occasions he turned and gave me a work he had just completed.

I am intrigued by one of them—a snow-covered mountain scene with a deep, emerald lake. It is dated 1957, leaving me to wonder what mysteries might be hidden in those brushstrokes, what troubles he had poured out; what emotions he had summoned and sorted and calmed as he applied the color. That was the year he assured the desegregation of Little Rock Central High School and Russia's Sputnik was launched—the first human-made satellite in space.

Like people responsible for finding coherence in a million moving parts, Eisenhower could often be found in silent retreat. During the White House years Jim Hagerty would from time to time find the president in his studio full of scattered paint tubes and half-finished daubs—just sitting, lost in thought, in front of a blank canvas. Even after his retirement, Jacqueline Cochran, a personal friend of Ike and Mamie, found the former president in a quiet office she had lent him, alone, not working, not phoning, not reading, just sitting.[6]

Observing Eisenhower directly, and in reading the Eisenhower scholarship and examining the issues that Ike had to address, I have come to realize that there is a curious factor in successfully providing consequential leadership. Authenticity is important, as the public or your specific audience is usually able, sooner or later, to spot a phony. But it also requires not just the command of one's inner self, but also a level of acting. One cannot imagine that Ike was optimistic all the time, but he understood, perhaps better than anyone else, pessimism's corrosive impact and the negativity it can produce in an organization and those associated with it.

Power brings with it, then, a certain kind of loneliness, even in the company of friends and trusted family. Eisenhower's role as supreme commander, and then as president with the power and capacity to launch a nuclear holocaust, required him to manage great burdens.

The wartime pressures are easier to imagine—making decisions with enormous consequences on the basis of inadequate information. But the loneliness of the presidency must have been every bit as acute, since people's goals differed and technology had made any wrong move even more potentially catastrophic with the advent of the hydrogen bomb and sophisticated delivery vehicles. When Eisenhower assumed the presidency, no real rules applied to the conduct of warfare or the management of a global rivalry capable of destroying in a matter of hours (with bombers) and minutes with (ICBMs) the United States, our allies, and even the world. Also, the beginnings of space exploration posed a whole new set of dangers, opportunities, and challenges that would wear on even the most farsighted, diligent, and organized of minds. These things all came in a period of rapid modernization, along with a shifting social landscape and rising demands for civil and later gender rights.

In 1960 Eisenhower gave a speech in which he eloquently recalled the airborne and the weather decisions he had made on the eve of the Normandy invasion, only sixteen years earlier. He noted that "for years thereafter I felt that only once in a lifetime could a problem of this sort weigh so heavily upon a man's mind and heart . . . but I know in this age the President encounters [such] soul-wracking problems many times in a single term of office."[7]

The nuclear equation had changed everything.

Throughout this dynamic period, Eisenhower's load got heavier in his second term, with the inevitable change in administration staff—the retirements of Treasury Secretary George Humphrey and Attorney General Herbert Brownell, as well as the death of John Foster Dulles and the unfortunate resignation of Sherman Adams on ethics lapses, which entailed accepting gifts from an old friend, even though nothing specific had crossed the legal line.

Ike also keenly felt the death of his close childhood friend Swede Hazlett, who had given Ike the idea of attending a military academy to get a free education. In this context he was faced with increasingly tough decisions without many of the people around him whose own leadership had been finely tuned with his during his first term.

Ike's other challenges were similar to those of people in positions of high-level responsibility—the distortion of personal relationships in the context of enormous authority. During his presidency he was the most powerful man in the world, so it is not surprising that people wanted his approval, craved his attention, and wanted him to be perfect. His outbursts of temper, whose frequency varied and were sometimes exaggerated, had many roots, but they can be easily understood.

First was Granddad's deep and unfulfilled desire for privacy. Although he never complained, as an adult I can see that he had been deprived of basic human things that many civilians take for granted, such as a life of some balance and a reasonable daily pace. Public life necessitated the absence of aloneness, bringing with it a distinct kind of loneliness instead. People hovered, his every word was quoted, diaries were kept of his every offhand utterance and action—and later bestselling books were based on these invasions of his privacy. And, during his illnesses the American public was privy even to his most intimate physical details.

He was aware of this, and I wonder if he may have sometimes regretted that he did not, until the last few years of his life, have time to enjoy more of the abiding love my grandparents shared—and the chance to rest deeply.

Even though he had to live with other people's endless, and often inaccurate, speculations regarding his own thinking and actions, he did not really know how to stand back and stop working. Even in retirement he was always thinking about the future.

Ike had his foibles. His critics said he could swear a blue streak or be profane, but his associates made note that his swearing consisted almost exclusively of "Goddammit!" and "What the hell!" It was a source of amusement to his colleagues that he never used the kind of four-letter words that are commonplace today—indeed, Ike could not even recount a proper dirty joke.[8]

Ike also expressed great annoyance in talking on the telephone, and could sometimes be abrupt. Sherman Adams remarked on this, but in his retirement I heard, more than once, Ike's very abbreviated answers to incoming calls. "What do you want?" or "Make it short!" He far preferred to meet his colleagues in person.

That's why I recall so vividly one Sunday morning in the latter half of the 1960s. We were reading the newspapers and watching television on the sunporch at the farm. Ike was glued to *Meet the Press.* That morning Gov. Mark Hatfield of Oregon, a candidate for the Senate, was on the show. As Hatfield answered the questions posed to him by the panel of journalists,

I noted Granddad leaning closer and closer to the television to make sure he did not miss a word. When the program was over I watched with amazement as Ike got out of his armchair and went to the telephone that was on a stand not far from the television set. I had never really seen him do such a thing.

When he made voice contact with someone on the other end of the line, it was clear he had called the television station. Ike asked to speak to Hatfield, and when the governor came to the telephone, the former president commended him for his excellent performance.

Years later, long after Ike had died and Senator Hatfield was nearing the end of his public life, I asked him if Ike had called him on the telephone after a television appearance. "He most certainly did!" Hatfield exclaimed. "You have no idea how much my credibility went up at the station when I was told that President Eisenhower was on the line and wanted to talk to me!"

Like anyone else, Eisenhower had human needs himself, which included the critical ones of satisfying relationships and friendships. In his marriage he was lucky. In his family he enjoyed love and mutual devotion—but all of us shared with him his isolation. As people at this level of acclaim and authority can attest, other relationships are disfigured by their proximity to this power.

Eisenhower returned to the United States the acclaimed victor—a man who was given ticker-tape parades across the country before millions of cheering Americans. In fact his ticker-tape parade in New York City after the war was the largest in American history at that time. Later he was elected president in two landslide victories. What he was unprepared for, as my father once explained to me, was the "use that others would try to make of him"—the subordinates who made money on their books professing to know what was in Eisenhower's heart; the politicians, like the rabid old right-wingers who hugged him at rallies and then knifed him in the back behind the scenes; and his successors, who irresponsibly blamed many of their own mistakes on him by implying that "Eisenhower had told them to do it." And then there were others: those who suffered from envy and a sense of "petty rivalry," fearing that Eisenhower's star might diminish their own. Earl Warren, his Chief Justice appointee, was one such man Ike's associates asserted.[9]

In 1959 Field Marshal Montgomery's memoirs came out—full of swipes at the former supreme commander. Though it was probably coincidental, Monty's editors must have marveled at the timing of his book. His critique hit the shelves in the post-hubbub period of Suez, Sputnik, and media and party political accusations that the president was failing at his job.

Eisenhower was not so much naïve about such things as he was simply a thick-skinned idealist who wanted everyone who loved this country and valued our long vital alliances to rise above attention-getting ploys, assume responsibility for their own choices, and avoid saying things that would undermine future cooperation.

Ike truly believed in the higher meaning of what had been accomplished through the United States' intimate cooperation with the British and our other wartime Allies. He was saddened to see the belittlement of this mighty alliance in some of the harder-hitting war memoirs. In his own, *Crusade in Europe*, according to Michael Korda, Eisenhower wrote "one of the clearest and least opinionated books to come out of World War II, and by far the least self-exculpatory and least judgmental."[10]

"Resentment was totally out of character for Ike," Gen. Lucius Clay once observed, "He was the least vengeful man I ever knew."[11] And General Goodpaster once observed to me: "Eisenhower had a remarkable ability just to 'move on.'" Still, "moving on" must have required enormous personal discipline to put the matter out of his mind. My father once told me that Ike learned "never to rewind the tape."

Staff assistants, in the presence of a person who wields such authority, are indispensable at organizing things in a way that fosters more straightforward decision making. And others, like household staff, can assure that the minor details of life disappear. But the boss's power also often distorts such relationships. My father loved to tell a story about just such a thing, which happened during the war. One day, General Ike said wistfully: "I wonder how John is doing," and said no more than that. The next day John was at supreme headquarters—and both were angry. "What in the hell are you doing here?!" Ike barked. "Why in the hell was I given orders to come!" John exclaimed. And then they both paused and realized that a well-meaning subordinate had heard the general muttering about his son. To please the boss, his subordinate had ordered John to SHAEF headquarters.

Given Eisenhower's desire to remain aloof from social relationships with his staff or his subordinates, it is not surprising that he found himself most comfortable in the company of other self-made men; individuals who enjoyed recreational sports as the president did—and who liked to relax and laugh. Many of them had run defense industries during the war or had some other role in the war effort.

John Kennedy once "acidly" remarked to his aide Arthur M. Schlesinger Jr. that Eisenhower had abandoned his army friends and now "all his golfing pals are rich men he has met since 1945."[12] Kennedy's barb was petty and inaccurate. Plenty of Eisenhower's army friends were around during those presidential times—from his personal physician, Gen. Doc Snyder, who had been with him since the war, to the nearly constant presence of Gen. Alfred Gruenther, an ace bridge player, who spent considerable time with the president and First Lady after his return from his supreme command of NATO in 1956 and during his time as president of the American Red Cross. Gens. Lucius Clay and John J. McCloy also went back to Eisenhower's earliest years in the military.

George Allen and Bill Robinson, arguably two of his closest friends, had met Eisenhower during the war. Since Ike simply did not like to mix business and pleasure, and many of his other wartime associates were still subordinates, he did not see many of them socially until after his retirement.[13]

If Ike kept a distance between those who worked for him and those who were members of his inner circle, there were conditions of entry for those closest to Ike and Mamie. According to Ellis Slater and George Allen, there was a sober understanding that there were no favors to be asked. My father once recalled that while on the porch of the Eisenhower farm, one of Ike's friends, a successful industrialist, lightheartedly asked the president when the nation could expect some tax relief. Ike must have thought that the question centered around the high tax rate being paid by his weekend guest, because he snapped: "How in the hell do you think we are going to pay for things!" It was unlikely that such a question was ever asked again.

At a Gridiron Dinner, Ellis Slater recalled that the emcee of the evening cracked: "These gentlemen are golfing cronies of the President, but we understand that it's after the golf game that the serious business starts." Slater wondered in his diary what kind of interpretation that comment might engender. Offended, he wrote: "Probably no one thought about it at all, but it might interest a lot of people to know that there isn't a friend the President has that wants a single thing from him or would ask him for even the slightest favor."[14]

This became evident to outsiders when a piece of legislation passed Congress in 1955 that would have limited the federal government's role, under the provisions of the Interstate Commerce Act, in regulating gas pipelines, as well as in setting prices for that gas. Eisenhower supported the aims of the bill, which in his view rectified the inappropriate role of the federal government in setting prices. Eisenhower also believed that the current regulatory environment discouraged new exploration for gas and "sowed confusion" in the industry.

During the debate on the bill in Congress, it came to light that some highly questionable lobbying activities had been under way, including an attempt to contribute to a senator's campaign expenses in exchange for his vote on this matter. Newspapers also quoted an oilman as saying: "He's in my pocket," referring to a powerful senator involved in pushing the legislation.

As much as Eisenhower agreed with the basic tenets of the bill, after exhaustive discussion with his aides and associates he decided to veto it, to what an aide called the "jeers of calloused Republicans."[15]

"I am unable to support H.R 6645 'To Amend the National Gas Act as Amended,'" Eisenhower declared.

> This I regret because I am in accord with its basic objectives. Since the passage of this bill, a body of evidence has accumulated indicating that private persons, apparently representing only a very small segment of a great and vital industry, have been seeking to further their own interests by highly questionable activities. These include efforts that I deem to be so arrogant and so much in defiance of acceptable standards of propriety as to risk creating doubt among the American people concerning the integrity of governmental processes.[16]

Privately Eisenhower wrote in his diary—clearly still fuming—"They make crooks out of themselves."[17]

Later at a press conference Eisenhower was asked again about his decision to veto the bill. Reporters wanted to know whether the president thought the veto would help or hurt his chances for reelection. The president replied that he didn't "have the slightest idea" of the veto's effect on his election prospects. But he did say that what had happened was "arrogant" and "indefensible."[18]

A number of Eisenhower's closest personal friends, part of "the gang,"[19] were engaged in the oil and gas industry and had stood to benefit from the legislation—these included W. Alton "Pete" Jones of Cities Service, Charles S. "Charlie" Jones of Atlantic Richfield, and Texas oilman Sid Richardson, one of Ike's friends from the early war years and among his earliest political supporters. "Not one had tried to use [our] friendship to persuade me to sign that gas bill," Eisenhower said.[20] And no doubt not one of them would have had the nerve to chide Ike for vetoing it.

I knew many of these men and their wives from their time with my grandparents. In addition to their own already achieved successes, most of them were generous philanthropists, and many of them funded an array of exchange organizations, such as the highly successful Eisenhower Fellows program and People to People, as well as think tanks that Eisenhower envisioned and created. All were initiatives that Ike hoped would make the world, in the depths of the Cold War, a more stable place.[21]

Among the other relationships that people normally rely on for honesty and intimate trust are those with one's doctors. But even these were distorted by Ike's power as president and by the strength of his personality.

According to Ellis Slater, for instance, Ike's doctors had known in May 1956—before his ileitis attack and just after he had thrown his hat into the election ring—that the president was likely to have another flare-up of this intestinal condition and that an operation would be required.

Slater confided to his diary that when Ike discovered that his doctors had kept him in the dark "for fear it would confirm the feeling in some of the public's mind that the President's health was not all that it should be," Eisenhower almost "blew his top" and threatened to get a new set of doctors if they were not more candid with him.[22]

This betrayal of trust would make it difficult for the president ever to think of "Doc" Howard Snyder in the same way again. The apparent manipulation had robbed the president of making a better-informed decision about running for reelection in 1956.

It is not surprising that Ike looked for ways to relax that would bring him pleasure, especially with the decisions he had to make constantly all day long. He got enormous satisfaction out of playing bridge, and was a formidable player. Eisenhower's favorite partner was Gen. Alfred Gruenther, a nationally ranked bridge master. They were both so good that they teamed up. Ike and Al, both normally fun-loving characters, were so serious about the pursuit of the game that, among Ike's circle, no one else wanted to partner with either of them.

But even in the context of such simple pleasures, Ike's doctors hovered, issuing orders that cut significantly into other things Ike enjoyed most. After his 1955 heart attack, for example, the president was prohibited from ever watching the Army-Navy football game in real time again—for fear of straining his heart: No doctor wanted *this* patient to die on his watch.

Decades after Granddad's death, one of his cardiologists told me they had noticed that—in his later years—when the former president watched golf on TV and his friend Arnold Palmer was playing, his heart tended to beat rapidly (and with some irregularity) and his blood pressure would rise. The doctors were on the verge of prohibiting Eisenhower from watching Palmer on TV anymore, but then decided that the former president did not have that long to live.

During Eisenhower's career, golf, which he had taken up in the 1920s, gave him some exercise and enormous physical relief. Aides often said that Eisenhower would have been like a "caged lion" had he not had a chance to work off the stress and the excess energy he carried with him.

"The gang" that would often convene with the Eisenhowers at Augusta National Golf Club assured that the presidential couple was able to make use of the club and feel at home. They generously decided to build "Mamie's Cabin" so that the president and First Lady had a home away from home on his favorite golf course. For proper ethical reasons, it was not until *after* Eisenhower left the presidency that he was furnished with the names of those members who had contributed to its construction, enabling him to thank each of them personally.[23]

Augusta was the place that really brought the president relaxation and a sense of perspective. There he had uncomplicated relationships and a private place to rest his mind and think things through. It is hard to explain adequately what a tonic it was for a man of action to be surrounded by activity-intensive friendships, even as he quietly contemplated issues of great importance. It was a lonely thing to work at the White House, Arthur Larson, then one of Eisenhower's speechwriters, once noted. On stepping off the family elevator, he recalled: "I discern what appears to be a very small figure sunk in the corner of a large sofa at the other side of a cavernous corridor that runs most the length of the building. By the light of a floor lamp, the President is hard at work scratching up a current draft. In this 'vast mausoleum . . . the tomblike silence is broken only by the scratch of a pen.'"[24]

As much a relief as Augusta was, even that place was not immune to the impact of Eisenhower's power as president. After the Little Rock desegregation crisis, Cliff Roberts, the founder and driving force of Augusta, got a call from Ike "wondering out loud if he would be welcome [there] in the future." The club was, after all, located in rural Georgia. Roberts tried to reassure the president, but he himself harbored "misgivings" about how people would react to their most visible member. It appeared that the club members, not all of them Southerners by any means, would put the matter out of their minds. However, when Roberts made an advance trip to Georgia before the president's planned visit, he was "shocked and discouraged by the bitter attitude of the local people."

When Ike and Mamie arrived at Augusta on November 15, 1957, for a six-day stay, none of the usual crowds lined the route from the airport, but out of respect for the American president, "a dozen prominent local leaders were on hand at the airport." Despite this, local papers that had "enthusiastically" supported the president in the past were now savaging him in editorials and op-ed columns.[25] Those members at Augusta National instinctively understood the weight that rested on Ike's shoulders and afforded him the privacy and camaraderie that gave him a badly needed change of pace.

In the end, relationships with family members are the bedrock of a powerful person's world. All are drawn into his or her orbit to provide trusted support. Often they are the only people on whom such a person can really rely unconditionally. In this Ike was most fortunate to have his son, John, and brother Milton as confidants; Mamie as his devoted life partner; his daughter-in-law, Barbara, whom he adored; and his grandchildren, on whom he lavished love and attention. Despite his burdens, my siblings and I enjoyed a deeply engaged relationship with him. He came to some of our baseball games, ballet recitals, and horse shows. He would also give each of us rides to Gettysburg from the White House—a one-on-one opportunity to chat. My sister Anne and I compared notes years later, and we both recalled a similar exchange on our trips with Granddad in the limo. "What do you think is the scourge of the countryside?" he had asked me once with some excitement near Emmitsburg, Pennsylvania, in the shadow of the beautiful Catoctin Mountains. "I don't know," I answered, uncertain of the comment's thrust. "Billboards!!" he responded with passion, as he looked out at the tacky signs for Civil War museums and souvenir shops, just miles from Gettysburg. Anne was similarly perplexed when asked the same question. But when Granddad said to her, "Billboards!" and then added, "Someone should pass a law," Anne said she thought at that moment, *Then why don't you!*[26]

Still, even what may have been events of normal family life could have an outsize impact on someone of Eisenhower's stature.

In 1955 Granddad had installed a putting green near the house in Gettysburg. This would enable him to practice his putting without the loss of privacy that would come if he practiced at the Gettysburg Country Club, where he would inevitably face crowds of enthusiastic onlookers. One early evening several years later, while my grandparents and parents were on the sunporch enjoying a cocktail and waiting for Ike's flags to be lowered from the sizable flagpole within easy sight, I changed my grandfather's lifestyle in a matter of moments.

Though only nine years old at the time, I rode Granddad's horses and was entrusted with considerable responsibility. That evening, while securing the horses for the night, four or five of them pushed me away from the gate—before I could secure the paddock lock. In no time they were running wildly up and down the roadway and over my grandparents' lawn—just in front of the sunporch, where the folks had gathered. In one final swoop all four of them galloped over Ike's beloved putting green. A number of us tried to catch them, and when we had finally rounded up all the horses, secured them in the paddock, and then replaced the divots on the green, I went to face the music. I was terrified.

My parents later told me that my grandmother was horrified as she watched the horses run over Ike's golf green—she knew what it meant to him. No doubt Granddad was deeply upset as well, but according to accounts he did not show it. When I finally arrived on the sunporch, Granddad swiveled around in his armchair and said to me (as I stood in front of him full of apprehension): "As I told your grandmother, I haven't seen horses run like that since I was a kid in Abilene, Kansas!"

That was the end of it.

My grandfather knew I would never make such a mistake again. He also knew the effect that his personal power, his personal energy, would have had over me. I was already devastated.

The aftermath of this incident made a significant difference to my grandfather's leisure hours. The putting green's finely cultivated grass subsequently caught a disease, not surprisingly where the horses had plowed up the turf, and the green had to be removed the following season. My failure to be diligent had cost my grandfather the privacy he badly needed and deserved. He had to go back to practicing his putts at the Gettysburg Country Club, where people would press him for autographs and watch every small move he made. He did so without any complaints—at least none that I heard of.

While Ike and his brothers may have had differing political views, they were bound together in extraordinary ways.

In December 1956, just after the election, the president got word that Edgar's son had died. Jack was old enough to have a family of his own, but his death was a crushing blow to Ike's older brother. In a moving condolence letter, the president offered his thoughts to Ed. After expressing his deepest regrets, he wrote:

> It is, of course, difficult to understand why so often the oldsters go on and on into the eighties and nineties, while the younger, more vigorous men are cut down in their youth. There is no way to explain it except that it is one of the accidents of living. It happens with the trees and the birds and everything that grows. No individual can have any possible explanation, and therefore it is one of those things that must be accepted and absorbed into the philosophy that a man develops as he goes along.

Ike encouraged his brother to try, despite his feelings, to be a support to those around him—"to provide an example that is not characterized by pessimism, cynicism and defeat."

Ike admitted, "This sounds like preaching," but went on to write: "My justification is that I lost a son of my own many years ago—the only one we had [at the time]. To this date it is not an easy thing to deal with when it comes fresh to my memory, but it is something that I had to learn to accept or go crazy."[27]

Embracing acceptance, with the confidence of honest, devoted, and diligent effort, is all a person can do in most situations. But the road to such wisdom, in Eisenhower's case, had taken him through some of the darkest places mankind has seen, and from the contemplation of that there arose his conviction that putting others first gives profound meaning to duty and self-sacrifice. As General Eisenhower wrote to a colleague during the war: "A man has to be able to forget himself and [his] personal fortunes."[28]

Painting would be the solitary undertaking that helped Ike retain that inner strength. And in some ways his paintings expressed not just his journey but his quest. They "were so placid, so gentle," wrote the author Bob Green. He "painted as if he had spent his whole life yearning for tranquility."[29]

The President poses with his valet and friends in the White House Rose Garden, June 11, 1957. John Moaney, devoted valet to President Eisenhower, beams proudly as he stands beside the president, posing with a group of his friends from the African Methodist Episcopal Church of Copperville, Maryland. Front row from left: Moaney's wife; his mother, Mrs. Ethel Moaney; and Mrs. Eisenhower. Foreground: Barbara Mills with purse around her neck. (National Park Service)

13

ESTABLISHING A BEACHHEAD

No postwar president has had more than eight years to shape the issues of his day. Eisenhower faced this short-term/long-term conundrum over civil rights and was acutely aware that he had little time to make progress without risking policy blunders that might perilously inflame emotions that might set back the cause.

In the case of equal opportunity in the United States, Eisenhower established a beachhead that would assure no future roll-back of the civil rights measures he advanced. To do this he used measures based on the federal authority he possessed, at the same time using the courts and the legislative process, thereby leveraging the strength of the coequal branches of government. By the time Ike left the White House, matters under federal jurisdiction had been largely desegregated. Together with Congress and the courts, few law-abiding Americans could reject the voice of their federal institutions.

In tackling the civil rights issue, Ike approached it the way he had undertaken other major challenges during the war.

In conversation with the Civil War historian Bruce Catton, Eisenhower told the famed author, "The principles of war are neither exclusive nor specialized. They are the principles of life which are fulfilled whenever an individual has a task or an objective to perform. They are a matter of common sense. Human nature is constant, as are the elements of political power, military power, economic power and morale . . . an army is not licked until it admits it."[1]

In the coming years it would be presumed by Eisenhower's critics that his measured approach to civil rights was a sign of indifference. It would take almost sixty years before historians could see that laying the groundwork for progress was as critical a contribution as making impassioned speeches and taking sides. In Eisenhower's case, fundamental to his philosophy and his objectives was to keep the country united and to assure a civil dialogue that might avert open rebellion and bloodshed. By choosing to desegregate the federal areas over which he had control, Eisenhower set legal precedents that would go a long way toward forcing the segregated part of the country to come to terms with the long-term futility of those ways.

The first true test of Eisenhower's civil rights commitment came to a head in September 1957.

On September 24, 1957, the president of the United States looked firmly into the television camera from his studio in the White House, his jaw tight, his eyes signaling that he meant business.[2] He had returned from Newport, Rhode Island, to speak to the nation—indeed the world—from "the house of Lincoln, of Jackson and of Wilson" to explain why he was authorizing the deployment of five hundred 101st Airborne paratroopers to one of America's cities. This would be the first imposition of federal troops in the South since Reconstruction, the period that came on the heels of the Civil War. Eisenhower's projection of overwhelming force in Little Rock, Arkansas, sent a powerful message to the people of that state and observers throughout the world: The rule of law would prevail.

Before coming to the presidency, Eisenhower had had varying exposure to racial issues. Growing up, he saw only episodic examples of it. Although his mother had migrated to Kansas from Virginia, the Brethren community had not been slaveholders.

As many as one hundred blacks lived in the town of Abilene in those years. While social clubs were segregated, Ike's own school was integrated. Years later he recalled an occasion when members of his school's football team made it clear they would not line up against the opposing team, which included an African American. According to accounts, Ike volunteered to line up across from the black player and shook his hand before and after the game—a gesture his teammates refused to make.

According to Ike's journal: "The rest of the team was a bit ashamed."[3]

The army was segregated as Ike came up through the ranks, so it was not until he was in charge that he confronted the issue of race relations directly. He would learn from experience the limitations placed on any open-minded leader.

Not long after Pearl Harbor, when our Allies in the Pacific region were under pressure to shore up their military capability, Eisenhower made some noteworthy advancements for soldiers of color. While still at War Plans, before being sent to Europe to take up command of American forces, Eisenhower identified and planned to deploy a black division to Australia. Australia's laws forbade the use of black troops. "All right—no troops" was Eisenhower's response.[4]

During the war he was insistent that the blood supply be integrated—a controversial proposition, especially among Southern units. He told Gen. Alfred Gruenther, responsible for implementing his decision, to "stand his ground."[5]

In Europe, Eisenhower desegregated many Red Cross Clubs and pushed hard to give blacks the chance to volunteer for combat. He was aware of the backbreaking work they were doing as support personnel and thought they should be given the right to move upward in the ranks.

Just before the Battle of the Bulge, Eisenhower ordered Gen. John C. H. Lee to see to it that African American troops were given the opportunity to serve in combat "without regard to color or race." Of those who volunteered from across the operation, however, preference was given to those troops who had already had basic training, a critical factor for combat survival.[6]

Under Eisenhower's command the military also experimented with using "Negro units" within white units; the supreme commander also replaced white GIs with black ones where appropriate. Given the exigencies of war, this was all he could do within the legal restrictions imposed by the military—that is, the federal government.[7]

On his return from Europe, Eisenhower testified before Congress about the bravery and competence of these troops, lauding the fact that nearly five thousand black soldiers had taken advantage of the opportunities that had been made available to them.

Stories were reported to the supreme commander of the successful utilization of these troops, even in units that came from America's South—despite initial concerns about racial tensions from a number of generals, including George Patton.

"There was not a single objection brought to my attention [regarding these black troops]. On the contrary from all sides there were heartwarming stories," Eisenhower recalled.[8]

Some of the black units had white leaders and others black—even in Southern squads. This experience convinced Eisenhower that with the right approach, desegregation could be peacefully implemented, "that the thing could be done."[9]

As the historian David Nichols pointed out: "Amid the stresses of a great war, Eisenhower had quietly undermined the myth that Negroes were unwilling and inadequate warriors."[10]

During the 1952 campaign, Eisenhower had spoken of the promise to "eliminate discrimination against black citizens in every area under the jurisdiction of the federal government." And by the fall of the campaign Eisenhower and his attorney general had ramped up his profile on the matter, noting decades of Democratic rhetoric on the subject of equal rights with no action behind the words.[11]

President Harry Truman had taken some steps during his presidency. In 1946, for example, he had established the President's Committee on Civil Rights, and on July 26, 1948, he had issued an executive order to desegregate the armed forces—but little had actually been done in the intervening years to implement the order.

"A Republican administration," Ike said during the campaign, "will not arouse false hopes of Negroes by promising what it never intends to deliver.[12] Truman was furious about these thinly veiled accusations, and such pronouncements put many of Ike's Southern supporters in an awkward position—but this had little effect on the candidate. He continued to highlight that gap between action and words. Eisenhower wanted to start with the District of Columbia, a city under federal oversight and jurisdiction.

"After 20 years of talk about moving mountains, [the Democrats have] not even brought forth a mouse," candidate Eisenhower had said. Truman defensively replied that the inexperienced Eisenhower should know "that the President can't get things done in the District of Columbia simply by waving a wand."[13]

Until his election as president, Eisenhower had no policymaking opportunity to change racial conditions in the United States beyond what he had already done. But rising to the presidency would give him an opportunity to lay the framework for civil rights. Now as president, he set forth on a strategy for progress.

In Eisenhower's first State of the Union address, he stated his objectives. Before a joint session of Congress, he declared his "dedication to the well-being of all our citizens and to the attainment of equality of opportunity for all so that our nation will ever act with the strength of *unity* in every task to which it is called."[14] In that same speech, Eisenhower specified measures to desegregate Washington, D.C. He continued:

Our civil and social rights form a central part of the heritage we are striving to defend on all fronts and with all our strength. I believe with all my heart that our vigilant guarding of these rights is a sacred obligation binding upon every citizen. To be true to one's own freedom, is, in essence, to honor and respect the freedom of all others.

A cardinal idea in this heritage we cherish is the equality of rights all citizens of every race and color and creed.

We know that discrimination against minorities persists despite our allegiance to this idea. Such discrimination—confined to no one section of the Nation—is but the outward testimony to the persistence of distrust and of fear in the hearts of men. . . .

Much of the answer lies in the power of fact, fully publicized; of persuasion, honestly pressed; and of conscience, justly aroused.[15]

Eisenhower then outlined his intention to use the office of the president to "end segregation in the District of Columbia, the Federal Government, and the Armed Forces." He went on to add that federal contracting would also be opened up for equal access to opportunity.

Eisenhower wanted the nation's capital to be a "showplace" of peaceful civil rights progress: "We expect to make true and rapid progress in civil rights and equality of employment opportunity."[16]

In consultation with Attorney General Herbert Brownell, the president believed that these stated goals could realistically be achieved, given the short four to eight years Eisenhower could have in office.

The response to this section of Ike's State of the Union address was noteworthy. Even though the president did not outline his full civil rights agenda, in the context of several desegregation cases before the Supreme Court in that term and his pronouncements on the campaign trail, there was concern in a number of corners that Eisenhower might be inclined to push too hard on civil rights. A number of visitors came to his office to warn about the potential repercussions.

One such visitor, Gov. James F. Byrnes of South Carolina, a Democrat, insisted on talking to the president. Eisenhower invited Byrnes to the White House for lunch, and during their meeting the governor told Ike that he was deeply concerned about the pending court decisions on desegregation.

In Eisenhower's private diary, on July 24, 1953, he wrote that Byrnes predicted that if desegregation were to happen, "a number of states would immediately cease support for public schools." Ike noted that several times during the meeting Byrnes made the point that the South

> no longer finds any great problem in dealing with adult Negroes. They are frightened at putting the children together.
>
> The governor was obviously afraid I would be carried away . . . and as a consequence take a stand on the question that would forever defeat any possibility of developing a real Republican or "opposition" party in the south. I told him that while I was not going to give my advance attitude toward a supreme court opinion that I had not even seen and so could not know in what terms it would be couched, that my convictions would not be formed by political expediency.

Then as an aside, Ike wrote his own thoughts about the matter, as he often did about issues he was trying to think through: "I do not believe that prejudices, even palpably unjustified prejudices, will succumb to compulsion. . . . Consequently, I believe that federal law imposed upon our states in such a way as to bring about a conflict of the police powers of the states and of the nation, would set back the cause of progress in race relations for a long, long time."[17]

Despite warnings issued to him by Democrats and Republicans alike, President Eisenhower and Attorney General Brownell made desegregating the District of Columbia a first order of business.[18]

There was an opening in the Thompson case, a legal measure brought to challenge the segregation practices of Thompson's Cafeteria in Washington, D.C. In 1872 and 1873 a measure had been passed that allowed blacks access to all public accommodations in Washington, D.C. Over the decades, however, due to the lack of enforcement, the black population had been deprived of these services. The management of the nation's capital was the responsibility of Congress, and Southern Democrats had run the House Oversight Subcommittee for decades. The failure to enforce the law was considered a "lost" measure, so the Eisenhower administration decided to challenge it. Herbert Brownell's Justice Department argued the case in the Supreme Court, and it unanimously ruled that such segregating policies were illegal.

The president responded immediately, calling together civic leaders and phoning Hollywood studio executives asking them to pressure local theaters to admit the city's blacks into what had been segregated movie houses. Eisenhower also put onto the district board of commissioners Samuel Spencer, a Harvard-educated lawyer and an outspoken advocate for desegregation.

Within the year Washington, D.C. was desegregated, without violence.[19]

Even in the social sphere things began to change. For instance, Mamie presided over desegregating the annual White House Easter egg roll in 1953 and visited a black women's sorority, Delta Sigma Theta, on May 28 of 1953, as an honored guest. These were only the beginning of the change that was under way.

Another critical part of the Eisenhower strategy was the determination to appoint only federal judges who were prepared to uphold the law—and its spirit—regarding equal opportunity. White supremacists were weeded out and rejected from any consideration.

In addition to this, Eisenhower directed Brownell to make a concerted effort to identify qualified African Americans for service in government. E. Frederic Morrow was selected to serve on the president's personal staff, the first black man in American history to do so. J. Ernest Wilkins Sr. was appointed assistant secretary of labor, the first black ever to participate in presidential cabinet meetings. In 1955 George E. C. Hayes was appointed to the Public Utilities Commission. He was a black attorney who had, incidentally, defended at least one "suspect" in the McCarthy hearings and had also managed a part of the segregation issue before the Supreme Court.

Concurrently Vice President Richard Nixon was assigned to chair a commission on employment for African Americans who were seeking to become government contractors. It would be the precursor to a 1955 Eisenhower measure that established a committee on government employment aimed at equal opportunity for all government employees.[20]

Even before Eisenhower was elected president, a challenge had been brewing to the Supreme Court's ruling in *Plessy v. Ferguson*. This 1896 decision had established the principle of "separate but equal" in public facilities, and it raised the question, decades later, of whether separate education could in fact be deemed "equal." The Supreme Court would rule on this matter, but it would be up to federal district courts to administer the findings of the court.

Chief Justice Fred M. Vinson, hinting at some dissention on the matter, asked the administration for its views on this pending case. Reluctant to cross constitutional lines with a reply, the administration soon found that the question was moot. On September 8, 1953, the chief justice died unexpectedly, leaving a vacancy at the very top of the court.

Nevertheless Attorney General Brownell filed an amicus curiae brief, which is a "friend of the court" document in which a nonlitigant may offer new information or some perspective on the case at hand. The administration's brief stated that the administration believed that "segregation of public schools was unconstitutional."[21]

Eisenhower nominated California governor Earl Warren—whom he admired and whose views were well known to him—for the position of chief justice. As soon as the appointment was made, the matter of *Plessy v. Ferguson* was promptly brought before the nation's highest court, the result of a challenge that came from a case known as *Brown v. Board of Education*, which originated in Topeka. A successful effort was made by Warren to assure a unanimous ruling, a crucial one given the far-reaching impact of the court's decision to eliminate segregation in the nation's public schools.

Lucius Clay, one of Ike's intimates and a close professional associate on the subject, noted that Eisenhower and Earl Warren "functioned as partners." Warren established the court's priorities, and Eisenhower, "by stressing compliance with *Brown*," lent the stature of the presidency to a ruling that was, in essence, "unsettled law," meaning that there had not been laws beforehand that had established a widely recognized precedent. The president's determination to enforce *Brown* effectively countered segregationists who opposed civil rights measures on states' rights grounds.[22] Clay went on to say that Eisenhower agreed with *Brown*, and viewed the landmark ruling as a "[political] burden, not a blunder."[23]

Clay did not believe, however, that Eisenhower's complicated relationship with Warren, which emerged not long after, had anything to do with civil rights or "even the appropriate role of the courts on civil rights matters." In due course Eisenhower came to fear that Warren, who harbored presidential ambitions, had found an outlet for his political frustrations on the court by "expanding" its authority "well beyond its traditional and appropriate limits." Others noted that the Warren Court "proceeded to discover new 'inherent rights' not enumerated in the Constitution."[24]

Later, in his memoirs, Earl Warren would blast Eisenhower for trying to affect the outcome of *Brown* negatively by failing to single out this decision for a public endorsement. Further, Warren reported bitterly, before *Brown* he attended a presidential "stag dinner," at which the president seated him next to a Southern segregationist—a gesture Warren interpreted as a go-slow on *Brown*. On the publication of this story a number of associates, including Attorney General Brownell (who had also been at the dinner), recalled that the evening had been about the Bricker Amendment, not *Brown*.[25]

In the coming decades much would be made of President Eisenhower's refusal to publicly voice his support for *Brown*, the court's landmark decision, beyond his usual pronouncements about upholding or "obeying" the law and his assertions about the importance of promoting measures to assure equal opportunities for people of all races, colors, and creeds. But there again the key to Eisenhower's approach was a principle:

> I believed that if I should express either approval or disapproval of a Supreme Court decision in one case, I would be obliged to do so in many, if not all, cases. Inevitably I would eventually be drawn into a public statement of disagreement with some decision, creating a suspicion that my vigor of enforcement would, in such cases, be in doubt. Moreover, to indulge in a practice of approving or criticizing court decisions could tend to lower the dignity of government, and would, in the long run, be hurtful. . . . In this case, I definitely agreed with the unanimous decision [in Brown].[26]

Another indication of Eisenhower's support for the measure—in an area where he did have authority—was, again, in the District of Columbia. After the Supreme Court ruled on *Brown*, Ike called the D.C. commissioners together and asserted that D.C. should "lead the way" to desegregate its schools "as an example to the entire country." By September 1954 the D.C. schools were integrated—again, "with no violence."[27]

Eisenhower and the White House staff had no illusions about the difficulties awaiting them. Brownell likened the "debate" over this issue as reminiscent of the passions that led to the bloody Civil War. Avoiding the prospect of violence was a key concern. Emotions were highly charged, and *Brown* had overturned the daily lives of "at least two generations of Americans." Until 1954 Southerners were in compliance with the 1896 Supreme Court ruling, and "separate but equal" had been the law of the land. "To expect a complete reversal of these habits and thinking in a matter of months was unrealistic," wrote the ever-pragmatic president.[28]

In this regard, a significant source of concern revolved around the potential for using troops to enforce the court decision. The conundrum was that while troops could be utilized to enforce the ruling, they did not have the authority to compel localities to operate the schools. There was always the danger that a school district would shut down the public schools and open private ones instead, as Senator Byrnes had warned.[29]

Violence had already begun to grip the nation. In 1955 a fourteen-year-old African American, Emmett Till, was murdered in Montgomery, Alabama, which was experiencing citywide boycotts. Shootings were jeopardizing public safety, bombs were being detonated, and police were working overtime to avert more bloodshed by providing convoys for buses as they made their way through the city.

This violence against the black population was "indefensible," the president later recalled, "and the administration, as well as all other sensible people, was outraged."[30]

Extremist groups promised more violence, and the South was already exacting revenge on innocent blacks by denying them credit, firing them from their jobs, and threatening their families. They promised more bloodshed if the black community "pushed the whites too far."[31]

Despite this, in Eisenhower's 1956 State of the Union address, he outlined his administration's determination to address voting rights. The president was mindful that the 1950 national census had revealed that fewer than one in four African Americans voted.

For that reason the Eisenhower administration proposed, in its 1957 civil rights legislation, a voting rights measure, a "legally constituted" commission with the power to subpoena witnesses and compel them to testify regarding allegations of voter infringement.

These initiatives, discussed by Eisenhower's full cabinet, also included the establishment of a Civil Rights Division in the Justice Department. The 1957 bill, which included these elements, would be the first civil rights legislation passed by Congress since the post–Civil War Reconstruction period, eighty-two years before.

Eisenhower later recalled that "these proposals were little less than revolutionary."[32]

On July 13 eighty-three Southern Democrat and four Republican representatives signed a manifesto deriding the bill, along with a pledge to "defeat this sinister and iniquitous proposal."[33] Nevertheless, the administration's civil rights bill passed the House of Representatives, with the votes of 168 Republicans and 102 Democrats. But the bill died in the Senate Judiciary Committee, which surprised the president. Democratic liberals, including Lyndon B. Johnson, John F. Kennedy, J. William Fulbright, Albert Gore Sr., and Mike Mansfield, to name just a few, opposed the bill. These prominent Democrats were insistent that on voting rights, any measures taken against possible racists who violated a voter's civil rights should be subject to a jury trial. It would be up to such juries to determine whether a defendant was in contempt of court—a method that had been used for centuries.

Eisenhower was against their position: "The basic purpose here would be to put into the hands of a local jury, who might be prejudiced, the determination of contempt of court." He favored giving that determination to a judge who could be more impartial.[34]

The next day, in a telephone call with Georgia senator Richard Russell, Eisenhower said that he understood the problems and the adjustments the South would have to make, but "I told him I could not yield in my purpose of protecting a citizen's right to vote. This was the overriding provision of the bill that I wanted set down in law; *with his right to vote assured, the American Negro could use it to help secure his other rights.*" (Emphasis is Eisenhower's.)[35]

The Democrat-controlled Senate voted to strip the bill of the voting rights section—threatening that if Eisenhower insisted on it there would be "no legislation whatsoever" for the rest of the term. Indeed, other threats were issued to the White House, letting the president know that there could also be retaliation over other pending bills important to the administration.

The Southern representatives were in fact threatening to engage in all-out war.[36]

Herbert Brownell recalled an episode in the midst of this contention. He and his wife were attending a Washington reception one evening at the American Bar Association. The attorney general of Georgia, Eugene Cook, and his wife, were in attendance. On meeting Brownell, Mrs. Cook "murmured" an outrageous epithet and "refused to shake hands."[37]

Eventually Eisenhower and Lyndon Johnson worked out a compromise over the hostile objections of the Southern Democrats. While the final bill was far from the president's liking, and many had urged him to veto it, Eisenhower wanted to get started on its other key provisions as soon as possible. In 1960 the president brought new legislation to Congress that would fix some of the problems with the original bill, including a first step toward voting rights, this time with Lyndon Johnson's support—though a broader measure remained a sticking point with Congress.

With the *Brown* decision, each school district was required to submit a plan for how it would implement the ruling's requirements. Many places around the country complied without incident. Such was also the case in Little Rock, Arkansas.

At the same time the National Association for the Advancement of Colored People (NAACP) had recruited nine schoolchildren and registered them to start at the high school that autumn. They were countered by a segregationist group called the "Mother's League," which applied for an injunction against the Little Rock school board to prevent those black students from attending the high school.

Only four days after the Senate approved the compromise on Eisenhower's landmark 1957 civil rights legislation, Arkansas governor Orval Faubus called out the state's National Guard to "preserve peace and good order" as Little Rock's students prepared to return to school. (It was later discovered that Faubus had not asked his law-enforcement officials for a public safety assessment before he did so.)[38]

On August 27, just as the summer of 1957 was fading and

the Little Rock schools were preparing to open their doors for a new year, the chancellor of the Pulaski County Chancery Court granted the Mother's League an injunction on the basis that "integration could lead to violence."

In a test of the validity of the school board's plan, Judge Ronald Davies, an Eisenhower appointee, who had been temporarily assigned to Little Rock, ruled that there was no reason to discard the original desegregation plan. On August 30 he nullified the injunction and ordered the authorities to proceed with integration. On the day the nine young African Americans tried to enter Central High School, a mob awaited them.

The school board again petitioned the court to suspend the integration plan. The judge refused, encouraging an injunction against the governor. Faubus called Eisenhower, pleading with the president of the United States for "understanding."

Eisenhower replied: "The only assurance I can give you is that the Federal Constitution will be upheld by me and every legal means at my command."[39] He later reflected: "I did not believe it was beneficial to anybody to have a trial of strength between the president and a governor. In any showdown, the Federal government would always win. . . . Surely there was a way to resolve this matter."[40]

Faubus's request to meet the president seemed likely to provide a face-to-face opportunity to settle the matter. But Brownell advised against it. Eisenhower nevertheless agreed, if the discussion would be based on a serious desire to resolve the situation. He must have reasoned that he would give Faubus one chance to do the right thing.

On September 14 Orval Faubus came to Newport, where the president was staying for a brief vacation. Eisenhower urged the Arkansas governor to revoke his orders to the National Guard and thus allow the black children to attend school. While Faubus said many of the things he knew the president was hoping to hear, when the Arkansas governor got back to Little Rock, he did nothing to change the National Guard's orders.

The president had had enough. He had given Faubus time, and the governor had failed to change the guard's orders. Ike would now use his full powers to ensure that the law would be followed.

Determined not just to enforce the court order but also to make an example of Little Rock, Eisenhower sent in the 101st Airborne—the paratroop division that had played such a key role in the invasion of Normandy. Overruling the expressed reservations of Joint Chiefs of Staff, the president, in Executive Order 10730, federalized the Arkansas National Guard. He then flew back to Washington.

On September 24, in that fateful speech, the president ordered the mob to disperse in and around Central High School, and explained, "where ever normal agencies prove inadequate to the task and it becomes necessary for the Executive Branch of the Federal Government to use its powers and uphold the Federal Courts, the President's responsibility is inescapable."[41]

On explaining his reasoning for the intervention, he left his viewers in little doubt about the critical nature of breaking the law. He also spoke of the impact these events were having on the nation's internal and national security:

> In the South, as elsewhere, citizens are keenly aware of the tremendous disservice that has been done to the people of Arkansas in the eyes of the nation, and that had been done to the nation in the eyes of the world.
>
> At a time when we face grave situations abroad because of the hatred that Communism bears toward a system of government based on human rights, it would be difficult to exaggerate the harm that is being done to the prestige and influence, and indeed to the safety of our nation and the world.
>
> Our enemies are gloating over this incident and using it everywhere to misrepresent our whole nation. We are portrayed as a violator of those standards of conduct, which people of the world united to proclaim in the Charter of the

> United Nations. There they affirmed "faith in fundamental human rights" and "in the dignity and worth of the human person" and they did so "without distinction as to race, sex, language or religion." . . .
>
> If resistance to the Federal Court orders cease at once, the further presence of Federal troops will be unnecessary and the City of Little Rock will return to its normal habits of peace and order and a blot upon the fair name and high honor of our nation in the world will be removed. Thus will be restored the image of America and of all its parts as one nation, indivisible, with liberty and justice for all.[42]

By invoking the international impact of these events, as well as reminding our citizens that the United States is a country of laws, Eisenhower used these key points because he knew that people could agree on them—and in doing so find some common ground. The president, however, was not indifferent to the human cost of these terrible events, especially on those who had borne the brunt of this grotesque display of violent racism.

On September 30 the president received a letter from the parents of the Little Rock Nine:

> *We the parents of nine Negro children enrolled at Little Rock Central High School want you to know that your action in safeguarding their rights have strengthened our faith in democracy. Now as never before we have an abiding feeling of belonging and purposefulness. We believe that freedom and equality with which all men are endowed at birth can be maintained only through freedom and equality of opportunity for self-development, growth and purposeful citizenship. We believe that the degree to which people everywhere realize and accept this concept will determine in a large measure American true growth and true greatness. You have demonstrated admirably to us, the nation and the world how profoundly you believe in this concept. For this we are deeply grateful and*

respectfully extend to you our heartfelt and lasting thanks. May the Almighty and all wise Father of us all bless guide and keep you always . . .

On October 4, Eisenhower sent a reply:

Dear Mr. Brown,
I deeply appreciate your September thirtieth telegram, signed also by other parents. The supreme law of our land has been clearly defined by the Supreme Court. To support and defend the Constitution of the United States is my solemn oath as your President—a pledge which imposes upon me the responsibility to see that the laws of our country are faithfully executed. I shall continue to discharge that responsibility in the interest of all Americans today, as well as to preserve our free institutions of government for the sake of Americans yet unborn.

I believe that America's heart goes out to you and your children in your present ordeal. In the course of our country's progress toward equality of opportunity, you have shown dignity and courage in circumstances which would daunt citizens of lesser faith.

With best wishes to you, Sincerely Dwight D. Eisenhower[43]

The military force provided by the 101st Airborne had the desired effect, and the sneering, fist-shaking, foulmouthed crowd around Central High School eventually dispersed, and the students were able to attend school until the end of the year. But the subject of Gov. Orval Faubus would always bring the president a special sense of frustration. Faubus had "stimulated resistance to integration for political and personal gain," he fumed.[44]

Consistent with the administration's fears, however, on February 20, the school board petitioned the district court to "postpone" the desegregation efforts because of the anger and hostility that had overtaken the community. The judge agreed to a two-and-a-half-year hiatus on the desegregation plan, barring the black students from attending the high school in 1958.

William Coleman Jr., a distinguished African American lawyer, brought this case to the Supreme Court. *Cooper v. Aaron* entailed a suit brought against the chairman of Little Rock school board and a Negro student denied admission to Central High School. "On September 29, the Court filed a compelling and dramatic unanimous opinion in favor of desegregation. In an unprecedented show of resolve," Coleman remembered, "the opinion was personally signed by each of the nine judges, three of whom were recent appointees of President Eisenhower. To my knowledge the signatures of nine justices have never—before or since—graced a decision of the Court."

In Coleman's assessment, *Cooper v. Aaron* assured that *Brown v. Board of Education* would not be an empty victory but truly "transformational."[45]

Criticism for sending in federal troops, however, rained down on the president, most notably from Southern Democrats, who saw the use of the 101st Airborne as an "illegal ill-advised use of troops [that] makes the United States a military dictatorship."

Sen. Olin Johnston of South Carolina even proposed that Faubus declare a "state of insurrection," and he called for reestablishing a national guard to confront federal troops—in what would amount to another civil war. And James Eastland, a Democrat from Mississippi, declared: "The president's move was an attempt to destroy the social order of the South."

A mass meeting in Kentucky put Eisenhower on mock trial for "treason." And a local politician from Georgia wrote to warn the president not to come to Georgia. If he did, he could expect "violence and physical injury."[46]

Days later Sen. Richard Russell sent the president a telegram blasting him for his actions, which he termed "high-handed," and accusing him of "illegal methods . . . [in] carrying out your order to mix the races."

Eisenhower wrote the senator a detailed defense of his actions, while taking exception to the senator's outlandish comparison with Nazi Germany: "I must say I completely fail to comprehend your comparison of our troops to Hitler's storm troopers," the president replied. "In one case military power was used to further the ambitions and purposes of a ruthless dictator; in the other to preserve the institutions of free government."[47]

Martin Luther King Jr., who the president would invite to the White House nine months later, wrote Eisenhower telling the president that the vast majority of Americans stood with him. "In the long run," he wrote, "justice must finally spring from a new moral climate, yet spiritual forces cannot emerge in a situation of mob violence."[48]

Coleman, over the span of years, would look back at this time and recall that the country was on the "precipice" of civil war. Resistance grew, lynchings were commonplace, and violence increased at the same time that "Congress was not helpful. It rejected an Eisenhower proposal to authorize the attorney general to intervene to protect the constitutional rights of any citizen. It rejected financial assistance to desegregating schools."[49]

Eisenhower said that he and his administration were determined that a fair, just, and moral America assume its responsibilities for the nation's less fortunate and for those who had been the victims of racism. Ike would face heavy headwinds, especially among Democrats, whose main political base consisted of Southern whites. Still, determined to be a president for the whole country, the Middle Way was, in his view, the only prospect the United States had for *sustainable* social and racial progress.

The objective of desegregating the areas controlled by the federal government had been difficult enough to attain, and they included measures of far-reaching impact such as progressive federal court appointments and the desegregation of federal contracting. But the attitudes prevalent in individual states would be harder to tackle, and they were outside any president's jurisdiction at that time.

To advantageously influence local affairs, "the President [had] endeavored to keep the trust of both sides so that when he acted he would be supported by the public," Herbert Brownell recalled.[50]

While Eisenhower's critics later blamed him for not doing more to create a new moral climate in this country, he realized that if the whole nation were to make good on its constitutional promise, it would require bringing the whole country along.

However, Eisenhower did avoid a potent problem that any other leader might have failed to confront: He managed to prevent furthering the Southern cause by falsely transforming Southerners "into martyrs."[51]

After his retirement Eisenhower remained in touch with his colleagues on this vital national issue. In *Going Home to Glory*, David Eisenhower noted that Eisenhower "strongly supported the Kennedy civil rights bill as it was developed, but he still disapproved of 'dramatic pronouncements' and demagogic appeals emanating from the right or left. His voice, as always, was one of moderation and restraint."[52]

In telephone discussions with his successor, President John F. Kennedy, Eisenhower "readily agreed" to pick up the phone and line up GOP votes for Kennedy's civil rights bill. In a letter to Kennedy on June 14, 1963, Eisenhower wrote: "As I then told you, I think this matter has become one that involves the conscience of the individual and the nation, and indeed, our moral standards."[53]

Eisenhower persisted in this theme, and while he generally avoided, after leaving office, trying to influence Republican votes, he did not hesitate to speak his own mind on this particular issue. He made it clear publicly that he supported the Kennedy measure: "With the passage of this law," he said, "Republicans should take upon themselves a moral commitment: to do their utmost to see this law is implemented not merely by the powers of legally constituted enforcement agencies, but by the hearts of a determined and free people."[54]

Eisenhower's willingness to help the Democrats pass legislation they themselves had opposed during his presidency was a notable example of his determination to put the country first, rather than his political party.

Eisenhower's civil rights record was a classic tale of being first. Emotions were high, as expectations and impatience grew. By the end of Eisenhower's second term many African Americans who had benefited from his efforts were restless and increasingly angry. They were not ready to hear that any level of "patience" might be required. Eisenhower had used this word, but for many it was frustrating to hear, even if it was not meant to be patronizing.

Perhaps Ike's critics thought they knew his thinking—but they certainly did not know his heart. He truly believed that actions always speak louder than words—as the wooden motto on his desk said: "Gently in Manner, Strongly in Deed."

"Although [such a] stance damaged his reputation for civil rights leadership," the historian David Nichols has written, "Eisenhower did not abandon his pledge that he not 'claim political credit for a simple matter of American justice.'"[55]

As Eisenhower later recalled: "The Administration had steered a difficult course between extremist firebrands and extremist diehards. This was due to conviction, not politics."[56]

It was also in keeping with Eisenhower's overall objectives—to build a platform on which the civil rights revolution could be built. Eight years would never be enough time to bring about a change of heart in the minds of millions—but by adopting such a strategy and putting in place people, such as the critical step of appointing enlightened federal judges who'd be there long after he was gone, he set the stage for civil rights progress in the years to come.[57]

"Eisenhower and the chief justice he appointed [Earl Warren] were men whose career accomplishments were anchored in relentless courage . . . the modern civil rights movement was launched," noted Bill Coleman, who had served on the legal defense fund of the NAACP.[58]

But perhaps most meaningful to Eisenhower was a message he received in October 1962 from the president of Harvard University, Dr. Nathan M. Pusey, notifying the former president that Harvard's first African American professor, Dr. William Hinton, who died in 1959, left all of his life savings—$75,000—to the university to establish a Dwight D. Eisenhower Scholarship Fund for graduate students at Harvard. The gift was made on the condition that it be done to recognize the progress toward equal opportunities that began in the Eisenhower administration.

Ike wrote Dr. Pusey to thank him and told the Harvard president that he could "not recall having been given a personal distinction that had touched me more deeply."[59]

President Eisenhower tours the George C. Marshall Space Flight Center of the National Aeronautics and Space Administration in Huntsville, Alabama, on September 8, 1960. (National Park Service)

14

PLAYING THE LONG GAME

After a power struggle in the aftermath of Stalin's death, and significant uncertainty with regard to the Soviet Union's primary leader, a reform-minded Stalin protégé emerged as the single focal point of power in that country. Nikita Khrushchev was ebullient, unpredictable, and sometimes crude, and his objective was to be accepted in the West among the great powers—by trying to demonstrate Soviet superiority in space and beyond.

Sputnik, the name of the Soviet Union's artificial satellite—and the reason for the USSR's status as "first in space"—was a turning point for the Eisenhower administration and for the country as a whole. Eisenhower, knowing full well what he was doing, would have to stand back and take a severe political hit for the Soviet Union's success if he was to meet other larger, more important security goals for the United States. He would also deftly use the "crisis" as leverage to make other key changes in the government; initiatives that would shape the world we live in today.

The race to achieve technical advantage, as new military capabilities such as rockets and nuclear warheads emerged, was the defining issue of the late 1950s. At the same time, Cold War tensions called into question extraterritorial matters that had yet to be fully addressed, and that needed resolution if the global community was to avoid having them become new flashpoints in the competition between Communism and democratic capitalism.

During the Eisenhower years, the principle of "freedom of space" was a critical issue that was, as yet, unresolved. Would low-earth orbit be an extension of sovereign airspace—with all the restrictions that implied—all the way out into the stratosphere? Or could freedom of space be established that would limit sovereign airspace, leaving low-earth orbit and beyond as an international commons, affording long-dreamed-of satellites the freedom to circle the earth? The resolution of these questions would affect military reconnaissance and verification, as well as commercial activity, into the future.

During this time as well, competing claims to Antarctica sooner or later had to be resolved, lest it too become an area of Cold War contention. The continent represented 10 percent of the world's landmass, larger than Europe and Australia.

The scientific community was at the forefront of these transformational questions, and in 1954 the International Council of Scientific Unions established the International Geophysical Year (IGY), which was set to take place in 1957–1958. Among the projects to be undertaken in that year of international exploration would be the launching of artificial satellites and the exploration of the polar regions. Along with many other nations, the United States and the Soviet Union signed on to the IGY objectives.

Under the IGY agreement both the United States and the Soviet Union agreed to launch artificial satellites. Under Eisenhower's chairmanship of the NSC, the subject of the impending Soviet launch of their IGY satellite came up numerous times after the

United States signed on, and it became even more relevant in the months leading to the actual launch. The CIA and the NSC were waiting for the Soviet launch of their satellite. Indeed, James Killian, at the time president of MIT, noted that the USSR was "quite open about the status of their satellite program."[1]

On June 22, 1957, the USSR reported to the IGY working group that it planned to launch a satellite within "the next few months." *The New York Times* printed the news on page twelve. A little more than a month later, on July 31, the president gave a news conference and mentioned the impending launch of a Soviet satellite; not one journalist asked a question about it. Furthermore there was "no great clamor" on August 27 when *The New York Times*—this time on page one—reported that the USSR had claimed it had successfully tested a multistage ICBM.[2]

A little more than a month later, on October 1, 1957, a front-page article in the *Times* appeared, though apparently few paid attention to Walter Sullivan's "Light May Flash in Soviet 'Moon.'" In it the author noted the impending Soviet launch.

The article began: "The Soviet Earth Satellite may contain a flashing light to mark its path across the night sky for all people of the world. This was revealed here today as Soviet scientists assiduously dodged all questions by their Western colleagues as to when they would fire their first sphere into orbit about the earth."

The dialogue had been part of a conference that opened on September 30 "to coordinate plans for the satellite firings."[3]

Then on October 4, 1957, it happened.

The Soviets put into orbit a 184-pound aluminum device that emitted beeps, traveling 560 miles above Earth and circling the planet every ninety-five minutes, calling it Sputnik, Russian for "traveling companion."[4]

While not at first a political issue, eventually the Soviet launch would provoke a new level of national hysteria, eventually creating a "feeding frenzy" that both encouraged and reflected the attitude of the political forces that seemed "surprised" by an impending event previously covered in the newspapers. From then on emotionalism ruled the story line, and the United States seemed sure that the Soviet Union was poised to win the Cold War and threaten our existence as a free people.

Interestingly, the American people themselves did not, at least at the outset, feel especially threatened. According to *Newsweek*'s "Listening Post," a public opinion survey found that there was "concern but not panic." Another *Newsweek* correspondent, in Boston, found: "The general reaction here indicates massive indifference." And later, on October 30, during Eisenhower's press conference only "one reporter asked a question that dealt directly with outer space."[5]

Unwilling to accept Eisenhower's calm assessment of this event, the media and the president's political opponents understood that this story could have "political legs."

"The media [became] just hysterical on the subject," recalled Arnold Frutkin, later an associate administrator at NASA. "The people in the Eisenhower administration spent a hell of a lot of time denying that there was any race on . . . but the press insisted we were in a race. So you're in a race whether you want to be or not."[6] Adding to the rising political temperature, Sen. Mike Mansfield, a Democrat from Montana, stated bluntly: "What is at stake is nothing less than our survival."[7]

Others, including the outspoken nuclear physicist Edward Teller, declared that Sputnik represented the most serious attack on the country since Pearl Harbor.[8]

Even Senate Majority Leader Lyndon Johnson spoke in ominous terms, calling for an immediate Senate-run investigation into the incident and America's military capabilities and preparedness.

The day before Sputnik, Bill Ewald recalled, Eisenhower was seen as a "champion of civil rights." Reporters praised his performance. "Twenty-four hours later he became what he would remain throughout his final years in office—a symbol of an America grown complacent, fat and unconcerned."[9]

The "combination" of the school crisis in Little Rock and Sputnik, wrote Michael Korda, "ended once and for all the notion that Ike was above or beyond criticism."[10] The Democratic Party at last had a slogan or a "theme," as Ewald called it, for attacking Eisenhower in the hopes of making political inroads into his popularity.

. . .

Despite press and political accusations, the administration knew exactly what it was doing, and it had calculated—for better or worse—the risk associated with its chosen path. While some in the White House worried that a "first" by the USSR would have profound repercussions politically, the president and many of his advisers underestimated the use that would be made of this issue by politicians with their eyes on the midterm elections in 1958, the emerging effects of a slowing economy and the upcoming 1960 presidential election.

Of all the public figures on the scene, however, nobody was more aware than Dwight Eisenhower of the fact that World War II had ushered in a new era in military-technological advances. The Allies had grappled with German rocket technology, first with their V-1s and later their V-2s during the war. These new weapons were, in effect, short- and medium-range missiles. It was not hard to understand the critical nature of advanced missile technology and its capabilities, if combined with nuclear warheads.

At the war's end the United States and the Soviet Union had rushed frantically to round up Hitler's missile men. It was clear to both countries that nuclear weapons and rocketry would define the postwar military posture.

The technologically advanced world was at a turning point—and the question was clear: Would these capabilities be used exclusively for national security purposes or would they also be applied toward human betterment? Scientists held the key.

Eisenhower, as a military man, understood the dual nature of such capacities and counted on his scientific advisers to help clarify and anticipate the technological advancements on the horizon. It was Nobel laureate Dr. Isidor I. Rabi, who helped the president and his administration think through how scientific expertise could be factored into political deliberation. As Rabi said: "We need to have people around the President who love the United States more than they hate the Russians."[11] Rabi also pointed out that at least some of the Sputnik hysteria arose from a country that was only three short years away from the demise of Sen. Joseph McCarthy.

Edwin Land, the founder of Polaroid, was also a member of the Science Advisory Council—a body that reported to the Office of Defense Mobilization. His was a high-tech company that had mastered the capability of instant photography.

Land and Rabi were the ones who had proposed the development of a high-altitude aircraft, the U-2, capable of photographing Soviet military installations, thus providing information that would help the president understand the potential for a surprise nuclear attack, and it had shown its utility in Suez.

This creative idea was welcomed in the small circle of people who knew about the proposal. But the U-2 would only be effective for so long—before advancements in aeronautics would make it possible to detect and shoot down such planes. Space, however, would open extraordinary technical vistas, and with the ability to launch satellites into orbit, these would include entirely new horizons for military operations. Given a satellite's global capabilities, it could provide a platform for reconnaissance of our adversaries' military infrastructure and provide early warning of their preparations for war. It could also provide verification of international treaties and would eventually incorporate defense support-and-guidance systems, and command and control communications.

This future was only possible if the legal principle of free access to space could be established.[12]

While the purpose of launching small satellites, as part of the IGY banner, was to explore the upper atmosphere of earth, the United States saw another advantage in this undertaking. In launching such a device into space, the satellites' orbits would establish that key legal precedent for freedom of space. But, if the United States was first to launch a satellite, the Soviets might become alert to the long-term implications for freedom of space, and turn the issue into another dangerous flashpoint.[13]

Four years before, on July 29, 1955, the United States publicly announced its intentions to build and launch a small satellite under the auspices of the International Geophysical Year. Only days later the Soviet Union made a similar announcement.

What now remained for the Eisenhower administration was the matter of assigning the task to one of the military branches that was currently developing missiles. The army's Redstone rocket facility in Huntsville, Alabama, was given highest priority to build the military's missile capability. The administration, however, intentionally separated this work from the IGY satellite program, which they placed under the auspices of the U. S. Navy. It's task was to develop and launch the Vanguard missile that would propel America's IGY satellite into orbit.

While developments were promising, there was no mistake that the Vanguard program, plagued by delays, was further behind than the Redstone's top-priority missile, the Jupiter-C. Furthermore, Vanguard "could not make full use of the all the advances made in our experimentation with military missiles," Eisenhower noted.[14]

The president was well aware of the discrepancies between these two missiles. The Jupiter-C was successfully tested in 1956—and could have put a satellite in orbit a year before the IGY kicked off—thus beating the Soviets into space. But the administration was also cognizant that launching our satellite in 1956 would have "contravened" space policy, undermined the IGY, and very possibly led to the weaponization of space.[15] "The fact that the United States deliberately did not utilize all means available to become the first nation in space is inescapable," wrote the scientific scholar Paul A. Berkman.[16]

While the administration had been anticipating the Soviet satellite, there were some unexpected aspects of it when it was finally launched: "The size of the thrust required to propel a satellite of this weight came as a distinct surprise to us," Eisenhower recalled. "Most surprising of all, however, was the intensity of the public concern."[17]

In his memoirs Eisenhower noted that the partisan attacks did not come without some irony. As chief of staff of the army, Eisenhower had warned the Truman administration that "we must keep abreast of the rest of the world" in missile technology.

We "lost six years" from 1945 to 1951 while the Russians worked on this capability. In fact, he noted, between 1947 and 1953 the United States programmed "less than 7 million dollars on long-range ballistic missiles." And delays and difficulties had plagued the program. "Some," Eisenhower reflected, were "created by the same legislators who later so quickly converted to impatience with our efforts."[18,19]

At his weekly press conference, five days after Sputnik, on October 9, Eisenhower started by congratulating the Soviet Union for putting a satellite into orbit, and he acknowledged that the Soviet Union, through Sputnik, "gained a great psychological advantage throughout the world." But, the president went on to say, there was "no reason to grow hysterical about it."[20]

At the same press conference he assured the United States that "we could have produced an orbiting satellite before now, but to the detriment of the scientific goal and our military progress."

With regard to Sputnik, Eisenhower said: "The American Space Program thus in no way began as a race or a contest with any other nation." The information from the project would be an international "gift," he continued, part of an "international engagement on our part to put up a vehicle of this kind during the period of IGY."[21]

Such reassurances did little to quell the outcry. Ike was shocked that people felt that "vulnerable," and also that the ensuing furor cast doubts on his leadership in this key area of his expertise.

But inside the executive branch, the situation looked far different to the defense professionals than it did to the media and the public. Donald Quarles, the deputy secretary of defense, told the NSC, four days after the launch of Sputnik: "The Russians have, in fact, done us a good turn, unintentionally, in establishing the concept of freedom of international space."[22]

Eisenhower's instincts had been right: It had been worth taking a short-term political hit for a long-term goal.

Sputnik, however, also turned out to be a gift for the president's opponents. Allusions were made to his illnesses in years past, which only seemed more relevant when Ike suffered a minor stroke on November 25, which did not affect his cognitive abilities but made clear speech difficult for a few days. While the president recovered right away, he again tested himself by going on a trip to visit NATO countries—which turned out to be an unqualified success. And in January, Eisenhower gave a forty-five-minute State of the Union address with virtually no speaking errors—a virtuoso performance that earned great reassurance and rave reviews from the press.

The public outcry over Sputnik, however, brought with it considerable and continuing political criticism, especially among Democrats—and their friends in the media. Wild ideas swirled around the political debate, with many jumping to the conclusion that if the Soviets could launch a satellite they could just as easily hurl a missile in our direction: "The potential of attacks from space," Lyndon Johnson said, would be like "kids dropping rocks onto cars from freeway overpasses."[23]

Eisenhower repeatedly made the point that launching a satellite like Sputnik and deploying an ICBM were technically different matters. Unlike satellites, ICBMs would need accuracy and sophisticated guidance systems.[24] This clarification did little to quell the outcry. But what grated most on the president was the accusation that he had been asleep at the switch.

"The idea of them charging me with not being interested in defense! Damn it, I've spent my whole life being concerned with the defense of our country," the president said with exasperation to one of his speechwriters.[25]

Sputnik was followed by a number of other Soviet firsts, including the launch, on November 3, 1957, of Sputnik 2, carrying a live dog. That project may have backfired somewhat from a PR standpoint—as some in the international community felt sorry for Laika, the dog, which could not, technically, be returned to Earth. But the apparent Soviet superiority was, to many people, undeniable.

Further difficulties for the president emerged when the Vanguard project tried to launch its U.S. satellite from Cape Canaveral on December 6 and, to the chagrin of the administration and the American public, the missile and its payload blew up on the launch pad.

More fuel was dumped on the political fire when on November 4, just one month after the launching of Sputnik, H. Rowan Gaither Jr., a lawyer, investment banker, and president of the Ford Foundation, came to the White House to brief the president on the report he and his committee had finished on fallout shelters and defense preparedness. One of the drafters of the report was Paul Nitze, the Truman adviser responsible for NSC 68—a hawkish directive from the postwar period that called for a massive buildup to counter the Soviet threat. The Gaither Report, reflecting much of Nitze's view, estimated that the United States was at a "time of deadly danger."[26] The USSR, the report argued, would be capable of delivering a "knockout blow" to the United States by 1959.[27] It recommended a steep rise in military expenditures that was even greater than the budgets that were run during the Korean War. Eisenhower saw the report as exaggerated and predicted it would have a negative effect on defense unification, which he saw as crucial, yet he refused to say so publicly.[28]

In the aftermath of Sputnik, however, the Gaither Report was leaked to the press—and it would have political consequences that lasted until the end of Eisenhower's term.

Finally, on January 31, 1958, the United States put its first satellite in space—followed in the months ahead by Vanguard 1 on March 17, which was the first solar-powered satellite.

Rather than assume an entirely defensive mode, Sputnik spurred the president to address the overall problems implied by its launch, but he did so through means that would address both short- and especially long-term needs. All would reap many benefits in the decades to come.

The president recognized the importance of taking a number of immediate measures—first, to call in the group of scientists who had served as advisers to the Office of Defense Mobilization and seek their advice. This meeting yielded a decision to move the scientific advisory apparatus from the Office of Defense Mobilization, an independent agency charged with planning and coordination in case of war, into the White House itself, to report directly to the president. Eisenhower renamed the committee the President's Science Advisory Council (PSAC) and appointed an assistant secretary, Dr. James Killian, who was given unprecedented access to him. Ike wanted only the best minds working on the scientific problems the government faced. So PSAC called upon other renowned scientists, including Dr. Isidor Rabi, Dr. George Kistiakowsky, and over time, Dr. Jerome Wiesner, Dr. Hans Bethe, Dr. Charles Townes, and other eminent scientists.

The administration also proposed, and Congress passed on September 2, 1958, a National Defense Education Act that constituted a major federal investment in STEM education in American schools. Many of the students educated through this program went on to make the United States a technical powerhouse in the decades to come.

At the same time, a new organization, the Advanced Research Projects Agency (ARPA, later known as DARPA), was established to do fundamental work on technical issues, on an accelerated schedule. Its pioneering work would lead the way to advances in computing and eventually the internet, among other important technological work.

Concurrent with these developments, to meet the needs of space exploration, the Eisenhower administration established an agency, distinct from the Pentagon projects that were intended only for military purposes. In 1958 the president signed into law the National Aeronautical and Space Administration (NASA), which further underscored that the United States in space would always be identified with peaceful progress. His singular decision to found it as a civilian space agency would, over time, make NASA the envy of the world.[29] Even decades later as I made countless trips to Moscow on space-related issues, Soviet scientists would express their longing for such a civilian space agency—an organization capable of transparency and liberation from classified work.

NASA would henceforth be the flagship of America's

commitment to peaceful pursuits in space. The Eisenhower administration eventually initiated the Mercury program, America's first human spaceflight effort. And the Saturn V rocket was also under development in 1960 as a high-priority Eisenhower administration project, which made possible Kennedy's envisioned 1968–1969 moon shot.

Through all of this, the IGY had another crucial role: to serve as an international platform for discussion of the exploration of the polar regions. On this agenda, the exploration of Antarctica offered an opportunity to begin discussions on its future, which until then had centered mainly among the claimants to this continent.

In 1948 seven claimants and the United States had circulated ideas that resulted in a "special regime" for Antarctica. However, Eisenhower and his administration believed that Antarctica held the potential to become a vast area of contention if the Soviet Union was not included in discussions about its future. He wanted the USSR brought in, with the clear objective to "demilitarize the entire area."[30]

The continent had enormous untapped resources and could potentially be exploited for that purpose. It could also, unless prohibited internationally, be used for nuclear testing and nuclear disposal. Scientific cooperation in Antarctica would not only serve our interests, it could also build more durable relations with the USSR.

The Eisenhower administration issued invitations to all nations with interests in Antarctica, including those IGY signatories who wished to pursue research and scientific exploration. In order to include the Soviet Union, Eisenhower had to overrule the Joint Chiefs of Staff and a group of skeptical allies—a decision that took courage, in light of the furor over Sputnik only months before.

The administration's statement of principles reiterated that the U.S. "is dedicated to the principle that the vast uninhabited wastes of Antarctica shall be used only for peaceful purposes. We do not want Antarctica to become an object of political conflict. Accordingly, the United States has invited eleven other countries, including the Soviet Union, to confer with us to seek an effective joint means of achieving this objective."[31]

On June 13, 1958, less than a year after Sputnik, after the leak of the Gaither Report, and before the actual founding of NASA, talks began on the future of Antarctica. For fourteen months, under U.S. leadership, ten IGY nations participated in sixty preparatory meetings. The result was a groundbreaking agreement: The participants declared that the entire continent would be set aside as a commons dedicated solely to the peaceful pursuit of scientific research. The protocol ensured that there would be no militarization of the continent, in effect denuclearizing it.

On December 1, 1959, the agreement was signed at the State Department in Washington, ratifying the measure and allowing for innovations in international inspection regimes for compliance with the agreement. Among these methods would be aerial and physical observation and verification.

The Treaty of Antarctica represented the first arms-control agreement of the Cold War period. In turn, it "reinforced the international status of the high seas"—and with its firm international foundation it also became "the precedent for outer space and the deep sea regimes, establishing those areas as international spaces."[32]

According to science historian Paul Berkman, "Because priority in space had not been pursued at any cost, [Eisenhower] preserved the leverage to establish the peaceful uses beyond sovereign jurisdictions."[33]

Finally, Eisenhower saw the potential to use the Sputnik "shock" to expose the dysfunctions within the Department of Defense itself—the overblown threat assessments, the politicized pitches to Congress, and the infighting among the services. This gave Eisenhower the impetus to make another effort to reorganize the military, to bring about the kind of change in the command structure for which he had long advocated.

The service chiefs had by tradition always been advocates for their own branches of the military. But after the end of World War II they appeared to have learned little about what had played the most effective role in our victory, beyond the obvious attributes of

Allied warfare. It was the unified command on D-day that had enabled General Eisenhower to synchronize, integrate, and leverage the capabilities of each service, under his own singular command.

Eisenhower suspected as early as 1949, when he was working with President Truman to enact some of these changes, that the problem was not just organizational, but also one of personal prestige. At that time the navy and the air force were at war with each other over jurisdiction, funding, and their own capabilities.[34]

Ike also recognized how corrosive it was for national security when the services routinely took their gripes and their pitches to Congress in this contest for more resources.

Some of this rivalry was on clear display after Sputnik. Eisenhower was enraged and repelled by the "goddamn three-star general" who had apparently—without "higher loyalty"—rejoiced that the navy's Vanguard rocket—a key part of our IGY contribution—had "fizzled" on the launch pad.[35] The president felt that a new attitude had to be fostered, duplication had to be reduced, and strategic coherence had to be achieved. Among those most effective at undermining the president were not only his political opponents but also military leaders who were not above leaking exaggerated estimates and doomsday scenarios to Congress and the press—men who were seething with frustration about budget restraints and the president's efforts to unify them. Inter-service rivalry, which continued uncontained, also fueled resentment that the Eisenhower administration was intent on prioritization and the determination to find what the president called his "Great Equation"—one that would balance military strength and spending with the growth of a healthy economy.[36] Defense represented the largest single item of the budget.

Eisenhower's tight budget was controversial in these circles, a debate made all the more intense because the president of the United States, a preeminent defense strategist in his own right, actually knew what he was talking about.[37] General Goodpaster confirmed this and said many times that no one knew more about the military budgets than Eisenhower—the product of his many long years of experience.[38]

To promote this change, Nelson Rockefeller was asked by the president to look into the general question of defense reform. In a draft called "Notes on the Reorganization of the Department of Defense," the future governor of New York and vice president under Gerald Ford, asserted that new weapons and technology had made traditional relationships among the military obsolete: "Today no service can achieve its primary mission without either trespassing on the role of the other services or calling on them for assistance." Rockefeller went on to say that the way things stood, each service demanded a big budget to "develop the capability for winning a war by itself."[39]

The desire for new weapons was "driven more by technology than by strategy" Goodpaster also asserted.[40]

In complete agreement with both sentiments, in the aftermath of Sputnik Eisenhower decided to take on his colleagues—and develop and pass legislation that would reorganize the Pentagon. At the time the bill was being developed, the armed forces had 130 liaison officers assigned to congressional affairs; a similar number were involved in public relations. This was a mind-bending number in the late 1950s, and spoke to the scale of influence the military sought to sustain on Capitol Hill.[41]

"Separate ground, sea, and air warfare is gone forever," Eisenhower wrote, "but our system, codified in law, [had] not kept pace with the change."[42]

It was not just the military that was resistant to change, much of the foot-dragging on organizational reform was coming from members of Congress themselves, and the military services associations. Those who did not want to adjust attacked Eisenhower, charging him with trying to "create a Prussian General Staff that would threaten liberty."[43]

Eisenhower wrote his old Abilene classmate Swede Hazlett:

> When each service puts down its minimum requirements for its own military budget for the following year, and [I] add up the total, I find they mount at a fantastic rate. . . . But someday there is going to be a man sitting in my present chair who has not been raised in the military services

> and will have little understanding of where the slashes in their estimates can be made with little or no damage. If that should happen while we still have the state of tension that now exists in the world, I shudder to think of what would happen to this country.[44]

Secretary of Defense Charlie Wilson could not manage this process; bureaucratically he did not have the authority. This led to an all-out effort by the president himself to secure a Defense Reform Bill in 1957–1958. It was a fight of epic proportions. Knowing how well connected the Pentagon was in Congress, Eisenhower undertook a letter-writing campaign, sending notes to more than 450 leading thinkers across the country asking for their help.

Eisenhower also spent considerable time on the wording of the bill, penning some of it himself. After great effort to lobby and cajole, on August 6, 1958, the Defense Reform Bill passed and was signed into law. This measure would empower the secretary of defense to streamline the military. Ike won this fight over the heads of his strongest critics, the Joint Chiefs, and the service chiefs themselves.[45]

While the president was unable to achieve a bill as radical and comprehensive as he might have liked, major changes were now assured. With its passage, the secretary of defense would finally have the authority to tackle further budgeting and decision-making processes. This would curtail the habit that the services had acquired of bypassing the secretary of defense and going directly to Congress—thus evading civilian authority within the executive branch.[46]

Sherman Adams later noted: "It was the dedicated and selfless work of a professional soldier to strengthen civilian control over the military."[47]

These fights over the force structure and its appropriations eventually fused with broader issues that emerged at the dawn of the space age: How much is enough to secure a credible deterrent?

And: How long could the U-2 be used before the Soviets had the capability of shooting it out of the sky?[48]

The U-2 program was *the* game changer: It revealed that the USSR was testing missiles but was not able yet to deploy them.

The political problem for the administration that attached to the Sputnik "shock" rested with the fact that Eisenhower, and only a handful of other key officials, knew about the top-secret U-2 program that was capable of providing aerial surveillance of the USSR's missile installations and other military capability.

Numerous U-2 flights since 1956 had showed Eisenhower and his small team that the Soviet Union was by no means ahead of the United States in any major capacity. Given this knowledge, the president fought back attempts to remedy our vulnerabilities with crash military programs—and the expenditure of more money—as the primary way to salve the nation's bruised ego.

As Eisenhower thought about how to manage the valuable U-2 program, he was convinced that it would be a more effective means of intelligence-gathering if it remained secret. Nevertheless, the information could have removed much of the political heat the president faced; even Secretary of State John Foster Dulles encouraged him to use the U-2 information as a way to reassure the public. But as Barry Goldwater later observed, "Ike took the heat, grinned, and kept his mouth shut."[49]

Isidor Rabi once observed that in the political realm, American pride is a greater driver than a true assessment of the nation's interests. Managing that pride and protecting the security of the country, while finding avenues for peace, would consume the last year and a half of Eisenhower's time in public service. Human beings, as he had always observed, are more emotional than they are intellectual or analytical.[50]

In this age of tension, Ike asserted, "what will . . . be needed is not just engineers and scientists, but a people who will keep their heads and, in every field, leaders who can meet intricate human problems with wisdom and courage."[51]

Eisenhower and Soviet premier Nikita Khrushchev arrive at Camp David, Maryland, September 25, 1959. (U.S. Navy Photographical Center)

15

A FAREWELL

With the end of Eisenhower's two terms drawing closer, the president had done a number of critical things. He had resisted advice to unleash "cheap money" to avert the post–Korean War recession of 1953, as well as that of 1958. As a result, inflation during his tenure in office averaged 1.4 percent over his eight years.[1]

Ike had balanced the budget and produced a surplus three times—in 1956, 1957, and in 1960—all while recalibrating and restructuring the national security apparatus for years to come and making monumental strides in the nation's infrastructure. U.S. GDP grew from $284.6 billion in 1950 to about $500 billion by 1960.[2]

"The essence of Eisenhower's immense fiscal achievement, an actual shrinkage of the federal budget in real terms during his eight-year term, is that he tamed the warfare state," wrote Ronald Reagan's budget director, David Stockman, years later.[3]

Relations with the Soviet Union, in the context of the "warfare state," would be another long-term matter, and one of a highly dynamic nature.

The one significant piece of this complex national security puzzle that was virtually unavailable to U.S. policy makers was the internal dynamics and priorities of the Soviet state itself. Aside from ambassadors who had been trained as sovietologists, among the political and military class few had had more exposure to the Russians than had Eisenhower during World War II and in its immediate aftermath. This was important for our country at this stage of the Cold War.

Firmly at the helm in Moscow was the outsize figure, Nikita Khrushchev. After a lengthy meeting with the Soviet leader in Moscow, Hubert Humphrey, a Minnesota senator at the time, concluded that Khrushchev was a "man who is defensive in an offensive way; insecure in a super confident way."[4]

Khrushchev, failing to realize at first the impact that Sputnik would have in the United States, was soon to understand that he could use such showy firsts to paint the image of a much more powerful, technologically advanced country than the USSR actually was. When the global anxiety about Sputnik's launch fully registered with him, Khrushchev ramped up his rhetoric with extravagant exaggerations about Soviet superiority—and they seemed real. "Only technologically ignorant people can doubt [Soviet superiority]," he blustered.[5]

His claims that Soviet intercontinental rockets could reach "any part of the world" were believed among America's chattering classes, and widely regarded with seriousness elsewhere.

Khrushchev was bluffing—just as Eisenhower suspected.

No one, not even the president, knew for sure the status of the rockets that launched Sputnik 1 and 2 into orbit, but they were not operational weapons, as Eisenhower had surmised.

In early August 1958, with midterm election campaigns and

a recession under way, Joseph Alsop, a columnist for the *New York Herald Tribune,* published a scathing column called "Our Government's Untruths." He accused Eisenhower and his administration of covering up our defense weaknesses—either by "consciously misleading" the American people or through the president's own administrative and personal shortcomings. Allegedly basing his knowledge on classified documents, Alsop wrote of the Soviet Union's imminent ability to overtake the United States, with the capability of fielding "1,000 and 2,000 ballistic missiles with suitable ranges to neutralize or destroy all overseas bases." He charged that the United States was also behind in missile production. The president was "gambling the American future," with the "indisputable" outcome of allowing the "Soviets to gain an overwhelming superiority in over-all striking power."[6]

In 1958, Sen. John F. Kennedy, without access to classified information, and relying only on public sources, was persuaded by Joe Alsop, a Georgetown neighbor and social friend, to make a speech on the floor of the Senate. It was there that Kennedy used the term "missile gap" for the first time, an expression that was a ringing indictment of Eisenhower's budget-conscious ways, accusing him of failing to provide adequate security for the United States. In his speech Kennedy asserted that the Soviet Union could destroy "85 percent of our industry, 43 of our 50 largest cities, and most of the Nation's population."[7]

Accusations by Alsop—and Kennedy, along with Stuart Symington, who had years earlier warned about a "bomber gap" that did not exist—were vehement and overwrought, creating a level of frenzy not seen since Joe McCarthy faded from view.

According to the historian and national security analyst Christopher Preble, "Alsop's numbers were misleading. They did not match official opinion within the intelligence community as expressed in several national security estimates."[8] And they certainly did not square with Eisenhower's studied conclusions. Top-secret work had been under way since Ike's first term, and progress—though halting and often frustrating—had produced the U-2 reconnaissance plane, and soon the development and deployment of reconnaissance satellites that had been proposed by Dr. James Killian and Dr. Edwin Land in a meeting with the president on February 7, 1958. At the same time the nuclear-armed submarine *Polaris* was under development, assuring that nuclear weapons launched from a moving submarine would make our retaliatory capability invulnerable to counterattack.

In fact it wasn't until the 1960s that the Soviet Union could boast of an ICBM—and only a "grand total of four . . . actually became operational," wrote Bill Taubman in *Khrushchev: The Man and His Era* (and that number included prototypes).[9]

By that time Khrushchev—gauging the debate in America—understood that "even empty nuclear threats could pay big dividends," Taubman wrote, "not just because . . . [he] was bluffing, but also because he cited mostly imaginary missiles as a justification for cutting back on [Soviet] conventional weapons of all sort."

The Soviets had come to many of the same conclusions that the Eisenhower administration had reached. Any new war would be different from the manpower-intensive World War II. Indeed, the strength of a country's economy was a key factor not just for survival, but for dominance as well. "Between 1955–1957, the USSR unilaterally reduced troop strength by more than two million men," noted Taubman. And in the last two years of the Eisenhower administration the Soviets reduced by as many as 1.5 million more.[10]

In the Soviet Union, Nikita Khrushchev was, in fact, under increasing pressure. Ever since his secret speech at the Twentieth Party Congress in February 1956, hard-liners were angered that he had railed against a "cult of personality" and denounced Stalin's crimes.

At least in part to impress his critics, on November 10, 1958, Khrushchev issued an ultimatum to the West to withdraw its troops from Berlin by May 27, 1959. If the West would not agree to negotiations beforehand, then they would have to fight their way across East Germany to gain access to West Berlin, by now a thriving capitalist zone. The United States and the other two occupation powers, Britain and France, had not recognized East Germany. In this there were shades of the 1948–1949 Berlin Airlift and of other tensions that had arisen, since the end of the war, over the status of the former German capital.

Again, the president believed Khrushchev was bluffing. The Soviet leader demanded a summit to discuss the matter. Eisenhower declined. To buy more time and to test his theory, Eisenhower said that a foreign ministers' meeting should occur first to discuss this difficult issue, and if progress was made, then a summit might be appropriate.

Eisenhower's political opposition in the United States again reacted with knives sharpened: "The chorus asserted that Eisenhower was under-reacting to the Berlin crisis," wrote the historian Stephen Ambrose. "The country as a whole grossly exaggerated the dangers," and "Senators Symington and Kennedy joined the Joint Chiefs of Staff, to demand increased spending." And the outlandish claims left "a general impression around the country, one that was assiduously spread by the huge Pentagon propaganda machine, the arms industry, the Democrats and columnists."[11]

As Ambrose noted, ordinary citizens "trusted" Ike but worried about how we could stay firm on Berlin and still proceed with planned reductions of the armed forces.[12]

On Berlin, Eisenhower used the same tactic he had used earlier in the 1954 and 1958 crises involving Quemoy and Matsu, two islands under contention between Communist China and Taiwan: *patience.* While privately the president did recognize the potential for these crises to spin out of control—and took contingency steps for such scenarios—in the case of Berlin, he gave Khrushchev enough room to maneuver and he damped down the domestic demands to throw billions more dollars into defense. He also reassured our allies.

Of these necessities, getting people to calm down may have

been the most difficult task of all. To the JSC, to Congress, and to the NSC, Eisenhower declared that it was necessary to avoid overreacting. "In doing so we give the Soviets ammunition," he told them.

The president made the point that Khrushchev's chief objective was to upset the United States [and its allies]—to "keep us off balance." This, he predicted, would be one of their long-term objectives, not a problem that could be solved in the short term, but over decades. "They would like us to go frantic every time they stir up difficulties," he told each group. The president also noted that anyone who had ever read Lenin knew that "the Communist objective is to make us spend ourselves into bankruptcy."[13]

Eisenhower had always been skeptical about the plans for postwar Germany, especially the four-power arrangement in Berlin. Even before the end of World War II, he had privately warned Roosevelt that the presence of Soviet troops in Berlin would make it unlikely that we could later get them out when arrangements called for a civilian administration. "The President made light of my fear," Eisenhower recalled. Ike had suggested that multinational forces might be more effective than the establishment of national zones. "On this point," President Roosevelt "had already decided," Eisenhower recalled.[14]

Indeed, the establishment of national zones was what had now become the central issue over Berlin. The Soviet Union wanted recognition for East Germany, and for it to take over full control of East Berlin; the Americans believed that the East German people should be given a vote, knowing this would extend our presence there. Given these differences, the USSR wanted all three powers out—and gave them a date for doing so, or else.

While the president waited, and diplomatic activity was under way between the occupying nations, in the last year and a half of the Eisenhower administration, Ike decided to take a series of round-the-world trips—thought of as goodwill tours. Jet aircraft made such audacious itineraries possible, and Eisenhower and his press secretary, Jim Hagerty, could see the potential for reaching people around the world not as a conqueror, but as a visiting friend.

The president's first trip—a three-week odyssey leading up to Christmas 1959—encompassed eleven nations. Mamie, for reasons of stamina, opted to stay in Washington. My parents, however, accompanied Ike on this far-reaching trip that included the capitals of Italy, Turkey, Pakistan, Afghanistan, India, Iran, Greece, Tunisia, France, Spain, and Morocco. Their stay in India was the longest—five days. The president and his entourage were mobbed by well-wishers in the cities they visited. In India, for instance, he recalled that a "human sea closed in upon us" and compelled the president's motorcade to stop for twenty-five minutes as the authorities, including Prime Minister Nehru himself, beat people off the official cars. Secret Servicemen were bruised and overwhelmed. People wanted to touch Eisenhower, creating a "hysterical fervor" that left Nehru observing that this was the largest demonstration of goodwill that India had seen since the day of its independence from Britain eleven years before.[15]

Ike was moved by his reception and later reflected that among the millions of people he had seen and spoken to on this three-week trip, he "never saw a hostile face."[16] The tour garnered other insights as well. In Afghanistan, for instance, the president learned firsthand of the inroads the Soviets were making in that country. His party traveled on a recently paved highway that he later noted had been laid "ironically with major Soviet assistance."[17] No doubt Eisenhower observed this with at least some frustration, as he had fought so hard to convince his fellow government officials—not to mention his brother Ed—that foreign aid was a crucial factor in gaining influence. The Afghan king, whose monarchy would be abolished in 1973, told Eisenhower that he did not fear "enslavement" in accepting Soviet help.

It was at times a rather dangerous trip. The president's helicopter, for instance, set a new altitude record, flying seven thousand feet above the mountainous terrain of Afghanistan. But it was an arduous one as well—often requiring Ike to board Air Force One in the wee hours of the morning—on a strict schedule, and based on the determination to arrive in time for the next country's official welcoming ceremonies. The president's exhausted appointments secretary, Tom Stephens, was heard muttering: "When this administration is over I'll never work for a farmer or an Army officer again."[18]

Though Vice President Richard Nixon's overseas travels had at times encountered anti-American riots, Eisenhower's subsequent trips to Latin America and Asia had huge popular appeal, though his planned trip to Japan had to be cancelled due to such security concerns.

In Latin America, Eisenhower wanted to demonstrate that the era of gunboat diplomacy was over. And, inspired by a letter from a young girl, the president came back to the United States to lay the groundwork and obtain the initial funding for what became popularly known as the Alliance for Progress, initiated to address some of Latin America's development issues.[19] John F. Kennedy would endorse this program once in the White House, and take it to the next level.

These trips were "unprecedented in peacetime," and they consolidated American support abroad. Eisenhower's Latin American trip would be groundbreaking; and in South Asia he was the first to visit Pakistan and other countries American presidents had bypassed before and after World War II. A striking example of this was Afghanistan: Eisenhower was the first and last president to visit Kabul until 2006—forty-seven years later.

In the midst of these trips, the Berlin crisis had evolved and changed. As weeks turned into months, it became increasingly clear that the real objective behind Khrushchev's desire to have a four-power summit meeting was to underscore the Soviet Union's importance as a global power.

British prime minister Harold Macmillan, after a trip to Moscow that winter, had returned with the news that the Soviet leader agreed to a foreign ministers' meeting as a precursor to a summit. Eisenhower was nonplussed, however, that no conditions of progress had been discussed as the benchmark for a summit. What did emerge, however, was at least some sign of flexibility on Khrushchev's part—he relaxed the ultimatum's deadline, leaving the actual date ambiguous.

Throughout this process Secretary of State Dulles was losing his battle with cancer. His absence from the job may have been the reason for some crossed signals at the State Department. On March 30, in a message utterly unanticipated by the Soviet officials, an invitation to Khrushchev to visit the United States was extended by the State Department, on behalf of the president of the United States. The invitation was issued without any conditions—a stance at odds with Ike's position. Nevertheless, Eisenhower made the best of the mistake and stuck by his staff. He reiterated the invitation to the Soviet leader by suggesting that his visit should be an informal one; a chance to see America, get to know its people, and hold informal discussions on the Berlin question and other issues of concern.

When Khrushchev discovered that the geopolitical discussions would be held at Camp David, he panicked, thinking it might be an internment camp (perhaps like those in the USSR) where he and his delegation would be held hostage. Russian diplomats had to reassure the Soviet chairman that Camp David was the president's *dacha*—the Russian word for "country house."[20]

At the end of September 1959, Khrushchev, his wife, Nina, and his children and some of their spouses, arrived in Washington. What a trip! After the official greeting, a state dinner at the White House, and a reciprocal one at the Soviet embassy, Khrushchev and his retinue—shepherded by our UN ambassador, Henry Cabot Lodge—were off on an extended tour of the United States, with visits to New York, Los Angeles, San Francisco, San Jose, Des Moines, Pittsburgh, and Camp David. The Soviet leader met businessmen, farmers, and other ordinary folk who came out to view the "road show," as it has been called.

When the official party got to Los Angeles, they saw the movie *Can-Can* being made, and later on another set the premier met Marilyn Monroe. (There was some confusion for the American star as she turned her cheek in anticipation of a kiss from Khrushchev.

To Monroe's embarrassment, the Soviet chairman didn't understand what he was supposed to do.)[21]

There were times when Khrushchev's temper flared, especially after he was told that for security reasons he would not be able to visit Disneyland. But with a few exceptions he was given a respectful and sometimes a warm welcome. The Soviet leader, as always, conducted himself with bravado, hypersensitivity, indignation, and enthusiasm. America was mesmerized.

At Camp David the informal style of the meeting between Khrushchev and Eisenhower lent itself to considerable discussion—some about earlier times during the war, as well as observations on the new and dangerous era that was now unfolding. The subject of Berlin, however, still remained a sticking point.

On the afternoon of September 25, Eisenhower, frustrated that little progress had been made, invited Khrushchev to the farm in Gettysburg. The exposure to cattle farming, the president's hobby, and his four grandchildren would, he thought, give both leaders a badly needed break. Khrushchev would enjoy every minute of the farm tour—accepting the president's spontaneous gift of a Black Angus cow from his herd.

As for the meeting that was held on my grandparents' sunporch—my siblings and I were full of excitement. The Soviet premier, who looked like Santa Claus without the red suit or white beard, was captivating as he flashed his wide toothy smile. He asked us questions, and he concluded with an invitation to the four of us—aged eleven to four—to come to the Soviet Union with the president sometime the following spring for a reciprocal visit. When I saw my father cross his legs at that moment, I understood that my siblings and I would never be allowed to go. My parents were sure that our place was in school, not traveling with the president—which would obviously set us apart from our schoolmates.

As it would happen, Eisenhower's trip—with or without us—was not to be. On May 1, 1960, the U-2, which the president had authorized for one last reconnaissance flight over Soviet territory to gather critical intelligence data before the four-power summit due to be held on May 14, was shot down by Soviet jets in the heart of Siberia.

If there was one Eisenhower principle that could be gleaned from this episode, it was his stubborn belief that he would never apologize for something that he had already offered.

Operating the U-2 was nothing more than "Open Skies," a proposal that had been made to the Soviet Union by the United States at a four-power summit in 1955. General Goodpaster recalls that Eisenhower thought that better communications and some transparency between the two superpowers were more stabilizing than the mutual recriminations that seemed to punctuate bilateral relations. In 1955 a study group had been convened to develop ideas on how to reduce tensions between the two countries. Open Skies would allow mutual overflights to monitor military activity in both countries, lessening the tensions around the existential dangers of a surprise attack. While this method might work for only a short time, Eisenhower felt it could be useful to take advantage of aerial reconnaissance that would later be overtaken by satellites.

According to Goodpaster, Eisenhower had surprised everyone at the four-power Geneva summit at which he unveiled this proposal: "I have been searching my heart and mind," he had told the conference, "for something I could say here that would convince everyone of the great sincerity of the United States in approaching problems of disarmament."[22] Michael Korda has observed that "Short of immediate and total world disarmament, this was about as radical a proposal as any president of the United States has ever made."[23]

The Soviet head of delegation at the talks, Nikolai Bulganin, had expressed interest in the proposal; it had been Nikita Khrushchev who had been against such transparency from the outset.

When the Soviet Union officially refused this offer of mutual overflights—ostensibly on the basis that the Americans wanted only to use this new program for intelligence gathering and targeting—Eisenhower began in earnest the development of the U-2 program. The first test flight took place on July 29, 1955, eventually leading to overflights of the USSR in 1956.[24]

Now the Soviet Union had shot down the U-2 over Siberia—a potential development that had always worried Eisenhower. He had been a reluctant consumer of the program, even if he understood its enormous value. He was now confronted with the worst-case scenario, and a way had to be found to keep the crisis from becoming a fatal complication in the Berlin talks.

Historians and policy makers who were there at the time debated why Khrushchev decided to shoot down the plane at that particular moment—with less than two weeks before the Paris summit. The Soviets had known about these flights for some time. Why now?

According to one theory, Khrushchev knew that the summit would not achieve his goals, so sinking it could be blamed on the Americans. Another was that Eisenhower's round-the-world trips had intimidated Khrushchev, and he worried he would not be received in the same respectful way in Paris. Still another theory had it that Soviet hard-liners were deeply unsettled by Khrushchev's visit to the United States, his enthusiasm for its president, and his apparent desire for some kind of détente. Probably all three of these theories played a role.

Whatever the Soviet leader's reasoning, for days after the incident Eisenhower was operating with inadequate knowledge. NASA announced, on May 6, that one of its weather satellites had gone missing on a routine mission over Turkey. This agreed-upon contingency cover story was released without the president's specific approval, and might have been effective if the Soviets had had no real evidence in their possession. But they did, and that official position did not last for long.

The president and others assumed at first that nothing had survived from the downing of the plane. The CIA chief, Allen

Dulles, had assured the president that the U-2, as a plane, could not survive such an incident, nor could a pilot survive the fall from seventy thousand feet. The plane had been designed to look distinctive—unlike any bomber. Rather, it was flimsy, constructed of exceedingly lightweight material.

But on May 7, six days after the incident, Nikita Khrushchev announced halfway through a rambling talk before the USSR's Supreme Soviet, their nominal legislature, that a U.S. plane had been shot down over Siberia. This was the first the public knew of the dilemma now facing the U.S. government.

Many advised the president to continue to maintain what we would call today "plausible deniability" and leave himself room for maneuver. But the Soviets paraded U-2 pilot Francis Gary Powers before television cameras, and displayed sections of the aircraft found near the scene of the crash. Furthermore, Khrushchev revealed that among the equipment recovered from the plane was a self-destruct button, and there were suggestions that poison tablets had been found that the pilot, in such circumstances, had orders to take. These revelations were a cruel surprise to the president. "In the event of a mishap," Eisenhower later wrote, he had been told that "the plane would virtually disintegrate."[25]

Ike decided he had had enough. He put out a statement of his own, accepting responsibility for the U-2 program. His reasoning was twofold. In the nuclear era it was critical for the international community—especially the Soviet Union—to know that the president of the United States had full control over the levers of power, including the national security apparatus of the military. Second, it was always his policy to be accountable—and given the gravity of the situation, had the president blamed someone else he would have had to fire at least one person, maybe more.

Milton Eisenhower later recalled that his brother would not blame those who worked for him for his decisions: It would be a "glaring and permanent injustice" to his subordinates. When my father suggested to Ike that he fire CIA chief Allen Dulles, the president responded: "I am not going to shift the blame to my underlings."

For years thereafter, however, there was some private defensiveness on Eisenhower's part. He was unhappy that he had bowed to the pressure for one last flight, and he was also deeply regretful that the CIA chief had misled him about what would happen if the plane were to be shot down. In fact, not long after the incident Eisenhower told Goodpaster and Gordon Gray, his special assistant for national security affairs, that he did not want—ever—to take a meeting alone with the CIA.[26]

On May 9—now fully cognizant of the story's details—Eisenhower told his team in the Oval Office, "We will now just have to endure the storm."[27]

Throughout the crisis Eisenhower remained unapologetic about the U-2 program. It was a peaceful program, meant to stabilize relations—even if it required violating sovereign airspace. He had offered the Soviet Union the opportunity to send aircraft over our own airspace for the purpose of assuring *them* that there were no preparations for a surprise attack, but they had refused. The president had simply instituted unilateral Open Skies.

The summit gathering, less than two weeks away, was convened as planned, and Eisenhower had to endure Khrushchev's emotional outbursts and demands that he apologize. When the president said to the assembled leaders that the U-2 flights would be suspended, it did little to mollify the Soviet strongman. Khrushchev was said to feel "betrayed."

Khrushchev's orchestrated anger later came with some irony. It is a little-known fact that in 1961 Khrushchev sent a secret message through John J. McCloy, a public servant and longtime friend of the president, offering Eisenhower the possibility of a conciliatory visit to the USSR at some undetermined date. Now retired, Ike felt no need to consider it.[28]

Years later—in 1990—it was with considerable trepidation that I met three of Nikita Khrushchev's grandchildren and great-grandchildren in Moscow. I think they, too, were nervous about our meeting. When we shook hands, one of his granddaughters started with an apology for Khrushchev's careless handling of the

U-2 incident. She thought he had overreacted. The Soviet leadership had also been of that view. Their complaint was that Khrushchev's unbridled emotionalism—genuine or staged—with regard to the U.S. overflights had been a strategically unsatisfactory way to handle a golden opportunity. In their view he should have used the incident to strengthen the USSR's hand in any negotiations, especially over Berlin. Khrushchev's outbursts in Moscow, but most especially his erratic behavior in Paris, would bring the summit to an unsuccessful end and later be among many reasons the Politburo dispensed with him as leader in 1964 and sent him into exile.

In this the Soviet leadership showed that they did not fully understand Eisenhower. Even if Khrushchev had tried behind the scenes to blackmail the United States over the U-2 matter, Eisenhower's public declaration, assuming responsibility for the program, gave the Soviets nothing to blackmail. At the same time Eisenhower also knew that making a vow to stop U-2 overflights of the USSR was no verification hardship since the Corona, America's new reconnaissance satellite, would, after many setbacks, achieve its first successful launch on August 10.[29]

The Berlin problem would persist well into the Kennedy administration—but such is the flow of the American system. No real presidential administration ever exists in a static period of time. Human problems and the issues that arise from them are ongoing. No one can solve any one thing in a matter of four to eight years—it requires the wisdom of those still to come to nurture and sustain the best of the policies any one president puts in place.

Throughout this period after Sputnik, as accusations of a "missile gap" persisted, Americans also bought the Soviet line that the USSR was on the verge of overtaking the United States economically. As with the Soviet Union's alleged military superiority, U.S. estimates of the Soviet economy were wildly off base. Administration spokespeople were unable to cool the hysteria even by citing

CIA statistics that showed that the USSR had a GNP that was approximately 40 percent of ours. Khrushchev's claims of economic growth were bluster. The Soviet economy was, in fact, in decline.[30]

These potent political issues grew in force as the presidential candidates were eventually identified. Vice President Richard Nixon for the GOP; John F. Kennedy for the Democrats. Some pushback to Kennedy's claims of the missile gap was evidenced among the GOP minority in Congress, but the Massachusetts senator and his forces mobilized the news media to press their case.

On February 6, 1959, the *Boston Herald* declared that the United States had essentially capitulated or "surrendered" to the Soviets. While not all the news media were by any means sold on the idea of an American "missile gap," the rancorous debate on this matter, even among inside experts, spilled into the public sphere. The president could only try to reassure the American public. However, Joseph Alsop and others, unrelenting, continued their campaigns, and egged on the Democratic presidential ticket. Any positive news that came from the administration, Alsop dismissed as "self-deluding." He and many of his journalist friends continued to hammer home the idea of America's vulnerabilities.[31]

"The people who irritated [the president the most] were the hard-sell technologists who tried to exploit Sputnik and the Missile Gap psychosis it engendered," recalled Herbert York, a weapons designer, physicist, and adviser to President Eisenhower. "They invented all sorts of technological threats to our safety and offered a thousand and one delights for confronting them."[32]

The president was sufficiently concerned by the damaging and inaccurate assertions about the missile gap that in July 1960, he arranged for Democratic candidates John F. Kennedy and Lyndon B. Johnson to receive classified briefings by the Joint Chiefs of Staff, Strategic Air Command, and the CIA, outlining no doubt a far more positive picture. Despite these sessions, Kennedy and Johnson continued to talk about the missile gap until the end of the campaign, at the same time ensuring that it appeared in the Democratic platform that year. They did so by alleging that the American military position was "measured in terms of gaps—missile gap, space gap, limited war gap."[33]

"In truth," wrote the scholar Yanek Mieczkowski, by August 1960, "the news on space was good." America had acquired a "commanding lead in scientific achievements" over the USSR. By October the United States had launched twenty-eight missiles to the Soviet Union's eight.[34]

Not long after Senator Kennedy narrowly defeated Vice President Nixon, and the new president's team was in place, Secretary of Defense Robert McNamara admitted that there was no missile gap. Jerome Wiesner, Kennedy's science adviser, also noted that when Kennedy was faced with this fact in the presence of his advisers, the new president considered his error more with "irritation than relief."[35]

The results of a 1961 study confirmed the findings that no gap existed. Kennedy, according to accounts, tossed it off, saying: "Whoever believed in the missile gap anyway?"[36]

Any real missile gap was in fact heavily to the United States' advantage. By the time of Eisenhower's departure from office, the United States had an enormous lead—with 160 operational Atlas ICBMs to just four R-7s in the Soviet arsenal. By late 1961, after Kennedy came into office, our satellite reconnaissance showed that the Soviets had only six ICBMs. Eighteen months into the Kennedy administration the balance was still overwhelmingly in our favor: 194 to 72.[37]

It is noteworthy that years later, after Lyndon Johnson became president, he said that because of the surveillance satellites, "we know how many missiles the enemy has and, it turned out, our guesses were way off. We were doing things we didn't need to do. We were building things we didn't need to build. We were harboring fears we didn't need to harbor."[38]

Had Kennedy not persisted in making these allegations after his classified briefing in July 1960, one wonders if it would have made a difference to the outcome of the election. Kennedy and

Johnson garnered 49.71 percent of the total popular vote; Nixon and Lodge, 49.55 percent. A reversal of merely 11,874 votes in five states—Missouri, New Mexico, Nevada, Illinois, and Hawaii—would have produced different winners.[39]

McGeorge Bundy, a Kennedy adviser, later asserted that "Eisenhower simply failed to do an effective job of communicating his position and persuading his adversaries" as to the presence of a missile gap. But such criticism leveled at Eisenhower for failing to make his case is largely disingenuous. The president used many occasions to try to calm those who were fearful of the Soviet's alleged superiority. But putting the public's mind completely at rest was all but impossible given the sensitive—indeed, classified—nature of the issue. Eisenhower was too good a strategist to tip his hand to the Soviet Union.

Many of these developments were, of necessity, top secret—even though the events just months earlier had revealed to the world that Eisenhower had had the advantage of aerial intelligence for some time. Nevertheless, the missile-gap issue was more about the military's desire for greater appropriations, perhaps, than it was about any actual threat. The leaked intelligence that Alsop used had come from those military sources—and their inaccuracies revolved around the notion of "intent" rather than the "facts" on the ground.

On these matters the president, who prized transparency, felt compelled to remain silent. Just as he would decline Dulles's advice to tell the public about the U-2 program after Sputnik, he was not about to signal to the Russians that America was either vulnerable or that we had attained superiority in military armaments, which we had verified by the U-2 and Corona programs. Had the USSR heard such pronouncements on the U.S. side, the Kremlin might well have redoubled its own effort in the area of weaponry to try and outpace us. *General* Eisenhower knew better than to answer his critics.

It was confirmed to my father many years later—by none other than Sargent Shriver, President Kennedy's brother-in-law—that the strategy of the Kennedy campaign had been to denigrate Eisenhower's achievements, and I would add character, as a way to confront the election challenge of Vice President Richard Nixon.

JFK's campaign managers could have, perhaps, made another choice during the campaign. They might have singled out the popular general and president for being an anomaly—which he was.

As an outsider—a military man—Eisenhower posed no real threat to the Democrats. He had worked with them, and the Congress they controlled often voted with him. Their unfounded challenge to his record brought him into the fray. The Democrats' persistence in pushing for significant increases in military spending, in the end, put them at odds with the former general and outgoing president.

It took decades before critics were ready to reassess Eisenhower's long-term impact on national security—and domestic policy. Even then it was not until later that historians and analysts took the long view, the timeline that drove Eisenhower's own decisions. As we are now ready to concede, the Eisenhower years were not the years of the "great postponement," but rather the years of recalibration and rebuilding—for the future.

Herbert Brownell, in his memoir, asserted that the reason this reevaluation took so long rested with a simple fact: "The members of the administration generally were not politicians; they were not ambitious for political advancement and had little desire for public acclaim or higher office. . . . Nor were individuals on the White House staff prone to engage in the kind of court-historian role" that was common in subsequent administrations.[40]

After Sputnik virtually the entire establishment demanded more money for defense. As the historian Stephen Ambrose once observed: "Ike said no, and in saying so he stood virtually alone. . . . In doing so he saved the United States billions of dollars in unnecessary duplication and wastage. . . . Eisenhower's calm, commonsense, and deliberate response to Sputnik may have been his finest gift to the nation, if only because he was the only man who could have given it."[41]

Eisenhower had also believed in the concept of nuclear "sufficiency," not "superiority." According to Ambrose, when Eisenhower first came to office he was told that we had the capability to hit seventy targets in the USSR. The number had gone up to seven hundred when Eisenhower left office. By the late sixties, the arms buildup during the Kennedy and Johnson years had brought that number to seven thousand.[42]

"We are taking counsel of our fears when we should indoctrinate ourselves that there is such a thing as common sense," Eisenhower said before leaving office. "How many times do we need to kill each Russian?"[43] This question would haunt the United States in the decades to come, as would many of the words Eisenhower left the nation in his farewell address on January 17, just days before leaving office.

Inter-service rivalry; resistance to fiscally responsible budgeting; the wastage of money on negative, inert, redundant weapons, rather than the prudent use of resources for education and investment—these concerns were included in his good-bye to the American people, after more than fifty years of service to our country. He regretted that he had not found a lasting peace, but he expressed gratitude for his productive working relationship with Congress while he also expressed concerns for the future—and at least two of his warnings would ring through the ages: "In the councils of government, we must guard against the acquisition of unwarranted influence, whether sought or unsought, by the military-industrial complex. The potential for the disastrous rise of misplaced power exists and will persist." He called for balance "in and among national programs," and he offered a stern warning about profligate spending, emphasizing the importance of sustainable stewardship:

> As we peer into society's future, we—you and I—and our government must avoid the impulse to live only for today,

plundering, for our own ease and convenience, the precious resources of tomorrow. We cannot mortgage the material assets of our grandchildren without risking the loss also of their political and spiritual heritage. We want democracy to survive for all generations to come, not to become the insolvent phantom of tomorrow.[44]

Eisenhower and his granddaughter Susan, at Westtown School, 1967.

16

WHEN NO ONE WAS LOOKING

The measure of a leader is more than the sum of his or her successful decisions: qualities of character, including empathy and fairness, are also central to any person worthy of that status. Sometimes these qualities can only be seen when the public is not looking.

In 1963 Dwight and Mamie Eisenhower and a small group of aides and friends crossed the Atlantic on the *Queen Elizabeth,* ultimately bound for the Normandy coast to film an upcoming documentary: " D-day Plus 20 Years: Eisenhower Returns to Normandy." It was the scene of what the military historian Carlo D'Este called Eisenhower's "greatest triumph." The conversation one evening had been focused on the events of those critical days, and no doubt the former supreme commander of Allied forces was effusively lauded for the singular role he had played during that fateful time. Always eager to deflect such accolades, Ike pulled a curling yellowed paper from his wallet and read it out loud. It was a poem—a ditty—that he carried with him and often recited to us kids—to remind us not to get too big for our britches. It was about putting your hand in a bucket of water and seeing what the result would be when you removed it. The last lines were this:

Be proud of yourself, but remember,
There is no indispensable man.[1]

A person of unchecked ego would have absorbed the credit offered him that evening and taken his bows, but Eisenhower would have none of it. A *team* of dedicated men and women had executed the events of that war, which had exacted an unconscionably high price on his country and the world. He remained humble at the memory of it.

Many of Eisenhower's critics would have scoffed at this story, or declared him a relic from the past: "too good to be true"—a "grownup Boy Scout." At the time many intellectuals simply could not believe that the conduct of his leadership and the relationships that he fostered could be so straightforward. However, they and others did not necessarily look behind the genial general and president to ponder Ike's spirituality, or the lessons of his simple Brethren upbringing. Indeed, some who have written about Dwight Eisenhower have said that he was hard to know, pejoratively suggesting some kind of inner complexity. If Ike had ever suffered from strains of two-mindedness, such thinking merged in his early years, forging an approach that even as a kid I thought to be extraordinarily straightforward and uncomplicated. You did not need to know Dwight Eisenhower's every thought to feel confident you knew who he was and what he stood for.

Nevertheless Ike's critics lacerated the president in his last years for his so-called do-nothing ways, culminating in a poll of historians, initiated by Kennedy friend and Harvard University professor Arthur Schlesinger Sr., ranking presidential greatness. Dwight Eisenhower stood twenty-eighth among the thirty-three presidents. While most intellectuals rejected Eisenhower's presidential years, the Gallup organization ranked him the most admired man in the world in 1960—a position he held twice more in his short post-presidential life. More important, throughout his presidency his public approval ratings averaged in the mid-sixtieth percentiles, the high—80 percent—just after the Geneva summit in 1955 and again after the resolution of the Suez crisis.[2] And today, he is ranked fifth in a poll of presidential historians.[3]

The American people thought they knew who Dwight Eisenhower was—and they did. It was his personal relationship with the American people that historian Robert Ferrell called "ineradicable, invincible, simply not subject to the erosions or buffetings that have knocked down so many American political reputations in the country's history."[4]

For a younger generation and those to come, the presidency would fuse with television, and politics with storytelling and drama. Eisenhower knew that leadership has many outward signs, but getting constant attention is not one of them. For Eisenhower patience and restraint were also critical attributes of sound leadership. He was confident enough to know that action—any action at all—may be satisfying in the short term but, if not justifiable, could bring with it untold consequences over the longer haul. This could be seen in his refusal to intervene in Vietnam, for example.

One day during Ike's presidency, the distinguished poet Robert Frost visited him at the White House. Eisenhower was under attack for "moving too slowly" on issues that people felt passionately about. After their meeting Frost thanked the president for his time and left one of his books of poetry as a gift. On the flyleaf, at the end of the inscription, Frost wrote: "The strong are saying nothing until they see."[5]

I learned many such things from my grandfather, as well as other qualities about him that still impress me today, though some of them were out of sight to reporters and historians. I have always been moved by his belief in this country and his fellow man. He also felt strongly about second chances. There are many examples of this, but perhaps the one that has stayed with me most is Mickey McKeogh's wartime account of how his boss, Ike, stepped in when he visited a camp for soldiers with battle fatigue, who were waiting to go home. On the discovery that the men were sitting idle before their departures, Eisenhower dressed down the captain in charge, remembering that such a form of warehousing had been the approach to those with what we called "shell shock" or "battle fatigue" during World War I. Many of them were left to feel worthless.

"The Boss said the men in the camp should be kept busy," Mickey recalled. "They ought to be made to understand that the Army did not think they were all washed up, and useless and no good. The Army ought to treat them in a way which would make them know that they had done a good job, and ought to be proud of it, and that they still had good jobs in them."

Eisenhower's orders to the captain were to give the men a schedule and put them to work around the camp—get them to install some shelves in the mess hall, assign them to paint and do other jobs like driving and hauling materials. It would let them know, Ike concluded, that "they could still be of use to the Army" and there were "things they could still do" when they reentered civilian life.[6]

I have also learned from Ike that strong individuals might have to be tough, but that strength is not defined entirely by it. Kindness, even softness, can also be a sign of strength. It takes courage to open oneself to seeing the world through other people's eyes—and this particular attribute was deeply imbued in him.

Over the years I noted literally countless things he did for people who could do nothing for him. A strong sense of empathy enabled him to connect with other people.

I recently learned of one such occasion, recounted to me by

a man who met General Eisenhower when he was a young boy. After the war, remembered Melvyn Bucholtz, a psychologist living in Santa Fe, New Mexico, Dwight Eisenhower came to the National Home for Jewish Children, where Bucholtz and other elementary-school-age children lived while receiving treatment for asthma. Melvyn had been sent there as part of a program hypothesizing that asthma could not be cured unless children were separated from their parents during their care—known as a "parentectomy." Perhaps the correlation between stress and anxiety, in the context of this condition, had spurred such a theory. In any case, according to Bucholtz, parents were allowed to visit their children only once a year.

Ike must have heard about this children's home while he and Mamie were in Denver. No doubt conscious that these children could not enjoy the kind of things a father would do with his kids on a Saturday afternoon, General Eisenhower arrived at the home to take the youngsters to the ballgame—the Denver Bears were playing that day.

Bucholtz recalls that the matron was very strict with the children, and admonished them to be good. Nevertheless, when Ike arrived one of the first things he did was ask the group if it was a "special day for anyone." Little Melvyn announced it was his ninth birthday. With that Ike invited him to ride to the ballpark with him in his car—the other kids followed in a van. On passing a toy store, the general stopped the car so that he and Melvyn could go in to select a birthday present. Young Melvyn chose a cap pistol and caps. Ike paid for it, and they proceeded on their way. At the game they enjoyed ballpark food, and afterward Melvyn and his classmates thanked the general profusely for a great day. Melvyn, however, was scolded by the matron for "speaking out" and "asking for things." He was spanked and sent to bed.

Ike's presence had a lasting impact on Melvyn. "I was struck by his presence," he recalled, "his softness, his firmness, and steadiness. There was no harshness about him, or cynicism—he was a good listener."

Bucholtz later became a psychologist who trains people in how to "embody stillness, awareness, and confidence"—all traits he attributed to this kindhearted stranger who came to take him and his classmates to the game.[7]

Another example of Ike's empathy occurred during his presidency. He was fishing in a stream at Camp David when his Secret Service detail saw a fisherman just outside the camp security perimeter. Ike started a conversation with the young man and realized that he had been a GI during the war. He advised the resident of nearby Thurmont that the better fishing was up closer to the presidential cabin. To the consternation of the Secret Servicemen the president made it clear that the young man could fish inside Camp David's security perimeter for a better catch.

And a few years ago, completely out of the blue, a man wrote me to tell me about his encounter with Ike, after he had left the White House and before Secret Servicemen for former presidents had been reinstated in the wake of the Kennedy assassination. He recounted that he had been an apprentice electrician at New York's Waldorf-Astoria Hotel.

One day the electrician was working on an outlet in one of the hallways when the former president came down the corridor. Eisenhower stopped and started talking to the man, asking him questions about his work and his family. The electrician said he had just gotten married. After their conversation Ike said goodbye, wished him luck, and asked him to go to the suite down the hall where he and Mamie were staying when he was done with his work—he wanted the young man to have something. When the electrician got there, a man opened the door and gave him two small white boxes.

The aide said: "President Eisenhower says he wants you to have these for your bride."

The electrician opened the boxes to discover that Ike had given him two orchid corsages for his wife.[8]

If Eisenhower was kind to strangers, he got enormous support from ordinary people in return. During the war, Mickey Mc-

Keogh's responsibilities included remembering to give the general his "lucky coins" that he carried with him in a small zipper purse. If Ike had an unexpected trip to make and the coins were not with him, Mickey would be sent back to their house to fetch them. They were coins, small medals, and "trinkets from the past"—sent to him by people back home.

One of these was a medal a little girl from Detroit had sent Ike when he and his SHAEF team were still in England: "She wrote a letter saying that she had adopted [Eisenhower] as her soldier and prayed for him every day." General Eisenhower wrote her back, Mickey recalled, and she wrote him back. This correspondence went on throughout the war: "The little girl was very special in his mind. He called her 'my little godmother.'"[9]

After Eisenhower's heart attack in 1955 and the other illnesses he suffered, the thoughtful, prayerful letters he received, as well as the kindnesses that people offered, buoyed the president's spirits. Among the most extraordinary of gestures were those that occurred in the last months of his life, in 1968. After another heart attack in August, as many as twenty people contacted Eisenhower's physicians and offered the former general and president their own beating hearts for transplant purposes. These unforgettable offers were graciously declined.[10]

In my youth, after my grandparents left the White House and retired to Gettysburg, my immediate family enjoyed living on a property adjacent to theirs. The Eisenhower farm, among other things, boasted a beautiful nineteenth-century Pennsylvania bank barn. By 1961 it was populated by those five overfed horses: two quarter horses, one Thoroughbred, and two Arabians. At some point in Ike's thinking, he decided to start breeding his horses to see if he could successfully combine their best attributes. I took a great interest in the discussion he was having with his farm manager, since by then I was the only one of us siblings still riding his horses, mucking out the stalls, and generally hanging around the barn.

There were two foals born in this experiment: wonderful mixes of quarter horse and Thoroughbred, Arabian and quarter horse. One was named Quinine and the other Sassy Sue (I felt especially attached to the latter, I guess because I figured she'd been named for me).

One day I remember asking my parents what had happened to Quinine. I was told only that she had been given away—but it wasn't until five decades later that I learned the full story.

After leaving the White House my grandfather was given what had once been the president's house at Gettysburg College, for writing his memoirs and pursuing public endeavors. A few years after Ike's presidential retirement, one of his secretaries died unexpectedly. Some months after her death, while everyone in the office still mourned her loss, Ike heard from one of his staff members that his late secretary's young daughter, Susan Markley—a girl about my age—had always wanted a pony or a horse. He wrote her a letter:

October 1, 1963

Dear Susan,
From Miss Brown I learned that you could give a good home to a horse that I should like to give you. Her name is Quinine and she is a cross between a registered Arabian and a registered Quarter Horse. I shall leave instructions at my Farm for the horse to be available at any time you might want to have her picked up and this letter will be your evidence of ownership.

I want nothing but a good home for her and this I am sure you will give.
With best wishes, Sincerely,

Some weeks later Susan Markley responded, accepting Ike's gift. She told him that ever since she could remember she had wanted to have a horse. When his offer arrived, she wrote: "I was speechless for quite a period." She reported that the animal had been picked up and that it was now in her possession. Quinine is "the most beautiful horse I have ever seen. . . . I promise to give Quinine the best of care and love."[11]

There was nothing maudlin about Ike's gift, and no one, not even I, knew that my grandfather had made this memorable gesture. Years later I would wonder how many people would give away a horse they had spent considerable money breeding to a little girl they'd never met.

Ike loved young people. He was not bored by them at all. He was interested in the small things as well as the big ones. In his retirement he would sometimes stay up late learning what we were being taught in school, like "new math," so he would be able to converse on it with knowledge and confidence when we got together.[12]

Many times he and I would talk at length about horsemanship. He had been an accomplished rider as a young soldier, and was fascinated by dressage. But he listened with attention and enthusiasm to my descriptions of my lessons—from walking and trotting in the early years to jumping and equitation later on.

In fact he was curious about everything we did, and he didn't have any "fixed ideas" about whom he could learn from. Bill Ewald, his longtime aide, once asked one of his sons (also Bill) if he recalled President Eisenhower. Young Bill, who would have been eight years old at the time, replied: "Of course. I taught him to weave gimp." Billy was excited about the weaving skills he had learned at camp. Ike asked him how it was done. In my mind's eye I can see Granddad listening and practicing this new skill as this youngster carefully—and literally—showed him the ropes. Bill Ewald, after many years with the president, noted that this scene was a good way to remember the president: "Blue eyes lively, willing to learn from anyone anything at all that was new, to his very end youthful."[13]

Ike always gave young kids a sense of support and validation, too. In 1949, as Eisenhower was juggling his work at Columbia with his frequent visits to Washington as an adviser to the Defense Department, he still found time to appear at gatherings that promoted leadership development in kids. Philip Fowler Jr. was twelve years old at the time and remembered an encounter he had with Ike. When he applied to become a Boy Scout, it turned out he was the five-hundredth youngster to be inducted, triggering his selection to represent his peers at the annual Dawn Patrol Breakfast in New York. More than a thousand guests were in attendance that day, as the whirs and the rapid-fire flashes of cameras mixed with the noise and energy of the crowd. Philip had already come to the event in a state of nerves, and now he felt panicky. Eisenhower was to speak at the gathering, and Philip later admitted that he had spent three weeks allowing his mind to run wild: He imagined that Eisenhower would be a "stiff, gruff military man coldly pinning on my tenderfoot badge."

By the time Ike mounted the stage that day, Philip's "knees were knocking." He recalled that he was so terrified by the attention that he wanted only to "turn and run away."

Eisenhower probably "sensed" the boy's anxiety, so he walked over to him to chat. "He said he was more nervous than I was and that we would comfort each other."

"As though that all wasn't enough," Fowler recalled, "I later received a letter from him that I will treasure as long as I live":

> *Dear Philip:*
> *For my part, I consider it a great honor that I was privileged to induct you into the Boy Scouts of America, and I must say that I found you a regular fellow, too. Stay that way and nothing will go to your head.*
> *Sincerely, Dwight D. Eisenhower*[14]

On a similar note, I was about six years old when I won my first riding trophy. It was a walk-trot competition at a local horse show in about 1957. The trophy was a tiny cup—consistent with the modesty of the endeavor—but Granddad treated it as if it was some huge deal. I failed to notice that the cup had disappeared, but some weeks later he presented it to me mounted on a carved wooden pedestal. He had designed it in a way that made the tiny cup look like the most important award ever.

Here was Eisenhower, a big man doing small things for all kinds of people; leaving memories and mementoes we still cherish. He designed jewelry for my grandmother, he painted portraits of his friends and associates as gifts, and he helped put one of his secretaries through college after her parents rejected the idea that a girl should seek higher education. He validated the lives and importance of strangers with keepsakes that, I hope, stayed with them always.

In the last months of his life, I called Granddad to say that I wanted to celebrate his birthday with him. I was at boarding school at the time—Westtown School in Westtown, Pennsylvania. I told him I wanted to bring him a cake. He was delighted, but he cautioned me that the doctors would not let him eat anything that contained salt. So I told him I would bake a cake from scratch and present it in person. To make this possible, however, I was told by the headmaster that I was required to get permission from all my teachers to take the day off. I was especially nervous about approaching my English teacher—as I was under deadline for an assignment. Isaac Green, known to everyone as "Ike" Green, was one of the school's two African American teachers. A recent graduate of Oberlin College, he was a tough but brilliant instructor.

I asked "Master Ike"—the nomenclature we used at this Friends' school—if I could be given the day off to take my cake to Walter Reed for my grandfather's birthday. Master Ike said I could, and then added, "October 14 is my birthday too."

During my memorable visit with Granddad that day, we discussed a range of things. At one point I mentioned Master Ike, and the coincidence that they both shared the same birthday. An hour or two later, when I finally had to leave to get back to school, Granddad whispered something to one of the nurses, and she returned with a white cake that said, "Happy Birthday, Ike." On the icing were also images of golf clubs and other sporting reminders of Eisenhower's outdoor days—obviously a gift to Granddad from one of his friends. He said, "Now, please give this cake to Master Ike and tell him I was thinking about him today and, from one Ike to another, I am wishing him a very happy birthday."

This I did. I lugged the cake all the way back to school and gave it to Ike Green as soon as I arrived. I don't have the words to describe the look on his face when he saw the cake and realized that the general and former president wanted to share his birthday with him.

It was my grandfather's last.

I look back on such stories, and I think about the sum of those years and what I learned from this man whom everyone knew yet few had ever met.

Though we were taught to compartmentalize our association with the president and our own relationship with him as a grandfather, there were many occasions when Granddad's other life would invade our private world—even if the backdrop of our youth had been hard to ignore. We were sometimes brought into Granddad's official life, providing, at times, the opportunity to use what I later called "the grandchildren strategy" to demonstrate to world leaders why they must find resolutions to difficult problems. Many of Granddad's speeches included the idea of "grandchildren," with exhortations to make decisions today that would one day lead to a better world for my generation and beyond.

As a young girl I was also more aware of Granddad's connection to World War II than most kids who were born in the early 1950s—yet in this regard he did not really talk about the war. In 1948 his book *Crusade in Europe* came out and was later turned into a documentary film. I remember seeing *Crusade* at least three times, though I am not sure I ever saw it with my grandparents. Granddad did not like war films, yet I knew the names Normandy and Battle of the Bulge before I had even left elementary school.

I can remember one memorable exception. In Gettysburg, I would often walk from my school to Ike's office on the Gettysburg College campus, and then he would drive me home—a small house adjacent to my grandparents' property.

That day I remember asking him about a big black-and-white photograph affixed to what looked like a large cupboard—a photo console that hung from the wall in a back study to his office. It was the famous photo of the Normandy invasion fleet unloading supplies, D-day plus 2, and it was affixed so that the console door would swing open. At my request Granddad told me about the liberation. Opening the console, he pulled down the maps that were inside and explained the events in a way he thought might be retained by a sixth-grader. I still remember at that moment a sense of awe in his presence—a few intimate minutes that allowed me to peer into this other life he had lived before I was born.

It was also on that day that I asked him about a letter from President John F. Kennedy, which hung on another wall. In it the new president reinstated Eisenhower's commission as an army officer, restoring to him the five-star rank he had relinquished when he ran for president in 1952. That was how my grandfather wanted to be remembered—as General Eisenhower.

Later, in my adulthood, I began to realize that I had lived my younger years surrounded by people who had played intimate roles in those epic events. There was Sergeant Moaney, my grandfather's beloved helper and valet who had been with him since the North African campaign, and Sergeant Dry, a man who had also followed Ike into retirement. He had served during the war as one of General Eisenhower's drivers and had been—so he later told me—the one who had taken General Eisenhower to meet the 101st Airborne Division the night they took off for the Normandy coast. And then there was Gen. Arthur Nevins, who managed my grandparents' farm. I knew him well, and yet throughout my youth he never mentioned to me that he had been on the SHAEF staff and had been there the night the decision was made to launch the assault on the Normandy coast.

I was late to know these things only because none of the people who had played either a major or minor role in these historic events felt the need to talk much about those transformational times—they were focused now on the future. What was clear to me then, however, is that the men I mentioned were devoted to my grandparents, especially their old boss. Together they had a kind of emotional shorthand. The bonds they'd established during the war were such that even their loving wives knew those ties could never be severed, let alone fully understood.

In this vein, Eisenhower's return to Normandy for "D-Day Plus 20 Years" (with Walter Cronkite) was so important in our family circle that my parents insisted I excuse myself from a friend's birthday party to watch the television program in her recreation room, as the other kids played outdoors.

I later found out that before his departure for Normandy to shoot the film, in 1963, my grandfather received a letter from a woman who had read about the upcoming special and wanted Eisenhower to stop by her son's grave in Colleville-sur-Mer, atop Omaha Beach. He was "Pfc. Herbert Kaufman, Plot B, Row 10, Grave 188. . . . When you go by," she wrote, "please say a silent prayer for our Darling Boy."

Ike's executive assistant wrote Mrs. Kaufman and said they did not know for sure whether the general's schedule would allow the Eisenhowers to include this stop, but that his on-site staff had been notified of the request. Several weeks later Ike's secretary, Lillian Brown, wrote Mrs. Kaufman again, enclosing photographs that had been taken of General and Mrs. Eisenhower at her son's grave. The Eisenhowers, Ms. Brown wrote, had visited it just before the filming of the TV special. They also left flowers at the grave site. Mrs. Kaufman responded with a note of heartfelt thanks, closing with appreciation for the "beautiful" flowers: "I simply can't find the right words to thank them both enough," she wrote.[15]

While Ike's boundless appreciation for the sacrifice of the ordinary fighting men and women was profound and deeply felt, he could be extraordinarily direct with his colleagues, exhorting them to sharper thinking, higher motives, greater sacrifice—never forgetting that they, like him, must be organized and prepared to do what they thought best for the country, and be ready for the fallout that might arise from the political environment in which they operated.

Though Eisenhower himself was tough, with the requisite thick skin when it came to doing his duty, I can only speculate that the nastiness, the personal attacks—which he had always tried to avoid making himself—must have had some effect on him in the last years of his life. He had never quarreled about sincere differences of opinion, but the petty, outright misrepresentations of his administration policy must have given him at least some pause about what was to come in American life. While he sometimes seemed pensive and withdrawn, he always retained his optimism, even if he was worried and perplexed about the chaotic new path on which our country had seemingly embarked.

Granddad did not talk much to our family about these things, nor did he rehash the horrors of the war. One simply cannot imagine what he had been through in his life—the full spectrum of human experience he had lived and observed. At Falaise, for example, a battle that was part of the larger Normandy campaign, the Allies eventually won the engagement by encircling the German position. It was one of the greatest "killing fields" of the campaign. The supreme commander had walked the grounds there after the battle and encountered "scenes that could be described only by Dante. It was literally possible to walk for hundreds of yards at a time, stepping on nothing but dead and decaying flesh."[16]

And during his presidency, Eisenhower struggled to convince his colleagues that the global Cold War could be waged in only two ways: by relationship management or the catastrophic end of human civilization. He knew firsthand of the fight for "hearts and minds" between two systems of government and two radically different ways of life. They could be seen in those overseas faces. Nixon and other administration officials had seen cheering crowds, but they had also encountered the anger fomented by Soviet-infiltrated mobs in such places as Venezuela and Japan; but Ike himself saw with his own eyes the yearning of millions around the world for freedom, and their hope for eventual prosperity and justice.

Eisenhower had processed those experiences, developed a philosophy about them and employed principles to address them. This may have been why a kind of inner ease lived within him. He had mastered the hardest part of consequential leadership. Despite occasional frustrations and low points, irritations and perhaps worries, inside, in his deepest self, he was at peace.

Leadership is about making strong, sound judgments, while at the same time building relationships with people—not just the favored few or the ones whose views you endorse—but connections with people, even forgotten ones.

Among the things I loved most about my grandparents as sincere public servants was their interest in those who had no voice or could do nothing to help advance my grandfather's career. Their relationships with the Secret Servicemen, as well as the butlers and maids at the White House, were examples of this. During the presidency, Ike and Mamie remembered each of them annually at Christmas and often on their birthdays. My grandmother knew their children's names and often sent gifts for them too. During Eisenhower's second term, they held an annual picnic for the White House staff, including the housekeeping employees, at the Gettysburg farm. Even after Granddad's death, a doorman and a few of the butlers from the White House would come to Gettysburg to visit my widowed grandmother. And some of my grandparents' Secret Servicemen also retired to Gettysburg, living close by.

Ike was not afraid to show his humanity to others, even in the conduct of his work—and that very act could have a powerful impact. I was reminded of this when we settled my father's estate. As my sister, Anne, and I were combing through piles of old letters, there was one that contained a string of beads and an undated, yellowed newspaper clipping. They came from John Simmons-Lee, the adopted son of American missionaries in China. The beads were a small gift for the president's grandchildren, as his way of saying thank you. John had taken his oath of citizenship nine days before he met Eisenhower, and the fifteen-year-old Chinese boy apparently never forgot it.

Simmons-Lee, born in Hankwo, China, in 1938, had experienced terror-bombing raids. He had also been in a concentration camp, where he was incarcerated with his adoptive parents. Finally making his way to the United States with them, he found his future filled with uncertainty. "Now he has the most important memory of his life," the old newspaper clipping said. "He knows what it is to see Ike grin, reach out his hand and bid him welcome as an American citizen."

His mother, Mrs. Simmons-Lee, concluded: "I regard [Eisenhower's] office as the most powerful in the world. [The president] was not too big or too great to take a minute for a little boy. That is the kind of Americanism that I want John to know and understand."[17]

Ike had spent his life committed to thinking and acting for "the long haul," in the hopes that the rising generations would benefit from the stewardship of his generation. After the war, in 1947, he wrote to his British comrade Gen. Frederick Morgan to say that he felt that it was up to their generation "to struggle toward stabilizing conditions so as to give our youngsters a chance to work out world improvements." And then he added with heartfelt optimism: "I incline to the view that we often overemphasize difficulties and obstacles. We forget the tremendous nature and size of the forces that work for decency, for stability and for a brighter future."[18]

At the core of humility is the acknowledgment of something larger than oneself—and the acceptance of one's own mortality. In the last year of his life, Dwight Eisenhower's mind remained extraordinarily sharp, but impending death was clear for all to see. My brother noted that "[Granddad's] illness had stripped away the exteriors exposing his spirit—serene, beautiful, and unafraid.[19]

On March 28, 1969, after a nearly a year in the hospital, Dwight D. Eisenhower died. He was seventy-eight years old.

After the general and president lay in state in the Capitol Rotunda, and his casket was taken to the National Cathedral for his state funeral, we boarded a train that took Granddad's body to Abilene for its interment. He would be buried in small chapel next to his and Mamie's first son, Doud Dwight.

All along the route, thousands of people came out, even late at night, to pay their respects as the train whistled through each station along the route. I remember being deeply moved by the diversity of the crowds: black and white, young and old, farmers and townspeople. All came to say good-bye.

One night, as the train broke the dark stillness of the midwestern farmland, I could not sleep. It was around three in the morning. Looking out the window as the countryside disappeared behind us, I noticed, just off in the distance, a solitary figure standing in a field, illuminated only by the moon. I watched as the man straightened to attention and saluted the general as the funeral train quickly passed.

On that same journey my father and I wanted to say our own good-byes. We were the last people to see what remained of Dwight D. Eisenhower. Granddad's body had been placed in a special railway car with an honor guard, not far from the family quarters. After making our way down the swaying companionway, we entered the dimly lit car. His coffin rested on a platform where two marines kept a solemn vigil.

My father asked them to lift the lid of his father's casket. Ike's body, laid out in a simple eighty-one-dollar GI coffin, was clad in his military uniform, which bore only one bar of ribbons and his five stars. This last sight of my grandfather has stayed with me ever since, and always will.

Unlike the remains of many people I have seen, and there have been many, this was not the Eisenhower I knew and loved. These were the remains of a stranger; someone I didn't know and almost didn't recognize. Until that moment I never fully realized the size of his indomitable spirit, the power of his persona, the depth and recesses of his humanity. It was then that I fully understood that when he uttered his last words: "I want to go, God take me," that the Almighty, whose presence I might have questioned, had taken him home.

EPILOGUE

On Eisenhower's death perhaps the most moving statement came from a Democrat, Lyndon B. Johnson, who had served as Senate majority leader while Ike was president. The fact that these two men came from different political parties mattered little. They respected each other, they worked together, and they became friends. On the news of Ike's passing, former president Johnson issued this statement:

> A giant of our age is gone. Dwight D. Eisenhower began his service to his people as a soldier of war. He ended as a crusader for peace. For both he will long be remembered by a scarred but hopeful world—a world that loved him well. The sturdy and enduring virtues—honor, courage, integrity, decency—all found eloquent expression in the life of

> this good man and noble leader. . . . I treasured him always as my close and lasting friend.
>
> . . . America will be a lonely land without him but America will always be a better nation—stronger, safer, more conscious of its heritage, more certain of its destiny—because Ike was with us when America needed him.[1]

Many people today think leadership is something that is conferred by some external validation. Instead it emanates from within. From his earliest years Eisenhower was driven to serve something bigger than himself—it came from his inner core. This enabled him to pursue his mission even when the personal cost had become high.

Dwight Eisenhower chose to devote his life to the unity and the security of our country—in war and peace—and to defend our Constitution and our American ideals. He exercised restraint, patience, and hardheaded realism in the pursuit of that goal, and he led with optimism and a determination to improve upon the promise of America. By the end of his years of service—more than fifty of them—he could rest in the knowledge that he had done his best and that everything he had undertaken had been in the service of *all* Americans, including his ardent pursuit of a just and lasting peace.

Ike's objectives had been simple: He sought unity of purpose—in the alliance whose forces he commanded during the war, and as president when he tried to bind the postwar wounds and build a Middle Way that would protect the country from the baleful influence of Communism and its foreign influence in our affairs. His nearly fanatical devotion to moderation was the platform he tried to build to ensure the growth of the American middle class—the bulwark of American democracy.

"The greatest virtue in civic life—and the ultimate factor determining political stability—has always been principled moderation, whatever the epoch," the public intellectual Robert D. Kaplan has observed. "The rarest and bravest of leaders" are the moderates—who stand against extremists—"the purveyors of rage and passion."[2]

Eisenhower was ill at ease with unbridled emotionalism; he knew how easy it would be for the wrong kind of leaders to manipulate such sentiments. During his years in authority, he had benefited from being an observer of men. Through his experiences during WWII he had also seen the sharp divisions between life and death, and pondered human beings' deepest weaknesses, as well as their soaring strengths.

Dwight Eisenhower truly loved this country, and believed in it, and was always positive about its future, even though he knew something of the human problems and the challenges we would eventually face. On his last visit to the Normandy beaches as part of "D-day plus 20," he noted—as he sat among the rows and rows of marble crosses and Stars of David—that these boys "gave us another chance."

Today we are facing the questions of what we have done with that opportunity and what we can now do to improve the conditions under which all Americans live, while demonstrating to the world, again, that the United States is a place of hope—a nation of immigrants who stand with the forces that seek global betterment.

I struggle today to retain the kind of optimism my grandfather would want to see in me, but I am determined to remain positive. As he would always say: "You've got to be *for* something" (not just be against what already exists). If I am to think of "what to be for" then, I want America to take stock of where we have been and where we are headed. I want to *be* for the renewal of America's promise and the can-do spirit that so characterized the country of my youth.

The unparalleled growth and prosperity that was generated after World War II produced national wealth and money to spend and to borrow. The allocation of vast financial resources means power. America became spoiled. The prosperity that we earned in the postwar period lulled subsequent generations into thinking that greatness could be easy; that it could be paid for rather than nurtured and demonstrated. And while the monumental sacrifices of those who fought in World War II, and the other wars that followed, are still a part of our heritage, they are now only the backdrop of a society that has become increasingly equated with glamour and celebrity over experience and substance, attention-getting over education and expert assessment. The imperative is to recommit ourselves to the "alert and knowledgeable citizenry" that Eisenhower called for in his farewell address. Without such an undertaking, the foundation of a thriving democracy will continue to feel shaky.

America's unrivaled position in the world has been, until recent years, seen by virtually everyone as a force for good. But today we no longer seem to know who we are as a people.

In essence we have a leadership crisis that actually favors factionalism, lack of accountability, and a complete misreading of what real leadership is. This is the other most urgent issue facing our nation. Before the crisis of September 11, 2001, our country still had some notion that leadership is the capacity to bring people along as one, while sustaining a dogged focus on a national goal. To do this requires exercising agility and flexibility in order to reach that point. If a leader *truly* has the nation's best interests at heart, then compromise is the only key to progress. No one group of Americans has a lock on the truth.

Today we have defined leadership as "standing your ground and digging in your heels," lest one look weak. If that is leadership, then civility is all but unattainable and there is no prospect for fostering national unity. In this light our citizens' differing views can only be cast as zero-sum confrontations, and a welcome sight to our adversaries.

Our culture no longer understands what was deeply ingrained in Eisenhower and many of his generation. Today we seem to think that strength is derived from winning every small fight, while raising ourselves up for recognition and advancement, even if others have to be diminished in the process. This is a trend that has been under way for many decades. To Dwight D. Eisenhower the exact opposite was fundamental to his beliefs. To Ike strength came from putting his own house in order, by exercising self-discipline and by putting others first and inspiring them to take up the cause as their own. At the same time he insisted that those "who should know better"—especially those connected to him in some way—understand there are "no excuses" for such things as pettiness and self-aggrandizement. It is easy to criticize your opponents, but it takes courage to hold your closest friends and associates to an equally high standard.

Strength, whether personal or national, derives from many other things too. Among them: the impulse to be fair and the willingness to be accountable. No true state of adulthood can really be achieved unless accountability is fully embraced. And no leader's power is legitimate without it.

Eisenhower was a constitutionalist who believed that the only way democracy can function is through governing practices based on principles rather than political expediency. He was a strategic leader who understood that the big themes are the ones that should drive organizations, and that such a leader must be focused on the present while anticipating the future.

What Ike feared most in his years as president, as the national cohesion from World War II began to fade, was the kind of tribalism we have today. That is why he kept articulating the things that we could all agree on—like the rule of law.

These simple approaches brought eight years of building—for the future—with "freedom of space" secured, Antarctica set aside for peaceful uses, statehood for Alaska and Hawaii, civil rights progress, the building of major infrastructure projects like the Interstate Highway System—three balanced budgets and a surplus for his successor with an inflation rate of no more than 1.4 percent per year—and a massive expansion in the economy. As Herbert Brownell also observed: "He obtained a lasting bipartisan international approach to world affairs."[3] And his achievements with NATO also bore the imprint of hard work and a commitment to freedom.

Perhaps his greatest achievement as president, however, was eight years of peace, with no American combat casualties after the end of the Korean War.

Ike would be the first to remind us that sound stewardship, however, is always under threat. His concerns are evident in much of his writing, especially with regard to the dangers of special interests and the potential for chaos if small parts of society are able to monopolize the policy agenda. He would be saddened that today's Americans are nearly paralyzed by the fear that our best days are behind us; that we are obsessed that foreigners are out to destroy us; and that we feel there is nothing we can do to reverse these trends. He would be shocked by our acceptance of cronyism, and by the fact that the shrinking middle class has few defenders. He would also oppose the special advantages that are seized by some while others lack access to opportunity. But most of all, he would be alarmed that common sense is often not even tried.

The historian Robert Ferrell once said that Eisenhower was "a man of judgment amid men of passion." It was his steadiness that made it possible for me and many of my generation to grow up feeling safe, secure, and ready to build on America's promise to our countrymen and the world.[4]

In those days my siblings and I often spent carefree summer evenings. We played hide-and-seek at the farm and caught fireflies in jam jars, before the dusk grew thick and the adults called us inside. There was always a sense of exhaustion and peace when we finally came indoors. We felt happy and very lucky to be Americans.

We sensed that the country was in good hands, and we knew that those in power were thinking of us kids and our futures, which were unfolding with each long, lazy summer evening. Such memories stand in sharp relief to today's ugly and undignified free-for-all.

In the years ahead will we manage to provide our children and grandchildren that sense of peace and security we felt as youngsters? Will the futures we are crafting for them ensure their chance to prosper without the fear of dislocation and national insolvency? Will we bequeath them a country that values and nurtures our democratic system—one that stands above all others as a beacon of tolerance, a land of equal opportunity? Or will we fail them and ourselves and choose expediency and self-serving over sacrifice and stewardship?

I reflect on this as I drive along the back roads of town near my grandparents' farm—on the famous ridges where America fought to become a nation of justice and equality. Our country urgently needs, again, a sense of national purpose and a vision for the future—and a commitment, I can still hear my grandfather say, to "leave the place better than you found it."

ACKNOWLEDGMENTS

Writing *How Ike Led* has been both a labor of love and an emotional sail through memory's long tributaries. I am grateful to so many people who helped me in this journey.

I am most grateful for the encouragement and guidance of my longtime agent, Ron Goldfarb and his associate Gerrie Sturman. I am grateful to him for introducing me to the great team at St. Martin's Press—Tom Dunne, Stephen S. Power, and Lisa Bonvissuto, Gabi Grant, as well as Joshua Rubins, Mac Nicholas, Paul Hochman, Laura Clark, and Sara Beth Haring. It has been a pleasure to work with them and to collaborate on bringing this book to life. As always, I am indebted to Tim Rives, deputy director of the Eisenhower Presidential Library, and Mary Burtzloff, photo archivist, who also worked closely with us. Mike Hill, an outstanding researcher, gave me indispensable feedback. I am grateful to Michael Korda for both that introduction and for his wise counsel and suggestions. My thanks also go to the historian David Nichols, who graciously gave me important feedback. I am also indebted to Richard Nelson for his important comments.

Determination to "carry on" is vital for writers, and I don't know how I would have finished this book without the enthusiasm and constant encouragement of Charles "Bucky" Clarkson. Ambassador Larry Taylor and George de Lama were also very helpful. My "Focus Buddy"—he knows who he is—also stepped in at crucial moments. Nathan Rabb gave me help with Edgar's correspondence with Ike, Peggy Ellis with stories about the Frieder brothers, and Bert O'Neil, for his generosity and reintroduction to McKeogh's memoirs. Thank you, Jed Lyons, for that introduction. I am also deeply appreciative of Col. Len Fullenkamp, Sam Holt, and Ambassador Gil Robinson for his memorable book *Why I Like Ike*. My gratitude goes to the Westtown School, especially Kevin Gallagher and Mary Brooks, who helped me with both the photograph of Granddad and me and our attempt to find Ike Green, who regrettably has died. And, I must thank the Dorchester Hotel in London, especially Bjørn Rydder, who helped me connect with the Eisenhower-related history there and the suite where Ike spent part of the war; just as I am grateful to Col. Jeremy Green, regimental secretary of the Royal Military Police, for his tour of Southwick House—the scene of the D-day decision—and for his history of the place.

Dr. Roald Sagdeev offered important feedback on the Soviet sections of the book and, along with Dr. Drew Baden, on the role of science. Dr. Paul Berkman's work, and his commitment to scientific diplomacy, made a vital contribution to my perspective on the IGY, including Sputnik and Antarctica.

Serendipity also plays a role in any book's fresh new takes. My gratitude goes to the Honorable Andrew Young, Nick Thomas, Renee Goldenberg, Melvin Bucholtz, and others who came unexpectedly into my life. I have Bill Milliken to thank for that wonderful introduction to Melvin Buchholtz; and Jesse Diner and Adele Stone for introducing me to Renee Goldenberg.

Ideas also came from unexpected places, and in this I would like to acknowledge Sam Sabin and John Popham, and other people on trains and planes who offered thoughts about the 1940s and 1950s in the context of today's problems.

And last, none of this would have happened without the support of Gettysburg College and its Eisenhower Institute. Special thanks go to President Robert Iuliano, Provost Chris Zappe, Dr. Rob Bohrer, Kevin Lavery, Darby Nesbit, and Patrick Cochran. But I want to add a special note of thanks to Lauren Cole for her indispensable help in pulling this together. She was amazing. Thanks, too, to Carol Hegeman of the Eisenhower Society.

To the "thugs"—as my father used to call my siblings and me—I give you a loving nod. You will remember much of what is contained in this book. Thanks for your never-ending encouragement and support.

In closing, I would like to note that I developed a deep appreciation for the books written by Ike's late associates. All were insightful and honest, and unafraid to express, candidly, their experiences. In memory of them, I would like to single out Mickey McKeogh for *Sgt. Mickey and General Ike,* for his wonderful observations of Eisenhower during the war; and Bill Ewald for *Eisenhower the President: The Crucial Days: 1951–1960* and his colorful recounting of those times, also for his revealing and disturbing account of the Church Committee hearings—specifically in relation to the Eisenhower years and the dubious assumptions that body embraced. I would also mention Arthur Larson's *The President That No One Knew,* for its fascinating account of the misplaced mythology that arose about Eisenhower and Vietnam, especially the popular misquote on Ike's advice to Lyndon Johnson to use nuclear weapons. These memoirists' own unmistakable voices can be heard as they recount the Dwight Eisenhower they knew, as well as the viewpoints of their associates at that time.

NOTES

INTRODUCTION

1 The Khrushchev visit helped avert a showdown over Berlin, and the Mateos visit led to a radar-tracking station in Mexico that was essential for NASA's Mercury program.

2 Dwight D. Eisenhower, *Crusade in Europe.* (Garden City, NY: Doubleday, 1948. Reprint, Baltimore, MD: Johns Hopkins University Press, 1998), p. 285.

3 It is noteworthy that after the failure, one of the first people Kennedy contacted for advice was Eisenhower.

4 Dwight D. Eisenhower, *At Ease: Stories I Tell to Friends* (Garden City, NY: Doubleday, 1967), pp. 185–86.

5 HEW later became the Department of Health and Human Services in 1979.

6 In trying to determine which case that might be, I presume it could be Gilligan v. Morgan 413 U.S. 1 (1973).

7 William Bragg Ewald, Jr., *Eisenhower the President* (Englewood Cliffs, NJ: Prentice-Hall, Inc., 1981), pp. 42–43.

8 Ibid., p. 7.

9 Ibid., p. 219.

1. ACCOUNTABILITY WITHOUT CAVEATS

1 Harry Butcher, *My Three Years with Eisenhower* (New York: Simon & Schuster, 1946), p. 610.

2 Ibid., p. 6.

3 Such accountability also preserved the larger objective—as he could then be fired without undermining the authority (in this case) of President Franklin Roosevelt and British prime minister Winston Churchill.

4 Robert H. Ferrell, ed., *The Eisenhower Diaries* (New York: W. W. Norton, 1981), November 28, 1959, entry, p. 369.

5 Marshall, "Ike the Warrior," *Eisenhower: An American Hero, the Historical Record of His Life,* edited by the editors of *American Heritage* magazine (New York: American Heritage Publishing, 1969), p. 73.
6 Ibid., p. 74.
7 Ibid.
8 Eisenhower, *Crusade in Europe*, p. 247.
9 Marshall, "Ike the Warrior," p. 73.; John S. D. Eisenhower, *Allies: Pearl Harbor to D-day* (Cambridge, MA: Da Capo Press, 2000), p. 448.
10 Eisenhower, *Crusade in Europe*, p. 245.
11 Ibid., p. 246.
12 Ibid.
13 Ibid.
14 Dwight D. Eisenhower to Trafford Leigh-Mallory, May 30, 1944 in *The Papers of Dwight David Eisenhower, vol. 3, The War Years*, edited by Alfred D. Chandler Jr. (Baltimore: Johns Hopkins University Press: 1970), pp. 1894–95.
15 Dwight D. Eisenhower to Bernard Law Montgomery, Omar Nelson Bradley, Bertram Home Ramsey, and Trafford Leigh-Mallory, May 26, 1994. Ibid., pp. 1890–91.
16 In *Ike: An American Hero* (New York: HarperCollins, 2007), p. 31, Michael Korda notes that two out of three soldiers who landed on D-day were British or Canadian. After the assault, when the cross-Channel transportation lines were open, those numbers became increasingly American.
17 Multiple personal interviews 2015-2019, with Gen. Richard Trefry; discussion with British historian James Holland, June 5, 2019.
18 Mickey McKeogh and Richard Lockridge, *Sgt. Mickey and General Ike* (New York: G. P. Putnam's Sons, 1946) p. 114.
19 Ibid., p. 116.
20 "D-Day Vet: We Made a Difference," *Baltimore Sun*, June 6, 2013—from a 1999 *Sun* article.
21 Butcher, *My Three Years with Eisenhower*, p. 558.
22 McKeogh and Lockridge, *Sgt. Mickey and General Ike,* pp. 116–117.
23 Marshall, "Ike: The Warrior," p. 74.
24 Ibid.
25 Gilbert Robinson, *Why I Like Ike* (New York: International Publishers, 2012), p. 121.
26 John R. "Tex" McCrary, "Personal Perspective: Powell? It Was Hard Persuading Ike to Run," *Los Angeles Times*, October 15, 1995.

2. INNER STRUGGLES

1 George W. S. Trow, *My Pilgrim's Progress: Media Studies 1950–1998* (New York: Pantheon, 1999), p. 152.
2 Eisenhower, *At Ease,* p. 181. Susan Eisenhower, *Mrs. Ike: Memories*

and Reflections on the Life of Mamie Eisenhower (New York: Farrar, Straus & Giroux, 1996), p. 309.
3 Ibid.
4 Ibid., p. 201.
5 David Eisenhower, *Going Home to Glory* (New York: Simon & Schuster, 2010), p. 141.
6 Michael Murray, *Jacques Barzun: Portrait of a Mind* (Savannah, GA: Frederic C. Beil, 2001), p. 162.
7 Edgar was at first known as "Big Ike" but later the name caught on and was solely used by Dwight. It is amusing that Ida Eisenhower, Dwight's mother, disliked the nickname "Ike." Once, after Mamie had written her to tell her mother-in-law about a road trip they had taken, Ida wrote back: "I am very glad you are having a fine motor trip, but who is this Ike you are traveling with?"
8 Edgar Eisenhower, "Growing Up," *Eisenhower: An American Hero,* p. 36.
9 Dwight Eisenhower to Edgar Eisenhower, June 30, 1953, in *The Papers of Dwight David Eisenhower,* vol. 15, *The Presidency: The Middle Way,* edited by Louis Galambos and Daun van Ee, p. 1349.
10 There were originally seven Eisenhower boys. Paul, born in 1894—four years after Ike—died before his first birthday.
11 McKeogh and Lockridge, *Sgt. Mickey and General Ike,* p. 43.
12 Ibid., p. 35.
13 Robinson, *Why I Like Ike,* p. 80.
14 Eisenhower, *At Ease,* p. 52.
15 Ibid.

3. BEYOND ETHNIC KINSHIP

1 Eisenhower ancestry, Eisenhower Presidential Library, July 25, 2019.
2 Susan Eisenhower, *Mrs. Ike,* p. 102.
3 Robinson, *Why I Like Ike,* p. 61. Jodl was head of the German High Command.
4 John S. D. Eisenhower, *The Bitter Woods* (New York: G. P. Putnam's Sons, 1969), p. 237.
5 Ibid., p. 238.
6 McKeogh and Lockridge, *Sgt. Mickey and General Ike,* p. 159.
7 Ibid., p. 164.
8 Korda, *Ike: An American Hero,* p. 29.
9 Eisenhower, *Crusade in Europe,* p. 407.
10 Ibid., p. 409.
11 McKeogh and Lockridge, *Sgt. Mickey and General Ike,* pp. 164–65.
12 Dwight D. Eisenhower to George C. Marshall, April 15, 1945, in *The Papers of Dwight David Eisenhower,* vol. 4, *The War Years,* edited by Alfred D. Chandler Jr., p. 2616. (Emphasis in original.)
13 "Inspection of the German Concentration Camp for Political Prisoners Located at Buchenwald on the North Edge of Weimar," preliminary

report by Brig. Gen. Eric F. Wood, April 16, 1945, Army War College, Carlisle, PA.

14 Dwight D. Eisenhower to George C. Marshall, April 19, 1945. *The Papers of Dwight David Eisenhower,* vol. 4, *The War Years,* p. 2623.

15 Ibid.

16 Eisenhower, *Crusade in Europe*, p. 409.

17 Dwight D. Eisenhower to George S. Patton Jr., April 18, 1945 on the discovery of Buchenwald, April 18, 1945, see *The Papers of Dwight David Eisenhower, vol. 4, The War Years,* p. 2621.

18 Walter Bedell Smith, "The Only Way It Could End" and "Epilogue to Victory," *Eisenhower's Six Great Decisions,* (London: Longman's 1956), pp. 205–11.

19 David Eisenhower, *Eisenhower at War: 1943–1945* (New York: Vintage, 1987), p. 802.

20 Dwight D. Eisenhower telegram to the Combined Chiefs of Staff, May 7, 1945. *The Papers of Dwight David Eisenhower,* vol. 4, *The War Years,* p. 2696.

21 Alexander Frieder to General Eisenhower regarding victory in Europe and the decision to allow inspections of the concentration camps, June 1, 1945. Dwight D. Eisenhower's Pre-Presidential Papers, Principal File, Box 43, Frieder Alexander. Eisenhower Presidential Library, Abilene, Kansas. Permission courtesy of Frieder Films.

22 Ibid.

23 War Department, Transcript of the press conference of General of the Army Dwight D. Eisenhower in the auditorium of the Pentagon, Monday, June 18, 1945. Eisenhower Presidential Library, Abilene, Kansas.

24 Henry B. Kraft, undated article, *Stars and Stripes*; personal interview with Claus Gruendl, September 16, 2018.

25 Stephen E. Ambrose, *The Victors: Eisenhower and His Boys: The Men of World War II* (New York: Simon & Schuster, 1999), p. 351.

4. "BORN TO COMMAND"

1 Brian Burnes, *The Ike Files* (Kansas City, MO: Kansas City Star Co., 2008), p. 14.

2 Ibid., p. 18.

3 Fred I. Greenstein, *The Art of Leadership* (Gettysburg, PA: Gettysburg College, 1990), pp. 42–43.

4 Burnes, *The Ike Files,* p. 14.

5 Eisenhower, *At Ease*, p. 4.

6 Carlo D'Este, *Eisenhower: A Soldier's Life* (New York: Holt, 2003), p. 151.

7 Ibid., p. 152.

8 Carrier pigeons were used extensively during the First and Second World Wars. Bombers often took the birds with them and released them if they crashed and could not radio back their location. Winkie,

a famous WWII pigeon, was awarded the Dickin Medal, the British equivalent of the Victoria Cross for animals. The hen received this award for a heroic flight the bird took, flying 120 miles from the North Sea to Dundee, that saved the lives of a bomber crew, that had crashed in the North Sea in 1942. www.bbc.com/news/uk-scotland-tayside-central-17138990.

9 Robinson, *Why I Like Ike*, pp. 28–29.

10 Captain Edward Beach in *A Pictorial Biography*, ed. William F. Longgood (New York: Time-Life Books, 1969), 138.

11 The only exception Eisenhower made to his insistence on wearing a hat rather than a helmet was when the theater commander in charge insisted on it, given their location.

12 McKeogh and Lockridge, *Sgt. Mickey and General Ike*. p. 122. McKeogh also wrote that Eisenhower preferred tents to villas or any other more spacious accommodations.

13 Ibid., p. 60.

14 Ibid., p. 51.

15 Korda, *Ike: An American Hero*, p. 497.

16 The editors of American Heritage Magazine and United Press International, *Eisenhower, American Hero* (New York: American Heritage, 1969), p. 75.

17 See transcript of a fascinating interview of Ike by journalist David Schoenbrun on Tuesday, August 25, 1964, at the Gettysburg farm. Obtainable at the Eisenhower Library and at www.eisenhower.archives.gov.

18 Jean E. Smith, *The Liberation of Paris: How Eisenhower, de Gaulle, and von Choltitz Saved the City of Light* (New York: Simon & Schuster, 2019), p. 205.

19 Dwight D. Eisenhower to Winston S. Churchill, August 11, 1944, *The Papers of Dwight David Eisenhower, vol. 4, The War Years*, p. 2065.

20 Ferrell, *The Eisenhower Diaries*, p. 52.

21 Ibid.

22 Ibid., p. 54.

23 John S. D. Eisenhower, *Allies*, pp. 140–141.

24 Ferrell, *The Eisenhower Diaries*, entry on Admiral King, pp. 50–51.

25 George Allen, *Presidents Who Have Known Me* (New York: Simon & Schuster, 1950), p. 111.

26 Ewald, *Eisenhower the President,* p. 251.

27 Greenstein, *The Art of Leadership,* p. 11.

28 Fred I. Greenstein, *The Hidden-Hand Presidency: Eisenhower as Leader* (New York: Basic Books, 1982), p. 37.

29 John S. D. Eisenhower, *Allies*, p. 461.

30 Dwight D. Eisenhower, "What Is Leadership?" *Reader's Digest*, June 1965, pp. 49–54.

31 Eisenhower, *Crusade in Europe*, pp. 179–180.
32 Stephen E. Ambrose, *Soldier and President* (New York: Simon & Schuster, 1960), p. 55.
33 Butcher, *My Three Years with Eisenhower*, p. 537.
34 Ewald, *Eisenhower the President*, p. 252.
35 Ibid.
36 Dwight D. Eisenhower to Mamie Eisenhower, February 15, 1943, *Letters to Mamie*, edited by John S. D. Eisenhower (New York: Doubleday, 1978), p. 95.
37 Eisenhower, *At Ease,* p. 26.

5. HUMAN PROBLEMS

1 This letter was sent to me by the psychology department at West Point.
2 For a fascinating account of this issue, see R. Alton Lee, "The Army 'Mutiny' of 1946," *Journal of American History* 53, no. 3 (December 1966): 555–571; Ferrell, *The Eisenhower Diaries,* introduction to "Chief of Staff," p. 134.
3 Ferrell, *The Eisenhower Diaries,* p. 136.
4 See Susan Eisenhower, *Mrs. Ike,* p. 243.
5 Stephen Ambrose, *Eisenhower: Soldier, General of the Army, President-Elect, 1890–1952* (New York: Simon & Schuster, 1983), p. 424.
6 Report, Earl G. Harrison, "Mission to Europe to inquire into the condition and needs of those among the displaced persons in the liberated countries of Western Europe and in SHAEF area of Germany—with particular reference to the Jewish refugees—who may possibly be stateless or non-repatriable," August 1945, Dwight D. Eisenhower's Pre-Presidential Papers, Box 116, Truman, Harry S. (4).
7 Dwight D. Eisenhower to Harry S. Truman, September 14, 1945, *The Papers of Dwight David Eisenhower, vol. 4, The War Years,* p. 469. It should also be noted that after Simon Rifkind returned to the United States in April 1946, he paid tribute to the U.S. Army for its "humanitarian efforts."
8 General Eisenhower to President Truman, telegram concerning the Harrison report and Jewish displaced persons, September 14, 1945. Dwight D. Eisenhower's Pre-Presidential Papers, Principal File, Box 116, Truman Harry S. (4).
9 From an email to the author, June 27, 2017.
10 Dwight Eisenhower to Alexander Wiley, November 4, 1945, *The Papers of Dwight David Eisenhower, vol. 6, Occupation 1945*, edited by Alfred D. Chandler Jr. and Louis Galambos, p. 504.
11 Ibid.
12 Letter from Dwight D. Eisenhower to senior commanders, quoted in *Mistreatment of Prisoners of War.* See Arthur C. Banks Jr.,"International Law Governing Prisoners of War during the Second World

War," Ph.D. diss. (Baltimore, MD: Johns Hopkins University, 1955).

13 Letter, Dr. Israel Goldstein to President Eisenhower in response, April 29, 1955. Dwight D. Eisenhower's Papers as President, Personal Files, Box 921, PPF 53-B-3 Jewish 1955. Presidential Library, Abilene, Kansas.

14 Eisenhower, *At Ease,* p. 317.

15 Lee, "The Army 'Mutiny' of 1946," p. 568.

16 I knew my grandfather's secretary, Sue Serafian Jehl, who took his dictation on this speech. Written by Ike himself, it remains one of the greatest speeches of his career.

17 Ferrell, *The Eisenhower Diaries,* p. 138.

18 Ibid., p. 136.

19 Ibid., p. 138.

20 Ibid., p. 137.

21 Eisenhower, *At Ease,* p. 334.

6. "I DON'T THINK HE HAS ANY POLITICS"

1 Sherman Adams, *Firsthand Report: The Story of the Eisenhower Administration* (New York: Harper & Brothers, 1961), p. 13.

2 Butcher, *My Three Years with Eisenhower*, p. 434.

3 Ferrell, *The Eisenhower Diaries, p.* 168.

4 Ibid., p. 165.

5 Dwight D. Eisenhower to Walter Bedell Smith, April 12, 1948 in *The Papers of Dwight David Eisenhower,* vol. 10, *Columbia*, p. 41.

6 Herbert S. Parmet, *Eisenhower and the American Crusades* (New York: Macmillan, 1972), p. 17.

7 And during the 1948 Republican convention itself, Ike got nearly five thousand letters.

8 Parmet, *Eisenhower and the American Crusades,* pp. 17–18.

9 Ibid., p. 19.

10 Ferrell, *The Eisenhower Diaries*, p. 147.

11 When asked to run for president, Civil War general William Tecumseh Sherman famously replied: "If nominated I will not run, if elected I will not serve."

12 Ferrell, *The Eisenhower Diaries,* p. 161.

13 Ibid.

14 Herbert Brownell, *Advising Ike*, (Lawrence: University of Kansas Press, 1993) p. 300.

15 Dwight D. Eisenhower to Senator Henry Cabot Lodge, February 23, 1949 in *The Papers of Dwight David Eisenhower,* vol. 10, *Columbia*, p. 502.

16 Ginzberg quoted in Robinson, *Why I Like Ike,* pp. 72–73.

17 North Atlantic Treaty Organization Online, *NATO Leaders: Dwight D. Eisenhower*, November 23, 2016. www.nato.int/cps/en/natohq/declassified_137961.htm.

18 Susan Eisenhower, *Mrs. Ike*, p. 259.

19 Brownell, *Advising Ike,* pp. 95, 300.
20 For details of the campaign see Stanley Rumbough Jr., *Citizens for Eisenhower: The 1952 Presidential Campaign: Lessons for the Future?* (New York: International Publishers, 2013).
21 Parmet, *Eisenhower and the American Crusades,* p. 44.
22 Korda, *Ike: An American Hero,* p. 641.
23 Ibid.
24 What a risk! By relinquishing his commission, Eisenhower lost all the perks that went with being a five-star general, along with his staff and his valet, Sgt. John Moaney. When Ike advised Moaney that he might want to start looking for a job, in case he failed to get the nomination or later the election, Sergeant Moaney replied that he thought they would both be able to find a job later if they had to.
25 Private collection.
26 Heather Cox Richardson, *To Make Men Free: A History of the Republican Party* (New York: Basic Books, 2014), p. 232.
27 Korda, *Ike: An American Hero,* p. 657.
28 Greenstein, *The Art of Leadership,* p. 12.
29 Adams, *Firsthand Report,* p. 9.
30 Ibid., p. 16. After the election Eisenhower offered Warren the opportunity to become solicitor general.
31 Ibid., p. 128.
32 Eisenhower, *At Ease: Stories I Tell to Friends,* p. 349.

7. SHAPING THE MIDDLE WAY

1 Eisenhower, "American Bar Association Labor Day Address," September 5, 1949 (St. Louis, Missouri. Eisenhower Speech Series, Box 3, Eisenhower Library, Abilene, Kansas).
2 Dwight D. Eisenhower to Edgar N. Eisenhower, May 5, 1953, in *The Papers of Dwight David Eisenhower, vol. 14, The Presidency: The Middle Way,* p. 211.
3 Robert R. Bowie and Richard H. Immerman, *Waging Peace: How Eisenhower Shaped an Enduring Cold War Strategy* (New York: Oxford University Press, 1998), p. 98.
4 Ferrell, *The Eisenhower Diaries,* p. 235.
5 Ibid.
6 Ibid., p. 236.
7 Ibid., p. 240.
8 Ibid., p. 227.
9 Greenstein, *The Hidden-Hand Presidency,* p. 112.
10 George Colburn interviews (Washington, DC: C-SPAN Video Library, May 15, 1991).
11 Years later my brother, David, sat next to Senator Barry Goldwater of Arizona at a dinner. Goldwater mentioned that Ike's nephew bore his name, adding merrily: "Your grandfather would roll over in his grave."

12 Edgar N. Eisenhower to Dwight D. Eisenhower, April 1, 1953 *The Papers of Dwight David Eisenhower,* vol. 14, *The Presidency: The Middle Way,* p. 142.
13 Adams, *Firsthand Report*, p. 374.
14 Richardson, *To Make Men Free,* p. 246.
15 Dwight D. Eisenhower to Edgar N. Eisenhower, November 30, 1957, from Gettysburg, PA. Nate Sanders Collection. Eisenhower recounts this conversation in a letter to Ed, 1957.
16 Dwight D. Eisenhower to Edgar N. Eisenhower, May 2, 1956, *The Papers of Dwight David Eisenhower,* vol. 17, *The Presidency: The Middle Way,* edited by Louis Galambos and Daun van Ee, p. 2156.
17 Chester Patch, *Dwight D. Eisenhower: Domestic Affairs (*Charlottesville: Miller Center, University of Virginia, 1986), pp. 2–7.
18 Andrew Glass, "Eisenhower Approves Expanded Social Security Coverage," *Politico*, September 1, 2018.
19 Eisenhower, *Waging Peace,* p. 295; www.ssa.gov/history/1950.html
20 Glass, "Eisenhower Approves Expanded Social Security Coverage."
21 Dwight D. Eisenhower to Edgar N. Eisenhower, November 8, 1954 in *The Papers of Dwight David Eisenhower,* vol. 15, *The Presidency: The Middle Way*. p. 1386.
22 Slater, *The Ike I Knew* (Ellis D. Slater Trust, 1980), p. 150.
23 Dwight D. Eisenhower to Edgar N. Eisenhower, November 8, 1954 in *The Papers of Dwight D. Eisenhower,* vol. 15, *The Presidency: The Middle Way,* p. 1387.
24 Richardson, *To Make Men Free*, p. xvii.
25 Ibid., pp. xvii-xviii.
26 Report from 1st Lt. E. R. Jackson to Col. L. B. Moody, "Report on First Transcontinental Motor Convoy, October 31, 1919 [U.S. Army, Transport Corps] (Eisenhower Library, Abilene, Kansas).
27 Robert H. Ferrell, *The Diary of James C. Hagerty: Eisenhower at Mid-Course 1954-1955*. (Bloomington: Indiana University Press 1983), p. 162.
28 Dwight D. Eisenhower to Edgar N. Eisenhower, June 27, 1957 in *The Papers of Dwight David Eisenhower,* Louis Galambos and Daun Van Ee, eds. vol. 18 *The Presidency: Keeping the Peace*, p. 282.
29 Richardson, *To Make Men Free*, p. 224.
30 Ibid., p. 225.
31 Robert W. Griffith, *Ike's Letters to a Friend 1941-1958*, (Lawrence: University Press of Kansas, 1984), p. 8.
32 While the effective tax rate was lower for many individuals, such high tax brackets encouraged philanthropic giving.
33 Dwight D. Eisenhower to Edgar N. Eisenhower, May 2, 1956 in *The Papers of Dwight David Eisenhower,* vol. 17, *The Presidency: The Middle Way,* p. 2157.
34 "Eisenhower . . . was no ideologist," Bill Ewald once wrote. "Again and again—before, during, and after his presidency—he would denounce

all labels, especially 'liberal' and 'conservative.' . . . On one issue, he claimed, 'I find myself siding with the liberals, on another issue with the conservatives. I think all you can do is try to look at the facts [and] use the sense the good Lord gave you.'" *Eisenhower the President: Crucial Days: 1951–1960*, p. 44.

35 Adams, *Firsthand Report*, p. 21.
36 Ibid., pp. 166–167.
37 Ibid., pp. 164–166.
38 Emphasis added.
39 Dwight D. Eisenhower to Edgar N. Eisenhower, November 8, 1954 in *The Papers of Dwight David Eisenhower, vol. 15, The Presidency: The Middle Way*, p. 1387–88.
40 Ferrell, *The Eisenhower Diaries*, p. 243.
41 Dwight D. Eisenhower, *Mandate for Change* (Garden City, New York: Doubleday, 1963), p. 11.

8. IKE'S RULES FOR GOOD GOVERNANCE

1 Milton S. Eisenhower, *The President Is Calling* (Garden City, New York: Doubleday, 1974), p. 340.
2 Greenstein, *The Art of Leadership*, p. 8.
3 Ibid., p. 178.
4 Brownell, *Advising Ike*, Foreword by John Chancellor, p. xiv.
5 Ibid., p. 178; Ferrell, *The Eisenhower Diaries*, p. 342.
6 Dwight D. Eisenhower to Edgar N. Eisenhower, March 23, 1956 in *The Papers of Dwight David Eisenhower: vol. 16, The Presidency: The Middle Way*, p. 2093.
7 This understanding was clearly seen in his approach to the renegade Senator McCarthy during his Communist "witch hunt."
8 Brownell, *Advising Ike*, p. 133.
9 Ibid.
10 Ibid., p. 296.
11 Arthur Larson, *Eisenhower: The President No One Knew* (New York: Scribner's, 1968). p. 19.
12 Adams, *Firsthand Report*, p. 333.
13 Even though Eisenhower appointed more women to administration posts than any president before him, I use the word "men" in the biblical sense—as in "Man"—simply for ease of reading.
14 Ewald, *Eisenhower the President*, pp. 66–67.
15 Adams, *Firsthand Report*, p. 164.
16 Brownell, *Advising Ike*, p. 296.
17 David Nichols, *A Matter of Justice* (New York: Simon & Schuster, 2008), p. 14.
18 Bowie and Immerman, *Waging Peace: How Eisenhower Shaped an Enduring Cold War Strategy*, Foreword by General Andrew J. Goodpaster, p. vi.

19 C. Richard Nelson, *The Life and Work of General Andrew J. Goodpaster* (Lanham, MD: Rowman & Littlefield, 2016), p. 119.
20 David Eisenhower, *Going Home to Glory*, p. 40.
21 Eisenhower wanted to be sure that what was said as part of a brainstorming session was not accidentally mistaken for a decision.
22 Adams, *Firsthand Report*, p. 8; see also Bowie and Immerman, *Waging Peace,* pp. 85–95.
23 See Ewald, *Eisenhower the President,* pp. 265–275, for a fascinating account of this, as well as the CIA's probable sandbagging of the president over its effort to assassinate Castro, and its role in the Congo crisis.
24 Greenstein, *The Hidden-Hand Presidency*, p. 29.
25 Ewald, *Eisenhower the President,* p. 71.
26 Slater, *The Ike I Knew*, p. 68.
27 Ewald, *Eisenhower the President*, p. 185.
28 Robert Ferrell, ed., *The Diaries of James C. Hagerty* (Bloomington: Indiana University Press, 1983), p. 177; Ewald, *Eisenhower the President,* p. 185.
29 Ewald, *Eisenhower the President*, p. 30: "In the analysis of the *Congressional Quarterly* cataloging the percentage of presidential victories on congressional votes where the President took a clear-cut stand, Eisenhower comes out with a record of 89 percent in 1953 and 82.8 percent in 1954." Ewald also notes the years 1955, 1956, 1957, and 1958 as, respectively, 75, 70, 68, and 76 percent. These figures were achieved during six years when control of Congress was held by the Democratic Party.
30 Larson, *Eisenhower: The President Nobody Knew*, p. 33.
31 When I was about six, I was questioned closely about why I had named my pet rabbit Humphrey. I guess I had just heard the secretary's name mentioned many times at the dinner table in positive terms. Anyway, I just thought it was a great name for a pet rabbit.
32 Brownell, *Advising Ike,* p. 302.
33 Ibid., pp. 290–291.
34 Milton S. Eisenhower, *The President Is Calling*, p. 273.
35 Brett Baier and Catherine Whitney, *Three Days in January: Dwight Eisenhower's Final Mission* (New York: William Morrow, 2017), p. 152.
36 Ferrell, *The Diaries of James C. Hagerty*, p. 167.
37 Ibid., p. 200.
38 Dwight D. Eisenhower to Paul Hoy Helms, March 9, 1954, in *Papers of Dwight David Eisenhower,* vol. 15, *The Presidency: The Middle Way.* pp. 938–939.
39 Larson, *Eisenhower: The President Nobody Knew*, p. 5.
40 Milton S. Eisenhower, *The President Is Calling,* p. 309.
41 Adams, *Firsthand Report*, p. 61.
42 Eisenhower, *At Ease,* pp. 167–168.

9. THE INTERCONNECTIONS BETWEEN WAR AND PEACE

1 Ferrell, *Eisenhower Diaries, p.* 176; John S. Rigden, *Rabi: Scientist and Citizen,* (Cambridge, MA: Harvard University Press, 1987), p. 238.
2 Parmet, *Eisenhower and the American Crusades,* p. 155.
3 Ibid., 156; Brownell, *Advising Ike,* pp. 138–139.
4 I have read varying accounts as to whether or not the president threatened the use of nuclear weapons. Some of his associates differ on the question.
5 William Hitchcock, *The Age of Eisenhower* (New York: Simon & Schuster, 2018), pp. 104–105.
6 Rigden, *Rabi: Scientist and Citizen,* p. 193.
7 Ibid.
8 Once, during my many years of travel to the USSR and Russia, I was privileged to spend a good deal of time with the Soviet physicist Dr. Andrei Sakharov, human rights activist and "father of the Soviet hydrogen bomb." Given the U.S. lead on the development of this superweapon, I asked him what was the breakthrough for him in the development of the Soviet H-bomb? He replied, "That it could be done."
9 Rigden, *Rabi: Scientist and Citizen,* p. 201.
10 Ibid., p. 194.
11 Atoms for Peace address before the General Assembly of the United Nations on peaceful uses of atomic energy. New York City, December 8, 1953.
12 The Soviet leader's real name was Iosif Vissarionovich Dzhugashvili. He assumed the name Joseph Stalin. The word "stalin" means "steel" in Russian.
13 Eisenhower, Chance for Peace speech, Miller Center, University of Virginia. April 16, 1953. www.millercenter.org/thepresidency/presidentialspeeches/april-16-1952-chance-peace
14 J. E. Smith, *Eisenhower in War and Peace,* (New York: Random House, 2013), p. 573.
15 Bowie and Immerman, *Waging Peace,* Foreword by General Andrew J. Goodpaster, p. v.
16 Nelson, *The Life and Work of Andrew J. Goodpaster,* p. 107.
17 Ibid., p. 108.
18 Ibid., p. 110; Goodpaster loved to tell this story. I am sure I heard him tell it at least a dozen times after Eisenhower's death and when the former president was still being criticized by historians for being intellectually second-rate.
19 Samuel P. Huntington, "The West: Unique, not Universal," *Foreign Affairs* (November/December 1996).
20 Nelson, *The Life and Work of Andrew J. Goodpaster,* pp. 107–108.
21 Ibid., p. 110.
22 Ibid., p. 118.
23 Ibid., pp. 110–112.

24 Evan Thomas, *Ike's Bluff: President Eisenhower's Secret Battle to Save the World* (New York: Back Bay Books, 2013), pp. 204–205.
25 Brownell, *Advising Ike,* p. 138.
26 It is also noteworthy that most of the bombing's victims were women, children and the elderly because the able-bodied men were at the front.
27 Nelson, *The Life and Work of General Andrew J. Goodpaster,* p. 125.
28 Captain Edward Beach in *A Pictorial Biography: Ike,* ed. William F. Longgood (New York: Time-Life Books, 1969), p. 137–138.
29 Rigden, *Rabi: Scientist and Citizen,* p. 240.
30 Ibid., p. 244.
31 Ibid.

10. A STRATEGIST TAKES ON A DEMAGOGUE

1 H. W. Brands Jr., "The Ghost of Yalta," *Foreign Service Journal,* vol. 63, no.4 April 1986 p. 17–21.
2 Brownell, *Advising Ike,* p. 255.
3 Ferrell, *Eisenhower Diaries,* p. 234.
4 Dwight D. Eisenhower to Edgar N. Eisenhower, November 8, 1954, in *The Papers of Dwight David Eisenhower,* vol. 15, *The Presidency: The Middle Way,* p. 1387.
5 Baier and Whitney, *Three Days in January,* p. 145.
6 Dwight D. Eisenhower to Edgar N. Eisenhower, November 8, 1954, in *Papers of Dwight David Eisenhower,* vol. 15, *The Presidency: The Middle Way,* p. 1386.
7 Ewald, *Eisenhower the President,* p. 129.
8 Parmet, *Eisenhower and the American Crusades,* p. 125.
9 Brownell, *Advising Ike,* p. 251.
10 Parmet, *Eisenhower and the American Crusades,* p. 126.
11 Brownell, *Advising Ike,* p. 252.
12 Adams, *First Hand Report,* p. 31.
13 Eisenhower, *Mandate for Change,* p. 318.
It should be noted that this incident did not negatively affect Eisenhower's relationship with Marshall. Many times during the White House years Marshall came to dinner and they remained in contact.
14 Greenstein, *Hidden-Hand Presidency,* p. 56.
15 See Adams, *Firsthand Report,* p. 258.
16 Parmet, *American Crusades,* pp. 254–255.
17 Larson, *The President Nobody Knew,* p. 13.
18 Eisenhower, *Mandate for Change,* p. 321.
19 Ferrell, *Diaries of James Hagerty,* p. 26.
20 Ewald, *Eisenhower the President,* p. 131.
21 David Nichols, *Ike and McCarthy: Dwight Eisenhower's Secret Campaign against Joe McCarthy.* (New York: Simon & Schuster, 2017), p. 33.
22 Eisenhower at Dartmouth. (Dartmouth College Library Film Collection, 1953).

23 Slater, *The Ike I Knew,* p. 53.
24 Ferrell, *Hagerty Diaries,* p. 25. Hagerty's exact words as printed were: "All these people want is to have President get down in gutter with Joe."
25 Ewald, *Eisenhower the President,* pp. 125–126.
26 Ibid.
27 Said in a campaign speech, 1952.
28 The press conference was March 1, 1954. Ferrell, *The Diaries of James C. Hagerty*, p. 23.
29 Ibid., p. 211.
30 Nichols, *Ike and McCarthy*, p. 142.
31 Ewald, *Eisenhower the President*, p. 135.
32 Ferrell, *The Eisenhower Diaries*, p. 280.
33 Ewald, *Eisenhower the President*, p. 140.
34 Brownell, *Advising Ike*, pp. 258–260.
35 Ewald, *Eisenhower the President,* p. 137.
36 Ferrell, *The Hagerty Diaries*, p. 58.
37 Eisenhower, *Mandate for Change*, p. 321.
38 Charles Bohlen's Oral History, Association for Diplomatic Studies and Training (adst.org/orla-history/fascinating-figures/chip-bohlen-thestate-department-has-always-been-a-whipping-boy/).
39 Ferrell, *The Eisenhower Diaries*, p. 242.
40 Greenstein, *The Art of Leadership,* p. 9.

11. PRINCIPLES AND TENACITY IN TIMES OF CRISIS

1 Ewald, *Eisenhower the President,* p. 167.
2 Milton S. Eisenhower, *The President Is Calling,* p. 347.
3 Captain Edward Beach in *A Pictorial Biography: Ike.* pp. 140–42.
4 Emmet John Hughes, *The Ordeal of Power* (New York: Atheneum, 1964), p. 154.
5 Nelson, *Andrew J. Goodpaster*, p. 134.
6 James Newton, *Eisenhower: The White House Years,* (New York: Anchor, 2012). p. 223.
7 Parmet, *Eisenhower and the American Crusades*, p. 474.
8 Smith, *Eisenhower in War and Peace*, pp. 694–704.
9 Nelson, *Andrew J. Goodpaster*, p. 134.
10 David Nichols, *Eisenhower 1956: The President's Year of Crisis—Suez and the Brink of War*, (New York: Simon & Schuster, 2012), pp. 134, 152, 279.
11 Smith, *Eisenhower in War and Peace*, pp. 686–687.
12 Ibid., p. 192.
13 Ibid., p. 694.
14 Ibid.
15 Newton, *Eisenhower: The White House Years,* p. 225.
16 Smith, *Eisenhower in War and Peace*, p. 694.
17 Ibid., p. 695.
18 Ferrell, *The Eisenhower Diaries*, p. 330.

19 Newton, *Eisenhower: The White House Years,* p. 231.
20 Smith, *Eisenhower in War and Peace,* p. 697.
21 Parmet, *Eisenhower and the American Crusades,* p. 493.
22 Smith, *Eisenhower in War and Peace,* p. 698.
23 Nichols, *Eisenhower 1956,* pp. 246–247.
24 Nelson, *Eisenhower: The White House Years,* p. 135.
25 Nichols, *Eisenhower 1956,* p. 264; Smith, *Eisenhower in War and Peace,* p. 697.
26 Smith, *Eisenhower in War and Peace,* p. 699.
27 Nichols, *Eisenhower 1956,* p. 271.
28 Dwight D. Eisenhower to Edward Everett Hazlett Jr., November 2, 1956 in *The Papers of Dwight David Eisenhower,* vol. 17, *The Presidency: The Middle Way,* pp. 2355–2356.
29 Nelson, *Andrew J. Goodpaster,* p. 133.
30 Ibid., p. 140.
31 Adams, *Firsthand Report,* p. 88. In fact, the exact words were "To aid by every peaceful means, but only by peaceful means, the right to live in freedom."
32 Smith, *Eisenhower in War and Peace,* p. 701.
33 Newton, *Eisenhower: The White House Years,* p. 231.
34 Korda, *Ike: An American Hero,* p. 693.
35 Isaac Alteras, *Eisenhower and Israel: U.S. Israeli Relations 1953–1960* (Gainesville: University Press of Florida, 1993), pp. 317–318.

12. THE LONELINESS OF LEADERSHIP

1 Richard Cohen, "A Visit with the Real Dwight Eisenhower," *Washington Post,* April 9, 2012.
2 Ewald, *Eisenhower the President,* p. 94.
3 I wrote about Sergeant Moaney extensively in *Mrs. Ike.* He was an African American who Ike elevated during the war from doing heavy outside work to becoming part of his household staff. Moaney stayed with Ike until his death. He died not long after the boss passed away. Sergeant Moaney was the first African American to serve as a pallbearer in a presidential state funeral.
4 Bob Green, "The President and the Art of the Oil Painting," *Wall Street Journal,* April 23, 2018.
5 Adams, *Firsthand Report,* p. 73.
6 Ewald, *Eisenhower the President,* p. 318.
7 Address in Pittsburgh at a dinner sponsored by the Allegheny County Republican Executive Committee, November 4, 1960. Public Papers of the President: Dwight David Eisenhower, 1960–1961, Washington, DC: U.S. GPO, 1961, pp. 846–851.
8 Larson, *Eisenhower the President Nobody Knew,* p. 182.
9 Ewald, *Eisenhower the President,* p. 82.
10 Korda, *Ike: An American Hero,* p. 613.
11 Ewald, *Eisenhower the President,* p. 57.

12 Michael Beschloss, "The Gang that Always Liked Ike," *New York Times*, November 15, 2014.
13 The pallbearers at Ike's funeral were his wartime comrades.
14 Slater, *The Ike I Knew*, p. 87.
15 Ewald, *Eisenhower the President*, p. 262.
16 Eisenhower, *Mandate for Change*, p. 555.
17 Ewald, *Eisenhower the President*, p. 262.
18 Eisenhower, *Mandate for Change*, p. 556.
19 This expression "the gang" was used by the Eisenhowers and their friends since the prewar period. When the Eisenhowers lived in Washington, DC, in the 1920s they used it interchangeably with "Club Eisenhower"—and Mamie regarded it as part of her end of the partnership to keep after hours lively and fun.
20 Eisenhower, *Mandate for Change*, pp. 555–556.
21 A number of these organizations still play a crucial role in bringing the international community closer together: The Eisenhower Fellows in Philadelphia, PA; People to People International, Sister Cities, The Business Council for International Understanding, The Center for the Study of the Presidency and Congress, to name a few. The Eisenhower Institute and the Eisenhower Foundation also continue to work on education and issues related to his legacy.
22 Slater, *The Ike I Knew*, p. 148.
23 Cliff Roberts, *The Story of Augusta National Golf Club*, (Garden City, NY: Doubleday & Company, 1976), p. 190.
24 Larson, *Eisenhower: The President Nobody Knew*, pp. 177–178.
25 Roberts, *The Story of Augusta National Golf Club*, pp. 178–179.
26 I am not sure whether or not it is an urban legend, and I have tried to find the answer, but it has been mentioned to me that there are no billboards on the Interstate Highway System. It was suggested to me by one associate that Ike may have had something to do with it.
27 Dwight D. Eisenhower to Edgar N. Eisenhower, December 14, 1956, in *The Papers of Dwight David Eisenhower*, vol. 17, *The Presidency: The Middle Way*, pp. 2443–44.
28 Eisenhower, *At Ease*, p. 254.
29 Bob Green, "The President and the Art of Oil Painting," *Wall Street Journal*, April 23, 2018.

13. ESTABLISHING A BEACHHEAD

1 Dwight Eisenhower in conversation with Civil War historian Bruce Catton in David Eisenhower, *Going Home to Glory*, p. 55.
2 It is noteworthy that this speech was delivered on the precise date that Eisenhower suffered his heart attack two years before. September 24 was also the date of his late son's birth—an emotional day in the lives of my grandparents.
3 Burnes, *The Ike Files*, p. 138.
4 Nichols, *A Matter of Justice*, p. 9.

5 Ibid.
6 Ibid.
7 It should be noted that the word "Negro" was used even in the black community. It was not until the 1970s and 1980s that the term "black" became common usage.
8 Nichols, *A Matter of Justice*, p. 10.
9 Ibid., p. 9.
10 Ibid., p. 10.
11 Ibid., p. 6.
12 Hitchcock, *The Age of Eisenhower*, p. 215; Nichols, *A Matter of Justice*, p. 19.
13 Nichols, *A Matter of Justice*, p. 22.
14 Emphasis added.
15 Public Papers of the President: Dwight David Eisenhower, 1953 (Washington, DC: GPO, 1960), p. 30.
16 Eisenhower, *Waging Peace*, p. 148.
17 Ferrell, *The Eisenhower Diaries*, p. 245.
18 Eisenhower, *Waging Peace*, p. 148.
19 Brownell, *Advising Ike*, pp. 186–187.
20 Nichols, *A Matter of Justice*, p. 111.
21 Eisenhower, *Waging Peace*, p. 150.
22 David Eisenhower, *Going Home to Glory*, p. 104.
23 Ibid.
24 Ibid., p. 105.
25 Ewald, *Eisenhower the President*, pp. 82–83.
26 Eisenhower, *Waging Peace*, p. 150.
27 Ibid.
28 Ibid., p. 151.
29 Ibid., p. 152.
30 Ibid.
31 Ibid.
32 Ibid.
33 Ibid., p. 154.
34 Ibid., p. 156.
35 Ibid. (Emphasis in the original was Eisenhower's.)
36 Ibid., p. 157.
37 Brownell, *Advising Ike*, p. 203.
38 Eisenhower, *Waging Peace*, p. 167.
39 Nichols, *A Matter of Justice*, p. 173.
40 Eisenhower, *Waging Peace*, p. 166.
41 DDE's address to the American people, September 24, 1957, on Little Rock, Arkansas. www.historymatters.gmu.edu/d/6335.
42 Ibid.
43 Burnes, *The Ike Files*, pp. 152–153.
44 David Eisenhower, *Going Home to Glory*, p. 109.
45 William T. Coleman, with Donald T. Bliss, *Counsel for the Situation:*

Shaping the Law to Realize America's Promise (Washington, DC: Brookings Institution, 2010), p. 163.
46 Hitchcock, *Age of Eisenhower*, p. 371.
47 Eisenhower, *Waging Peace*, p. 173.
48 Nichols, *A Matter of Justice*, p. 206.
49 Coleman, *Counsel for the Situation,* p. 164.
50 Brownell, *Advising Ike*, p. 200.
51 Eisenhower, *Waging Peace*, p. 172.
52 David Eisenhower, *Going Home to Glory*, p. 109.
53 Ibid., p. 110.
54 Ibid., p. 110–111.
55 Nichols, *A Matter of American Justice,* p. 281.
56 Eisenhower, *Waging Peace,* p. 154.
57 This evaluation was confirmed to me by the civil rights activist and former mayor of Atlanta and UN ambassador, Andrew Young, in a personal interview, April 2019.
58 Coleman, *Counsel for the Situation,* p. 164.
59 Eisenhower, *Mandate for Change*, p. 236.

14. PLAYING THE LONG GAME

1 James Killian, *Sputnik, Scientists and Eisenhower: A Memoir of the First Special Assistant to the President for Science and Technology* (Cambridge, MA: MIT Press, 1982), p. 2.
2 Ewald, *Eisenhower the President,* p. 285.
3 Dateline September 30, 1957, *New York Times,* October 1, 1957, p. 1.
4 Soviet scientists, a Russian once told me, had an incentive to be the first to put their satellite into orbit. Unlike the conditions facing American rocket men, the failure of Soviet scientists to be first to launch one, even under IGY, would have imperiled their lives with the sure punishment of time in the gulag.
5 Yanek Mieczkowski, *Eisenhower's Sputnik Moment: The Race for Space and World Prestige* (Ithaca, NY: Cornell University, 2013). p. 21.
6 Ibid., p. 22.
7 Ibid., p. 16.
8 Killian, *Sputnik, Scientists and Eisenhower,* p. 8.
9 Ewald, *Eisenhower the President*, p. 285.
10 Korda, *Ike: An American Hero*, p. 701.
11 Rigden, *Rabi*: *Scientist and Citizen,* p. 254.
12 See Cargill Hall, "The Origins of Space Policy," p. 2.
13 Paul A. Berkman, "President Eisenhower: The Antarctic Treaty and the Origins of International Spaces," *Science Diplomacy: Antarctica, Science, and the Governance of International Spaces.* (Washington, DC: Smithsonian Contributions to Knowledge, 2011), p. 21.
14 Eisenhower, *Waging Peace,* p. 209.
15 Berkman, "President Eisenhower: The Antarctic Treaty and the Origins of International Spaces," p. 22.

16 Ibid.
17 Eisenhower, *Waging Peace,* pp. 205–206.
18 Ibid., p. 210.
19 On May 14, only months before Sputnik was launched, House Minority Leader Joseph W. Martin had told legislative leaders that the House would "probably cut the Pentagon's appropriation by about $2 billion, mostly in missiles and aircraft." The president had reacted with force: "To cut the Defense Department budget further now is to take a gamble with our national safety," he said.
20 David Jablonsky, *War by Land, Sea, and Air* (New Haven, CT: Yale University Press, 2011), p. 261.
21 Eisenhower, *Waging Peace,* pp. 208–209.
22 Berkman, "President Eisenhower," p. 22.
23 Mieczkowski, *Eisenhower's Sputnik Moment,* p. 16.
24 Smith, *Eisenhower in War and Peace,* pp. 732–33.
25 Jablonsky, *War by Land, Sea, and Air,* p. 261.
26 In 1954, Nitze and other had declared the period to be one of "maximum danger." See Mieczkowski, p. 244.
27 Killian, *Sputnik, Scientists and Eisenhower,* p. 6.
28 Adams, *Firsthand Report,* p. 413; Ewald, *Eisenhower the President,* p. 250.
29 For a general thesis on this, see: Susan Eisenhower, *Partners in Space: US-Soviet Cooperation after the Cold War* (Washington, DC: Eisenhower Institute, 2004) pp. 1–21.
30 Berkman, "President Eisenhower," p. 23.
31 Ibid.
32 Ibid., p. 25.
33 Ibid., p. 22.
34 Ferrell, *Eisenhower Diaries,* p. 155.
35 Ewald, *Eisenhower the President,* p. 321.
36 Ibid.
37 Bowie and Immerman, *Waging Peace,* p. 98.
38 Eisenhower's problems with the military, Goodpaster recalled, began just after the war when Eisenhower was presiding over the Joint Chiefs of Staff. Truman had given him a budget figure as a ceiling, and General Ike had used his credibility with the services to finally bring their requests down to that level. When Truman took another half billion dollars out of the allocation—a lot of money on those days—General Eisenhower had to break his agreement with the services. He was privately furious, and so were the service heads.
39 Jablonsky, *War by Land, Sea, and Air,* p. 264.
40 Nelson, *Andrew J. Goodpaster,* p. 121.
41 Ibid.
42 Eisenhower, *Waging Peace,* p. 246.
43 Nelson, *Andrew J. Goodpaster,* pp. 121–22.
44 Dwight D. Eisenhower to Swede Hazlett, August 20, 1956, in *The*

Papers of Dwight David Eisenhower, vol. 17, *The Presidency: The Middle Way,* p. 2255.

45 Adams, *Firsthand Report,* p. 418.

46 Ibid., p. 419.

47 Ibid., pp. 420–421.

48 Sputnik's influence would be felt not just in the remaining years of Eisenhower's presidency but through the decades.

Beginning in 1955, the trend lines of attacks from Capitol Hill could be seen. Senator Stuart Symington, President Truman's first air force secretary, sensed an opportunity going into the 1956 election year. According to *U.S. News & World Report,* "Stuart Symington is becoming known as the most outspoken challenger of President Eisenhower's reputation as a military planner."

From the floor of the Senate, Symington had warned of a "Bomber Gap." The "Reds," he asserted, had "thousands more" jet fighters and jet bombers than the United States did. And, he warned, they "probably" exceed this country in long-range jet bombers and guided missiles. Symington's message had been that the president was making a fatal mistake to reduce the strength of the armed services. (This claim was, as General Goodpaster liked to say, "a fiction.") (*U.S. News & World Report*, July 1, 1955, pp. 16-18).

49 Jablonsky, *War By Land, Sea, and Air,* p. 266.

50 Scientists, Eisenhower had discovered, were one such group. He remembered for the rest of his life the indispensable role they had played during those contentious times. In fact, during the last months of Ike's life, Dr. James Killian, his onetime PSAC chairman, visited the former president at Walter Reed. Surrounded by the "paraphernalia of a cardiac intensive care unit," Eisenhower asked Killian about the health and well-being of "my scientists"—naming many of those who had been on his team. "You know, Jim," Eisenhower said to Killian, "this bunch of scientists was one of the few groups that I encountered in Washington who seemed to be there to help the country not help themselves." (Killian, *Sputnik, Scientists and Eisenhower*, p. 241).

51 Ewald, *Eisenhower the President*, p. 322.

15. A FAREWELL

1 Ewald, *Eisenhower the President,* p. 294.

2 Brian W. Clark, "Eisenhower's Common Sense Leadership on National Security and the Economy," *Eisenhower Leadership*, July 15, 2012. Eisenhowerleadership.com/2012/07/15/eisenhowers-common-sense-leadership-on-national-security-and-the-economy.

3 David Stockman, "Yes We Can: How Eisenhower Wrestled Down the U.S. Warfare State," *The Globalist*, April 29, 2014.

4 William Taubman, *Khrushchev: The Man and His Era* (New York: W. W. Norton, 2004), p. 408.

5 Ibid., p. 378.

6 Christopher Preble, *John F. Kennedy and the Missile Gap* (DeKalb, IL: Northern Illinois University Press, 2004), pp. 55–57.
7 Mieczkowski, *Eisenhower's Sputnik Moment*, p. 244.
8 Preble, *John F. Kennedy and the Missile Gap*, p. 57.
9 Taubman, *Khrushchev*, p. 379.
10 Ibid.
11 Ambrose, *Soldier and President*, pp. 481–482.
12 Ibid., p. 283.
13 Ibid., p. 484.
14 Eisenhower, *At Ease*, p. 268.
15 Eisenhower, *Waging Peace*, p. 500.
16 Ibid., pp. 489–527.
17 Ibid., p. 497.
18 Ibid.
19 Ibid., pp. 528, 530, 539.
20 Michael Beschloss, *May Day: Eisenhower, Khrushchev, and the U-2 Affair* (New York: Harper & Row, 1988), p. 178.
21 The Marilyn Monroe anecdote was related to me by a Russian who had been friends with the Khrushchev family.
22 Nelson, *Andrew J. Goodpaster*, pp. 126–127.
23 Korda, *Ike: An American Hero*, p. 702.
24 The invaluable information that came from this program was also used during the Suez crisis, and later during the Soviet military and nuclear buildup in Cuba.
25 Eisenhower, *Waging Peace*, p. 546.
26 Ewald, *Eisenhower the President*, p. 271.
27 For more on this story see Milton Eisenhower, *The President Is Calling*, p. 335; and Jean Edward Smith, *Eisenhower in War and Peace*, p. 753.
28 See John S. D. Eisenhower, *Strictly Personal*, appendix C, pp. 390–391, in which Khrushchev expresses "regret" and the hope that DDE might make a trip to the Soviet Union after all.
29 See Philip Taubman's outstanding book *Secret Empire: Eisenhower, the CIA, and the Hidden Story of America's Space Espionage* (New York: Simon & Schuster, 2004).
30 Ewald, *Eisenhower the President*, p. 288.
31 Preble, *John F. Kennedy and the Missile Gap*, p. 73.
32 Herbert York, *Making Weapons, Talking Peace: A Physicist's Odyssey from Hiroshima to Geneva* (New York: Basic Books, 1987), p. 126.
33 Mieczkowski, *Eisenhower's Sputnik Moment*, p. 246.
34 Ibid., p. 244.
35 Ibid.
36 Ibid., p. 246.
37 Ibid.

According to some historians, our superior numbers were one of the reasons that Khrushchev was emboldened, during the new administration, to place missiles in Cuba.

38 Ibid., pp. 246–247.
39 Ewald, *Eisenhower the President,* p. 308.
40 Brownell, *Advising Ike*, p. 291.
41 Gettysburg College, *The Art of Leadership*, p. 40.
42 Ibid., p. 41.
43 Ibid.
44 "Transcript of President Dwight D. Eisenhower's Farewell Address (1961)" *Our Documents,* n.d. https://www.ourdocuments.gov/doc.php?flash=false&doc=90&page=transcript.

16. WHEN NO ONE WAS LOOKING

1 D'Este, *Eisenhower: A Soldier's Life*, p. 705.
2 Longgood, *Ike, A Pictorial Biography,* pp. 110–11.
3 Rachel Gillett and Allana Akhtar, "These Are the Top 20 US Presidents," *Business Insider,* July 4, 2019. www.businessinsider.com/the-top-20-presidents-in-us-history-according-to-historians-2017-2
4 Ferrell, *The Eisenhower Diaries*, p. xii.
5 Eisenhower, *At Ease*, p. 168.
6 McKeogh and Lockridge, *Sgt. Mickey and General Ike*, p. 161.
7 Interview with Melvyn Bucholtz, April 23, 2019.
8 Email to author, n.d.
9 McKeogh and Lockridge, *Sgt. Mickey and General Ike*, p. 85.
10 This also appears in David Eisenhower, *Going Home to Glory*, p. 260.
11 Burnes, *The Ike Files*, pp. 244–245.
12 David Eisenhower, *Going Home to Glory,* p. 27.
13 Ewald, *Eisenhower the President*, p. 323.
14 Robinson, *Why I Like Ike*, pp. 89–90.
15 Burnes, *The Ike Files*, p. 240.
16 Merle Miller, *Ike the Soldier* (New York: G. P. Putnam's Sons, 1987), p. 677.
17 Esther Young, *Atlanta Chronicle* staff, n.d.
18 Dwight D. Eisenhower to Frederick Edgworth Morgan, December 26, 1947, *The Eisenhower Papers,* vol. 9, *The Chief of Staff*, ed., Louis Galambos, p. 2165. Eisenhower goes on to say that underestimating the power of the positive is also the same in warfare, noting the naysayers just before Operation Overlord.
19 David Eisenhower, *Going Home to Glory*, p. 271.

EPILOGUE

1 "General Eisenhower Is Dead." *Evening Star*, March 28, 1969, p. 1.
2 Robert Kaplan, "Why We Need Someone Like Ike," *Wall Street Journal*, July 18, 2019.
3 Brownell, *Advising Ike*, p. 302.
4 Ferrell, *The Eisenhower Diaries*, p. 1.

BIBLIOGRAPHY

Adams, Sherman. *Firsthand Report: The Story of the Eisenhower Administration*. New York: Harper & Brothers, 1961.

Alteras, Isaac. *Eisenhower and Israel: U.S.–Israeli Relations 1953–1960.* Gainesville: University of Florida Press, 1993.

Ambrose, Stephen E. *The Victors.* New York: Simon & Schuster, 1998.

———. *Eisenhower: Soldier and President*, New York: Simon & Schuster, 1960.

Baier, Brett, with Catherine Whitney. *Three Days in January: Dwight Eisenhower's Final Mission*. New York: William Morrow, 2017.

Becker, Ralph. *Miracle on the Potomac.* Silver Spring, MD: Bartleby Press, 1990.

Berkman, Paul Arthur. "President Eisenhower, the Antarctic Treaty and the Origin of International Spaces," *Science Diplomacy*, January 2011.

Beschloss, Michael. *Mayday: Eisenhower, Khrushchev, and the U-2 Affair.* New York: Harper & Row, 1986.

Bowie, Robert R., and Richard H. Immerman. *Waging Peace: How Eisenhower Shaped an Enduring Cold War Strategy.* New York: Oxford University Press, 1998.

Brownell, Herbert. *Advising Ike.* Lawrence: University Press of Kansas, 1993.

Burnes, Brian. *The Ike Files: Mementoes of the Man and His Era*. Kansas City: Kansas City Star Books, 2008.

Butcher, Harry C. *My Three Years with Eisenhower.* New York: Simon & Schuster, 1946.

Coleman, William T. *Counsel for the Situation*. Washington, DC: Brookings Institution, 2010.

D'Este, Carlo. *Eisenhower: A Soldier's Life*. New York: Henry Holt, 2002.

Donovan, Robert J. *Confidential Secretary: Ann Whitman's 20 Years with Eisenhower and Rockefeller*. New York: E. P. Dutton, 1988.

———. *Eisenhower: The Inside Story*. New York: Harper & Brothers, 1956. Partially published as "Eisenhower in the White House," *New York Herald Tribune*. 1956.

Editors of *American Heritage* magazine. *Eisenhower: An American Hero*, American Heritage, 1969.

Eisenhower, David. *Eisenhower at War*. New York: Random House, 1986.

———. *Going Home to Glory*. New York: Simon & Schuster, 2010.

Eisenhower, Dwight D. *Crusade in Europe*. Garden City, NY: Doubleday and Company, 1948.

———. *Mandate for Change*. Garden City, NY: Doubleday, 1967.

———. *Waging Peace*. Garden City, NY: Doubleday, 1965.

———. *At Ease: Stories I Tell to Friends*. Gettysburg Eastern National (with permission of New York: Doubleday and Company), 1967.

Eisenhower Papers Series. Louis Galambos, et al., eds. Baltimore, MD: Johns Hopkins University Press.

Eisenhower, John S. D. *The Bitter Woods: The Battle of the Bulge*. New York: G. P. Putnam's Sons, 1969.

———. *Allies*: *Pearl Harbor to D-day*. Cambridge, MA: Da Capo Press, 2000.

———. *Strictly Personal*. Garden City, NY: Doubleday, 1974.

Eisenhower, Milton S. *The President Is Calling*. Garden City, NY: Doubleday, 1974.

Eisenhower, Susan. *Mrs. Ike: Memories and Reflections on the Life of Mamie Eisenhower*. New York: Farrar, Straus & Giroux, 1996.

Ewald, William B. Jr. *Eisenhower the President: The Crucial Days: 1951–1960*. Englewood Cliffs, NJ: Prentice-Hall, 1981.

Ferrell, Robert H. *The Eisenhower Diaries*. New York: W. W. Norton and Company, 1981.

———. *The Diary of James C. Hagerty: Eisenhower in Mid-Course 1954–1955*, Bloomington: Indiana University Press, 1983.

Gellman, Irwin F. *The President and the Apprentice: Eisenhower and Nixon, 1952–1961.* New Haven, CT: Yale University Press, 2015.

Gettysburg College. *Eisenhower and the Art of Leadership*, compendium of speeches on the Eisenhower Centennial, 1990.

Greenstein, Fred I. *The Hidden-Hand Presidency: Eisenhower as a Leader.* New York: Basic Books, 1982.

Hall, R. Cargill. "The Origins of Space Policy: Eisenhower, Open Skies, and Freedom of Space," National Reconnaissance Office, Department of Defense, USAF Historical Research Center, 1998.

Hitchcock, William I. *The Age of Eisenhower: America and the World in the 1950s.* New York: Simon & Schuster, 2018.

Jablonsky, David. *War by Land, Sea, and Air: Dwight Eisenhower and the Concept of Unified Command.* New Haven, CT: Yale University Press, 2010.

Killian, James R. Jr. *Sputnik, Scientists and Eisenhower: A Memoir of the First Special Assistant to the President for Science and Technology.* Cambridge, MA: MIT Press, 1977.

Larson, Arthur. *Eisenhower: The President Nobody Knew.* New York: Scribner's, 1968.

Longgood, William F. *Ike: A Pictorial Biography.* New York: Time-Life Books, 1969.

McKeogh, Michael J. and Richard Lockridge. *Sgt. Mickey and General Ike.* New York: G. P. Putnam's Sons, 1946.

Mieczkowski, Yanek. *Eisenhower's Sputnik Moment: The Race for Space and World Prestige.* Ithaca, NY: Cornell University Press, 2013.

Miller, Merle. *Ike The Soldier: As They Knew Him.* New York: Perigee Books—Putnam Publishing Group, 1988.

Murray, Michael. *Jacques Barzun: Portrait of a Mind.* Savannah, GA: Frederic C. Beil, 2001.

Nelson, C. Richard. *The Life and Work of General Andrew J. Goodpaster: Best Practices in National Security Affairs.* Lanham, MD: Rowman & Littlefield, 2016.

Newton, Jim. *Eisenhower: The White House Years.* New York: Doubleday, 2011.

Nichols, David. *A Matter of Justice.* New York: Simon & Schuster, 2007.

———. *Eisenhower 1956: The President's Year of Crisis: Suez and the Brink of War.* New York: Simon & Schuster, 2011.

———. *Ike and McCarthy: Dwight Eisenhower's Secret Campaign against Joe McCarthy*. New York: Simon & Schuster, 2017.

Parmet, Herbert S. *Eisenhower and the American Crusades*. New York: Macmillan, 1972.

Preble, Christopher A. *John F. Kennedy and the Missile Gap*. Dekalb, IL: Northern Illinois University Press, 2004.

Richardson, Heather Cox. *To Make Men Free: A History of the Republican Party*. New York: Basic Books, 2014.

Rigden, John S. *Rabi: Scientist and Citizen*. Cambridge, MA: Harvard University Press, 2002.

Roberts, Clifford. *The Story of the Augusta National Golf Club*. Garden City, NY: Doubleday, 1976.

Robinson, Gilbert A. *Why I Like Ike*. McLean, VA: International Publishers, 2012.

Rumbough, Stanley, Jr. *Citizens for Eisenhower*. McLean, VA: International Publishers, 2013.

Shinkle, Peter. *Ike's Mystery Man: The Secret Lives of Robert Cutler*. Hanover, NH: Steerforth Press, 2018.

Slater, Ellis. *The Ike I Knew*. Ellis Slater Trust, 1980.

Smith, Jean Edward. *The Liberation of Paris: How Eisenhower, de Gaulle, and von Choltitz Saved the City of Light*. New York: Simon & Schuster, 2019.

———. *Eisenhower in War and Peace*. New York: Random House, 2003.

Smith, Walter Bedell. *Eisenhower's Six Great Decisions*. New York: Longmans Green, 1956.

Stans, Maurice. *One of the President's Men: Twenty Years with Eisenhower and Nixon*. Washington and London: Brassey's, 1995.

Taubman, Philip. *Secret Empire: Eisenhower, the CIA, and the Hidden Story of America's Space Espionage*. New York: Simon & Schuster, 2003.

Taubman, William. *Khrushchev: The Man and His Era*. New York: W. W. Norton, 2003.

Thomas, Evan. *Ike's Bluff: President Eisenhower's Secret Battle to Save the World*. New York: Little, Brown, 2012.

Trow, George W. S. *My Pilgrim's Progress: Media Studies 1950–1998*. New York: Pantheon, 1999.

York, Herbert F. *Making Weapons, Talking Peace: A Physicist's Odyssey from Hiroshima to Geneva*. New York: Basic Books, 1987.

INDEX